Caring for the poor is an obvious priority to followers of Jesus. But how do we help without hurting? Fikkert and Mask's new book, *From Dependence to Dignity*, explores groundbreaking ideas on how to help the poor through microfinance ministries. The result of years of research, field experience, and prayerful insight, this latest book from the Chalmers Center will empower the body of Christ to make a significant difference in the lives of the poor worldwide.

—Craig Groeschel
Senior Pastor of LifeChurch.tv and coauthor of *From This Day Forward: Five Commitments to Fail-Proof Your Marriage*

In this highly anticipated book, Brian Fikkert and Russell Mask of the Chalmers Center go beyond the call for charity by equipping the church to respond in ways that make a lasting impact. HOPE International has used the Chalmers Center's training and curricula in our own church-centered microfinance ministries with amazing results, so I am delighted to see the global church being equipped on an even larger scale through this outstanding book and the resources on the associated website. I couldn't recommend it more highly!

—Peter Greer
President and CEO of HOPE International and coauthor of *Mission Drift: The Unspoken Crisis Facing Leaders, Charities, and Churches*

Filled with first-rate theology and practice, Fikkert and Mask present a set of proven solutions to help people overcome vulnerability. Practical and sound, this book enca[...] worldwide microfinance movement. I highly c[...]

Stephan Bauman
[...]EO of World Relief

This is an excellent book for those engaged in the task of breaking the "dependency syndrome" that some NGOs have inadvertently created among the poor and marginalized that they have sought to help through long-term engagement. The book makes a strong case for the important role of the local church in poverty alleviation by being balanced in how it proclaims and demonstrates the gospel, in the spirit of what true integral mission is all about. Just as *Helping without Hurting in Short-Term Missions* had a significant impact on the uninitiated "short-term visitors" into the developing world, this book has a message for transforming the "long-term settlers"!

—Dr. Ravi I. Jayakaran
Senior Associate for Integral Mission,
Lausanne Movement

Churches around the world have attempted to harness the power of microfinance to reduce poverty, empower dignity, and bring Christ-centered transformation to their communities ... but the results are often disappointing. As a Rwandan pastor once told me, "It's hard for a pastor to be your loan shark," expressing the frustration of grace-centered churches attempting to enforce repayment (which often requires coercion-centered measures). In *From Dependence to Dignity,* Fikkert and Mask have empowered the church with a great resource—providing a gospel-centered framework, economic best practices, and easy-to-understand tools for churches to use microfinance for the glory of God and the transformation of the world.

—Joshua Ryan Butler
Pastor of Local and Global Outreach,
Imago Dei Community church

Drs. Fikkert and Mask extend the groundbreaking approach of *When Helping Hurts* into the practice of microfinance. Their prescriptions remain biblically sound, practically effective, and generously humane—in a word, Christ-centered. If the Church is going to lead internationally in poverty alleviation that works on the ground, this is the book that must be read first.

—Scott Maclellan
Chair of the Maclellan Foundation

Thank you, Brian and Russell, for sharing these stories and awesome resources about the power of dignity. Poor women and communities could have never dreamed how belonging to a church-based savings program could so radically change their lives, their family, and community. This is a book on what integral mission looks like today. This is a book about the Great Commission and how some of the poorest people and churches are loving God, loving their neighbor, and loving themselves through microfinance.

You will not read this practical, how-to book just once, but will refer back often to look at models of what Good News looks like to the poorest amongst us and those partnering with them in seeing God's kingdom come in this generation.

—G. Stephen Goode
YWAM Ambassador for Compassion/Justice,
Bangkok, Thailand

Once again Fikkert and Mask are providing a pragmatic, exciting path forward to help us learn how to meet the needs of the world's poorest people—without creating dependency. Their solution, based in the local church, is supported by strong theology, real world examples, and practical steps on how to move forward. This book is must reading to understand how to bring healthy, Christ-centered, lasting change in the interesting, complex financial world of the very poor.

—Peter Ochs
Cofounder and Board Chair of First Fruit Inc.

I am honored to heartily endorse the work *From Dependency to Dignity* by Brian Fikkert and Russ Mask. They are making a great contribution to the church and benefiting the poor in the hardest places around the globe. Through the insights of this book, they are—with sound biblical reasoning and application—helping us to tackle poverty alleviation in the fullest sense. I am confident that the result of their labor will be helping the Church of King Jesus to be more fully the Church that Christ intended. And their work will help "the poor to see and be glad" (Psalm 69:32). Do yourself, the poor, and your church a favor by putting into practice the wisdom contained in these pages.

—Gary Edmonds
President and CEO, FH/Food for the Hungry

A Follow-up to the Bestselling *When Helping Hurts*

FROM DEPENDENCE TO DIGNITY

How to Alleviate Poverty Through Church-Centered Microfinance

BRIAN FIKKERT
RUSSELL MASK

FOREWARD BY RICK WARREN

ZONDERVAN®

ZONDERVAN

From Dependence to Dignity

This title is also available as a Zondervan ebook.
Visit www.zondervan.com/ebooks.

Requests for information should be addressed to:

Zondervan, 3900 *Sparks Drive SE, Grand Rapids, Michigan 49546*

Library of Congress Cataloging-in-Publication Data

Fikkert, Brian.
From dependence to dignity / Brian Fikkert and Russell Mask.
pages cm.
Includes bibliographical references and index.
ISBN 978-0-310-51812-9 (softcover)
1. Church work with the poor. 2. Poverty—Religious aspects—Christianity.
3. Microfinance. I. Title.
BV639.P6F55 2015
261.8'325—dc23 2014044781

Cover design: Studio Gearbox
Cover photography: The Chalmers Center
Interior design and composition: Greg Johnson/Textbook Perfect

Printed in the United States of America

15 16 17 18 19 20 21 22 23 24 25 26 /DCI/ 18 17 16 15 14 13 12 11 10 9 8 7 6 5 4 3 2 1

CONTENTS

FOREWORD

Did you know that God has favorites? He does. The Bible has over 2,000 verses that call them, by name, "the poor." And in Luke 4, Jesus tells how to love the poor when he utters his first public words: "The Spirit of the Lord is upon me, because he anointed me to preach the gospel to the poor." If you're going to follow Jesus, you'd better love the poor.

In 2003, at a church conference in Johannesburg, I wanted to see for myself if I truly followed Jesus' command to love the poor, so I asked to see a typical church in rural Africa. I was taken to a little village in the middle of nowhere. No water, no electricity. It was a little tent church of 75 people—50 adults and 25 children orphaned by AIDS—the poorest of the poor. The poverty was all around me, and yet I saw a little garden growing by the tent church that fed this extended family group. They showed me a couple of old, run-down school buses where the kids went to school and the ragged tents where they slept because there was no home for them. I saw a little, under-resourced church doing more to help the poor than my rich megachurch. It was like a knife in my heart, and I said to myself: "I need to repent."

That's how God broke my heart for the poor and birthed the vision for the PEACE Plan, our mission model at Saddleback Church. The PEACE Plan is about bringing the hope of Jesus Christ to those without a voice by taking on the five global giants: spiritual emptiness, self-serving leadership, poverty, disease, and illiteracy.

In 2005, we partnered with Rwanda—a country at the time ranked by the World Bank as the 174th poorest country in the world—to test and refine the Plan's focus to fulfill the Great Commandment and the Great Commission. The success of PEACE in Rwanda has been God-sized because of the cooperation of the Rwandan government and businesses partnering with local pastors' churches and communities.

Orphans are finding homes with local families, health care is on the rise, churches are growing, education is available, and the Rwandans are becoming self-sufficient.

One of the most successful programs launched in Rwanda has been the church-centered savings and credit associations designed by the Chalmers Center. Any church—and I do mean *any* church, *any*where—can use these methods to engage the extreme poor in their community.

I urge you to read Fikkert and Mask's book, *From Dependence to Dignity*. You will learn some practical ways your church can get started on The PEACE Plan Mission Model for assisting the poor. Their proven methods are now standard curricula for all of our Saddleback PEACE ministries and for our Global Purpose Driven Church Network.

Whether you're a pastor, leader, or lay member of your church—be it a church of 25 or 25,000—and whether you're in a major metropolitan center or the most rural of towns, start a savings and credit group ministry. It just takes one person with a heart broken for the poor in your local church to get started.

Rick Warren
Senior Pastor, Saddleback Church
Founder, The PEACE Plan

PREFACE

Since its beginning in 1999, the Chalmers Center for Economic Development at Covenant College (www.chalmers.org) in Lookout Mountain, Georgia (USA), has been equipping the local church—including its missionaries to unreached regions—to declare and demonstrate among people who are poor that Jesus Christ is making all things new. In particular, the Chalmers Center trains churches to implement gospel-centered ministries that empower poor people to glorify God through sustaining work. In the process, the church restores poor people to their rightful dignity as image bearers of the Triune God, and it gives a foretaste of that great day when Jesus Christ will usher in a new heaven and a new earth. Come quickly, Lord Jesus!

In order to fulfill this mission, the Chalmers Center first designs gospel-centered ministries that churches and missionaries can use, then implements those strategies in field tests, and finally trains churches, missionaries, and church-equipping organizations to use those ministries on their own. In all of this, the hope is that poor people will never hear of the Chalmers Center, but rather that they will experience in the local church the very embodiment of Jesus Christ, the only one who can truly alleviate all of our poverty.

From its inception, the Chalmers Center has been designing and developing models, training, and curricula in the area of church-centered microfinance, and the authors have been privileged to be heavily involved with this part of the Center's work throughout that time period. Hence, this book reflects fifteen years of the Chalmers Center's research and experiences along with those of its ministry partners and of numerous scholars and practitioners from around the world.

The book builds on an earlier book from the Chalmers Center, *When Helping Hurts: How to Alleviate Poverty Without Hurting the Poor ... and Yourself*, which argued that good intentions are not enough. It is possible to hurt poor people in the process of trying to help them. This is true in general, and it is definitely true in the field of microfinance.

Moving from Theory to Practice

This book is intended to help the global body of Christ understand both the possibilities and potential pitfalls of using microfinance as a ministry of the church. Although the book includes a fair amount of theory, the ultimate goal is to move readers into more effective practices. Toward that end, the book includes several features:

- Key principles are boldfaced and repeated throughout the text in order to reinforce central concepts. Appendix 2 provides a complete list of all these key principles.
- Application questions and exercises at the end of chapters help readers to apply the content to their ministry contexts.
- A website provides access to additional tools, resources, and curricula to enable readers to implement the microfinance ministries described in this book. Create an account at www.chalmers.org/dignity.

A Multidisciplinary Approach

Although the world often seems fragmented and incoherent, the fact that Jesus Christ is the Creator, Sustainer, and Reconciler of all things implies that the entire cosmos holds together in him (Colossians 1:15–23). Hence, although both academics and practitioners tend to focus narrowly on their areas of specialization, in reality the world is both multifaceted and integrated. Thus, this book is necessarily multidisciplinary, integrating theory, empirical evidence, and practices from disciplines that are rarely considered together: theology, missions, the social sciences, community development, and microfinance. As a result, this is likely the only book in the world that discusses both the Trinity and microfinance!

Therefore, readers may find some portions of the book a bit more difficult to understand than others. For example, some pastors might struggle with the finance theory, and some microfinance practitioners may wonder why they need to think so much about theology. But do not despair. The book is designed to be accessible to nonexperts. If you are passionate about the kingdom, the church, and the poor, this book is for you. So stretch yourself a little. Spend a bit more time reading those portions that are not as easy for you to understand. For in the process you may grow just a bit closer to understanding the complexities of God's world, thereby making you better equipped for kingdom service.

The book is divided into four parts:

- Part 1 lays the groundwork, exploring the unique challenges facing the global church in the twenty-first century due to the coexistence of unprecedented wealth and grinding poverty within the body of Christ. How can wealthy Christians partner well with poor churches without creating unhealthy dependencies either on the part of those churches or on the part of the poor people to whom those churches are ministering? In addition, chapter 4 introduces readers to the field of microfinance in order to provide a context for the following sections.
- Part 2 explores the nature of poverty and its alleviation, arguing that most relief and development efforts are rooted in the materialism and rationalism of the Enlightenment worldview. This section then introduces a holistic theory of change that is rooted in a biblical understanding of God, the cosmos, and human beings, applying this theory of change to the design of microfinance ministries.
- Part 3 introduces the key terms and financial principles needed to understand microfinance. A failure to understand and faithfully apply these principles can do considerable harm to everyone involved, especially the poor.
- Part 4 introduces and evaluates three possible models that churches and missionaries can use to pursue microfinance ministries and discusses the surprising difficulty of getting them the training and curricula that they need.

PART 1

REPLACING DEPENDENCY WITH DIGNITY

CHAPTER 1

MASAI MISSIONS

> Brothers and sisters, think of what you were when you were called. Not many of you were wise by human standards; not many were influential; not many were of noble birth. But God chose the foolish things of the world to shame the wise; God chose the weak things of the world to shame the strong. God chose the lowly things of this world and the despised things — and the things that are not — to nullify the things that are, so that no one may boast before him.
>
> — *1 Corinthians 1:26–29*

> Because of the [savings and credit association] and through the teaching we are receiving, I have accepted Jesus as my Lord and Savior. And he has changed my life.
>
> — *Member of a church-centered microfinance ministry in Togo, West Africa*[1]

A missionary stands in the front of the church gathering and shares her vision for her ministry in rural Kenya: "I want to be able to help the Masai girls far in the interior regions. The Masai fathers do not want to invest in their daughters' education because their daughters will be lost to other families when they get married. I want to teach the girls living in the interior regions, so that I can empower them to be just like us."

And what would it mean to be "just like us"? All of the women in this church gathering — *including the missionary* — are Masai, a seminomadic tribe in East Africa. Their ears strain under the weight of their heavy earrings. In fact, their entire bodies seem to strain under the weight of their difficult lives. Masai women are viewed as property by their husbands, relegating them to a second-class social status. They are subjected to backbreaking work, female genital mutilation, polygamy, and low levels of education. Indeed, the strain of this reality is evident on the faces of all the women gathered in this small church in rural Kenya.

But there is hope in their faces as well, hope that has come from the church's ministry, a ministry that the women run themselves: a *microfinance ministry*. Lacking access to formal banking services, these women have always struggled to save and to borrow, and are often forced to go to loan sharks, who charge them exorbitant interest rates. As a result, they have had a hard time accumulating the money they so desperately need to start small businesses, pay school fees, purchase medicine, and respond to other opportunities and needs.

Microfinance addresses these problems by providing poor people with access to the financial services that they lack, services like savings, loans, insurance, and money transfers, in the hope of helping them to improve their economic situation and to get out of poverty. In the past several decades the microfinance movement has experienced explosive growth, becoming one of the leading strategies for alleviating poverty in the Global South (Africa, Asia, and Latin America). Therefore, in 2006 the Nobel Peace Prize was awarded to Muhammad Yunus, the founder of the microfinance movement, and to the Grameen Bank of Bangladesh that he founded.

In the case of the Masai church, the women are engaging in a simple—but powerful—form of microfinance, a savings and credit association that has enabled the women to save and lend *their own money* to one another. No loan capital from outsiders is needed. This is a very poor church using its own human, financial, and spiritual resources to restore oppressed women and to send them out as missionaries to other oppressed women.

Savings and loan services can do all of that? No, not on their own. But this savings and credit association does far more than provide beneficial financial services. Group meetings consist of Bible study, prayer, singing, and fellowship, providing these "second-class citizens" with a profound encounter with the ultimate solution to all of our needs: Jesus Christ.

Indeed, the women share how God has used the savings and credit association to bless their lives in multiple ways. Despite being born into an inferior social status, each of these Masai ladies now resembles the woman described in Proverbs 31, whose hard work, entrepreneurship, and faith resulted in praise from her husband and children. They hold their heads high as they describe how the association has provided them with the capital and the dignity they need to start and expand their own small businesses and to meet a variety of economic needs. This is ministry—powerful, holistic, restorative, microfinance ministry.

One lady testifies, "I bought a cow with my loan of 20,000 Kenya shillings (approximately $300 US) and then sold it. I got good profit! When I finished this loan, I took another loan of 20,000. I am so happy. This has really uplifted me. I have now started another business of selling practice tests to students to help them prepare for the national exams. With the profits I am able to pay the school fees for my children."

Another lady shares, "Some Masai women look at all my business activities and wonder if I am a pure Masai. They do not believe that a Masai woman can do all these things. But I am a pure Masai."

How do the Masai men view the empowerment of these women? One lady, who became a cattle trader as a result of the microfinance ministry, beams as she states, "Because we are born-again Christians, the Lord has helped this group of ladies. My husband is very proud of me. The Masai men don't think we women can do anything. But because I have been working so hard, my husband sees that I am a very important person." Another woman states, "As a result of this group, my husband is proud of me. Even my children are proud. I am doing business and paying school fees for my children. I am even paying the tuition for my husband to get more education. All the family members are happy."

And Masai outside the church are taking note. Seeing the improved economic and social status of these ladies, unbelievers are asking if they can join this microfinance ministry. The women anticipate that after these unbelievers join the savings and credit association, they will eventually become Christians and join their church.

And now the ladies are sending out one of their own as a missionary to other Masai girls far in the interior regions, so that those girls can be "just like us": namely, restored image bearers who are seeking to restore others.[2]

The Upside-Down Kingdom Meets the Internet

This is more than just an inspiring story, for the Masai church's microfinance ministry represents a highly significant development with both theological and strategic implications for the church and missions in the twenty-first century. Later chapters will unpack these implications in greater detail.

But for now, consider this: As the center of Christianity shifts from the West (North America and Western Europe) to the Global South, grinding poverty is on the front doorstep—and in the front pews—of the church of Jesus Christ. The Global South includes 2.6 billion people who live on less than two dollars per day, and it is amongst these very poor people that the church is experiencing its most rapid growth. As church historian Philip Jenkins notes, "The most successful new denominations target their message very directly at the have-nots, or rather, the have-nothings."[3]

Moreover, as the church's missionaries strive to take the gospel to unreached people groups, they will necessarily be doing so amongst the poorest people on the planet. According to one estimate, more than 80 percent of the "poorest of the poor" live in the "10/40 Window," the band of countries that contain the vast majority of the remaining unreached people groups. "The poor are the lost, and the lost are the poor."[4]

Reflecting on these developments, missiologist Andrew Walls states that the church of the twenty-first century will be a "church of the poor. Christianity will be mainly the religion of rather poor and very poor people with few gifts to bring except the gospel itself. And the heartlands of the Church will include some of the poorest countries on earth."[5] Similarly, Jenkins notes, the typical Christian in the world in the twenty-first century is not a businessperson attending a megachurch in an American suburb but rather a poor woman in a slum in Sao Paulo, Brazil, or a poor woman in a village in Nigeria[6] ... or a poor Masai woman in rural Kenya.

The Great Commission has been given to the church, and in the twenty-first century this church will largely consist of very poor people bringing the gospel to other very poor people.

Stop and think about this amazing reality: *The advancement of the*

Great Commission in the twenty-first century is largely in the hands of some of the poorest people on the planet.

Can they possibly move things forward? The evidence from the Masai church and its missionary is a resounding "Yes!" Indeed, there is no better missionary to poor, oppressed Masai women than a formerly poor and oppressed Masai woman, whose entire life has been transformed through the power of Jesus Christ.

None of this should be too surprising, for God has chosen "the lowly things of this world and the despised things—and the things that are not—to nullify the things that are, so that no one may boast before him" (1 Corinthians 1:28–29). The kingdom of God is upside down; it has always been this way.

Coexisting with these materially poor churches is another group of people: Christians in wealthy nations who possess vastly greater financial, human, and technological resources than Christians have at any other point in history. Even the *average* Christian in North America or in other wealthy regions is one of the richest people ever to walk the face of the earth.

Indeed, there are greater disparities of wealth within the global body of Jesus Christ than at any time in its history. Moreover, due to the forces of globalization, these disparate portions of the body are coming into regular contact more than ever before. Indeed, short-term mission trips, email, the internet, Facebook, Skype, and Twitter have made our highly unequal world much smaller. As a result, poverty is on center stage for the entire body of Christ on a daily basis. And in the midst of all of this, 1 John 3:17–18 rings out across the ages:

> If anyone has material possessions and sees a brother or sister in need but has no pity on them, how can the love of God be in that person? Dear children, let us not love with words or speech but with actions and in truth.

All of these realities raise two profound questions for the body of Christ at the start of the twenty-first century:

1. *How can materially poor churches and indigenous missionaries in the Global South advance the Great Commission in the context of widespread poverty inside their congregations and communities?*

2. *What are the roles of financially prosperous churches, mission agencies, Christian relief and development organizations, church-equipping ministries, and donors in this process?*

From Dependence to Dignity

Unfortunately, all too often the answer to this set of questions is this: well-meaning churches and organizations from wealthy countries pursue strategies that either ignore churches in the Global South or that make them chronically dependent on foreigners for human and financial support.[7] In the process, these well-meaning outsiders hinder the ability of these materially poor churches to use their own gifts—*which are actually quite substantial*—to help fulfill the Great Commission.

And a second dependency is also quite common. Poverty alleviation efforts in the Global South often undermine the dignity of poor individuals and communities, making them highly dependent on the churches and organizations that seek to serve them.[8] Therefore, the capacities of the poor are weakened, and their poverty is actually deepened by the very churches and organizations that are trying to help them.

Hence, the body of Christ needs to move away from dependency-creating strategies and toward dignity-enhancing strategies with respect to two parties in the Global South: (1) materially poor churches, and (2) materially poor individuals and communities. This requires changes in both the paradigms and practices of the body of Christ. In particular, churches and organizations from wealthy nations need to step back, listen more, follow, and be a servant.[9] And they need to use their financial resources very strategically, placing a greater focus on training, equipping, and leadership development than on buildings and other material resources.[10] Most importantly, they need to recognize that while many churches and individuals in the Global South possess few material resources, they are tremendously gifted in ways that are not immediately obvious to people from wealthy nations. It is essential that these gifts be recognized, strengthened, and mobilized in order to advance the Great Commission in the twenty-first century.

As the Masai church's microfinance ministry illustrates, this is all possible! Christians from wealthy nations played a vital role in this story, providing consulting, training, and some financial resources. But all of these were offered in a nuanced, backstage, complementary, and supportive role rather than a front-stage, implementing, and controlling role.[11] And it was a role that assumed that "churches of the poor with few gifts" were actually "churches of the King with *many* gifts," gifts that they could use to minister in ways that no foreigner ever could.

As a result, the approach avoided the two common dependencies mentioned earlier: in poor churches and in the poor people to whom these churches are ministering. In addition, it reaffirmed two dignities. First, the Masai church was able to equip and mobilize its members to use their own human, financial, and spiritual resources for "works of service" (Ephesians 4:11–13). This is the church being the very embodiment of Jesus Christ, a role that is of the highest dignity. Second, in the process, oppressed women were given dignity as well, becoming productive entrepreneurs, respected mothers, and pioneering missionaries to interior regions where no foreigner would even dare to go.

It is possible for the global body to work together in such a way that both materially poor churches and individuals in the Global South experience dignity rather than unhealthy dependency. In fact, it is not only possible; it is imperative.

Helping without Hurting in Microfinance

This is a book about the global church and holistic ministry. In particular, the focus is on microfinance ministry, which can be a powerful tool for advancing the Great Commission in the Global South.

Indeed, the story of microfinance has become almost legendary: *Lend money to poor people so that they can start or expand microenterprises in order to earn a living. As a result, the incomes of the poor borrowers go up, lifting them and their families out of poverty. Moreover, as the loans are repaid, the money can be lent over and over to lift even more people out of poverty. If one is looking for a sustainable approach to poverty alleviation, it does not get much better than this!*

The story of microfinance is truly inspiring, so inspiring that for the past several decades providing loans to aspiring microentrepreneurs has been one of the leading strategies—perhaps the premier strategy—for alleviating poverty in the Global South. Major secular and Christian organizations have established large-scale microfinance programs, the total number of borrowers exceeding 204 million.[12] The repayment rates on loans from these organizations have been remarkably high, and poor people, who were previously considered "unbankable," are increasingly gaining access to financial services and to associated business development interventions. Moreover, donors see their money having a perpetual impact, as the capital from repaid loans can be relent time and again.

Churches and missionaries (and small parachurch organizations) on all continents have taken note of this movement and are using microfinance as part of their own ministries. From remote churches in rural Africa to the short-term missions programs of megachurches in the United States, churches and missionaries are plunging into microfinance, trying to emulate the apparent success of the large-scale organizations.

Unfortunately, these churches and missionaries often find that microfinance initiatives are far more difficult than they had imagined. For reasons that will be discussed in this book, repayment rates on loans from churches and missionaries are often extremely low, which can lead to the complete collapse of the program. Indeed, the landscape is covered with the carcasses of failed microfinance ministries. Everybody gets hurt in the process: poor people, churches and missionaries, donors, and other microfinance organizations. And most importantly, all of this does tremendous damage to the very name of Jesus Christ.

These realities raise another set of questions:

- What challenges do churches and missionaries (and small parachurch ministries) in the Global South face when they attempt to replicate the *apparently* successful microfinance programs of large-scale organizations?
- How can churches and missionaries in the Global South implement holistic microfinance ministries without succumbing to the risks of doing harm?
- How can the churches, Christian relief and development organizations, and donors from wealthy nations link arms with churches and missionaries in the Global South in this endeavor?

This book seeks to address these issues by articulating the basic principles that are necessary to make a microfinance ministry successful. Using those principles as a guide, we then explain why it is extremely difficult for churches, missionaries, and small parachurch ministries to implement the standard microfinance model of lending money to poor microentrepreneurs. Drawing on best practice research and experience, we then chart several appropriate paths for churches, missionaries, and parachurch ministries to pursue, paths that minimize the risks of harm, that rely on local resources as much as possible, and that enable even the poorest churches in the Global South to use microfinance to minister in powerful ways to the spiritual, social, and economic needs of some of the poorest people on the planet.

This book is based on the research and experiences of the Chalmers Center for Economic Development at Covenant College (www.chalmers.org), its ministry partners, and numerous scholars and practitioners from around the world. It builds on an earlier book from the Chalmers Center, *When Helping Hurts: How to Alleviate Poverty Without Hurting the Poor . . . and Yourself*, which argued that good intentions are not enough. It is possible to hurt poor people in the process of trying to help them. This is true in general, and it is definitely true in the field of microfinance.

We want to see many more stories like that of the Masai church's microfinance ministry, *and that is entirely possible*. But stories like this do not happen automatically; there is far more nuance in the design and execution of the Masai church's microfinance ministry than meets the eye, and small mistakes can have disastrous consequences. In fact, several recent incidents have shown the entire world that bad microfinance does real harm. In one highly publicized case, the government of the state of Andhra Pradesh in India virtually shut down the microfinance programs in that state due to reports of suicides amongst microfinance clients.

In other words, the purpose of this book is to equip the church to "help without hurting in microfinance." The theology, philosophy, and principles articulated in *When Helping Hurts* are the foundation for the design of the microfinance ministries described in this book. Those principles are not just theoretical. Indeed, by God's grace alone, they are working in the Masai church, and they are working all over the globe. And with God's help, you can make them work in the context in which you are ministering.

Recalibrating Expectations

One of the central themes of this book is that microfinance may not be what you think it is. In particular, microfinance offers both so much less and so much more than most people realize. It offers less, because the vast majority of poor households are unlikely to experience dramatic increases in their incomes through starting their own microenterprises. It offers more, because microfinance can play a tremendous role in helping to stabilize poor households, removing them from the brink of disaster and enabling them to make the changes that are conducive to long-run progress. Moreover, when combined with evangelism and discipleship, microfinance can be a powerful tool for holistic ministry.

Thus, if the global church recalibrates its expectations about microfinance, it can unleash materially poor churches—churches like the Masai church—to implement microfinance ministries that are truly restorative for poor people in the Global South. And it can do so in a way that avoids creating dependencies on the part of either these churches or the poor people to whom they are ministering.

And that is where you come in. Although we hope you will find this book interesting, our goal is not just to write an interesting book. Rather, the goal is to equip you to help create more stories like the Masai church story. Although this book is not a detailed implementation manual, it explains the key issues and ministry options to enable you to take the next steps, and it points you to additional learning resources and tools. As such, we pray that God will use this book to assist pastors, missions committees, ministry leaders, strategists, practitioners, trainers, and funders who are interested in implementing holistic, gospel-centered microfinance ministries in churches and frontier missions across the Global South.

Summary

The spread of the gospel in the twenty-first century requires the church to address poverty head on. As the next chapter argues, this is not a new phenomenon. Indeed, it has always been the case. What is novel are two things: First, the center of Christianity has shifted to the Global South so that the Great Commission is largely in the hands of churches comprised of people with very few material resources. Second, coexisting with these materially poor churches are Christians from wealthy nations, believers who possess unprecedented economic and technological resources. Indeed, there are greater disparities of wealth within the global body of Christ than at any time in history. The global body needs holistic strategies that enable materially poor churches to minister effectively without creating unhealthy dependencies for them or for the poor people to whom they are ministering. A microfinance ministry, if designed and executed properly, is one such strategy.

CHAPTER 2

WHAT IS THE MISSION OF THE CHURCH?

In the first century, mission strategy was always congregationally based.... There were no mission societies, mission boards, or parachurch organizations.... Today, most local churches are sidelined and uninvolved when it comes to missions. The message from most mission and parachurch organizations to the local church is essentially "Pray, pay, and get out of the way." ... I believe the proper role for all the great parachurch and relief organizations is to serve local churches in a supportive role, offering their expertise and knowledge, but allowing the local churches around the world to be the central focus and distribution centers.

—*Rick Warren, pastor of Saddleback Community Church*[1]

Jesus Christ has risen from the dead. That is what this savings and credit association is all about.

—*Lay leader of a church-centered microfinance ministry in Togo, West Africa*[2]

This book is fundamentally about the church and the Great Commission in the twenty-first century; hence, this book is necessarily about materially poor churches and materially poor people. Therefore, before we delve into the details of microfinance ministry, it is important to first consider theologically the very nature of the church. Specifically, what is the mission of the church? What is the church supposed to do about poverty? Is there a role for parachurch ministries, including Christian relief and development agencies?

This chapter explores these theological issues and argues that the Masai church's microfinance ministry represents a highly significant development for the church and its mission in the twenty-first century.

The Mission of Jesus Christ

What is the mission of the church?[3] Because the church is the "body" and "fullness" of Jesus Christ, its mission is rooted in the mission of Jesus Christ (Ephesians 4:1–13). Therefore, in order to appreciate the theological significance of the Masai church's microfinance ministry, it is important to first consider the nature of the mission of Jesus Christ.

Jesus's earthly ministry began one Sabbath day in a synagogue in Nazareth. Week in and week out, Jews gathered in this synagogue to worship under the chafing yoke of the Roman Empire. Aware of Old Testament prophecy, these worshipers were longing for God to send the promised Messiah who would restore the kingdom to Israel and reign on David's throne forever. But centuries had gone by with no Messiah, and the Romans were in power. Hope was probably in short supply. It is in this context that the son of a carpenter from that very town stood up and was handed a scroll from the prophet Isaiah:

> Unrolling it, he found the place where it is written: "The Spirit of the Lord is on me, because he has anointed me to proclaim good news to the poor. He has sent me to proclaim freedom for the prisoners and recovery of sight for the blind, to set the oppressed free, to proclaim the year of the Lord's favor." . . . The eyes of everyone in the synagogue were fastened on him. He began by saying to them, "Today this scripture is fulfilled in your hearing." (Luke 4:17–21)

A shiver must have gone down the spine of the worshipers that day. Isaiah had prophesied that a King was coming who would usher in a kingdom unlike anything the world had ever seen. Could it be that Isaiah's prophecies were really about to come true? Could it really be that a kingdom whose domain would increase without end was about to begin (Isaiah 9:7)? Was it really possible that justice, peace, and righteousness were about to be established forever? Would this King really bring healing to the parched soil, the feeble hands, the shaky knees, the fearful hearts, the blind, the deaf, the lame, the mute, the brokenhearted, the captives, and the sinful souls, and would he proclaim the year of jubilee for the poor (Isaiah 35:1–6; 53:5; 61:1–2)? Jesus's answer to all these questions was a resounding "YES," declaring, "*Today* this scripture is fulfilled in your hearing."

The announcement of the arrival of the kingdom of God was the central theme of Jesus's ministry. Indeed, just a few verses after Jesus's declaration in the synagogue he declared, "I must proclaim the good news of the *kingdom of God* to the other towns also, *because that is why I was sent*" (Luke 4:43, emphasis added). The mission of Jesus was to preach the good news of the kingdom of God, to say to one and all, "I am the King of Kings and Lord of Lords, and I am using my power to fix everything that sin has ruined." As pastor and theologian Timothy Keller states, "The kingdom is the renewal of the whole world through the entrance of supernatural forces. As things are brought back under Christ's rule and authority, they are restored to health, beauty, and freedom."[4]

Of course, Jesus did not just *speak* the good news of the kingdom; he *demonstrated* the good news of the kingdom through acts of healing and compassion amongst the blind, the lame, the leper, the deaf, the dead, and the poor (Luke 7:18–23). And as people watched Jesus do these things, they got a foretaste of what his kingdom will look like on that great day when it comes in its fullness, a day in which all of the effects of sin will be permanently defeated (Revelation 21:1–5).

Note that Jesus's miracles were acts of reconciliation—that is, acts that restored people to what God created them to be. Jesus did not simply show off his immense power by making trees walk or by sending lightning bolts to destroy things. Rather, his miracles helped restore the blind, the lame, and the leper to what they were created to be. In these acts of restoration, Jesus gave a preview of that day when his kingdom will come in its fullness, a day in which there will be no more blind, or lame, or lepers, because full restoration will have come to the entire cosmos (Colossians 1:19–20). Come quickly, Lord Jesus!

Given some current misunderstandings in the church, it is important to emphasize that the cosmic scope of the kingdom of God does not replace the need for people to be individually saved through faith alone in the substitutionary atonement of Jesus Christ. Indeed, when people encounter the good news of the kingdom, they are called to submit to it: "Repent, for the kingdom of heaven has come near" (Matthew 4:17). The "good news" is only good for those who put their faith in the King, while punishment awaits those who do not (Matthew

25:31–46; John 3:16; Romans 6:23; 2 Thessalonians 1:5–10). In other words, the only proper response to the good news of the kingdom is to trust and obey the King.[5]

The Mission of the Church

The mission of the church is rooted in the mission of Jesus Christ.[6] Indeed, the Bible teaches that Jesus continues "to do and to teach" through his church (Acts 1:1).

Hence, it is not surprising that when Jesus sent out his twelve disciples, he sent them out as he was sent: "He gave them power and authority to drive out all demons and to cure diseases, and he sent them out to proclaim the kingdom of God and to heal the sick" (Luke 9:1–2). Similarly, when Jesus sent out seventy-two of his followers, he commanded them, "Heal the sick who are there and tell them, 'The kingdom of God has come near to you'" (Luke 10:9). The message of Jesus and his followers was the "kingdom of God," and it was communicated through both words and deeds.

Moreover, when the New Testament church was established, the concern for both word and deed ministry, particularly amongst the poor, was part of the very fabric of the church (Acts 2:42–45; 4:32–37; 6:1–7; 2 Corinthians 8–9; Galatians 2:1–10; 6:10; James 1:27; 1 John 3:17–18). Paul described the relationship of words and deeds in the New Testament church in this beautiful way:

> So Christ himself gave the apostles, the prophets, the evangelists, the pastors and teachers, to equip his people for works of service, so that the body of Christ may be built up until we all reach unity in the faith and in the knowledge of the Son of God and become mature, attaining to the whole measure of the fullness of Christ. (Ephesians 4:11–13)

Apostles, prophets, evangelists, pastors, and teachers are all primarily engaged in the ministry of the Word with the goal of equipping the members of the congregation for "works of service." The Greek word that is translated as "works of service" in this passage is *diakonia*, the same word that is commonly translated as "deacon," i.e., church officers who engage in practical deeds of service, especially caring for the poor. And what happens when the church ministers in both words and deeds? It becomes the "fullness of Jesus Christ," because this is how he ministered while he was on earth, and it is how he continues to minister through his body, the church.

In recent decades, the global body of Christ has been rediscovering the intimate relationship of word and deed ministry in its mission, an approach that is increasingly being referred to as "integral mission." For example, the global gathering of the Lausanne Movement in Cape Town, South Africa, in 2010 declared "integral mission" as inherent to the church's task:

> Integral mission is the proclamation and demonstration of the gospel. It is not simply that evangelism and social involvement are to be done alongside each other. Rather, in integral mission our proclamation has social consequences as we call people to love and repentance in all areas of life. And our social involvement has evangelistic consequences as we bear witness to the transforming grace of Jesus Christ. If we ignore the world, we betray the Word of God, which sends us out to serve the world. If we ignore the Word of God, we have nothing to bring to the world.[7]

Jesus Christ engaged in integral mission; as his body and fullness, the church must engage in integral mission as well.

The Unique Role of the Local Church

The church of Jesus Christ is necessarily global in nature, as reflected in the phrase "the holy catholic Church" in the Apostles' Creed.[8] Thus, the global body is to engage in integral mission *together*.

At the same time, it is profoundly important to recognize the theological significance of the local church, i.e., the particular congregation in any context. The Bible indicates that *each* local congregation is to have elders in it to equip every member for "works of service," making the local congregation the primary manifestation of Jesus Christ and his kingdom in its community (Acts 14:23; Ephesians 4:11–13; Titus 1:5).[9]

Although this is not a new idea, theologians, missiologists, and development practitioners are increasingly emphasizing the special role of the local church in God's kingdom mission.[10] There are multiple reasons for this increased emphasis, but one of the primary factors is the recognition that biblical *contextualization* is essential in order for the gospel to be fruitful in each cultural setting. In his book *Center Church: Doing Balanced, Gospel-Centered Ministry in Your City*, theologian and church planter Timothy Keller explains contextualization as follows:

> Contextualization is not—as is often argued—"giving people what they want to hear." Rather, it is giving people *the Bible's answers*, which they may not at all want to hear, *to questions about life* that people in their particular time and place are asking, *in language and forms* they can comprehend, and *through appeals and arguments* with force they can feel, even if they reject them. Sound contextualization means translating and adapting the communication and ministry of the gospel to a particular culture without compromising the essence and particulars of the gospel itself. The great missionary task is to express the gospel message to a new culture in a way that avoids making the message unnecessarily alien to that culture, yet without removing or obscuring the scandal and offense of biblical truth. A contextualized gospel is marked by clarity and attractiveness, and yet it still challenges sinners' self-sufficiency and calls them to repentance. It adapts and connects to the culture, yet at the same time challenges and confronts it. If we fail to adapt to the culture or if we fail to challenge the culture—if we under- or overcontextualize—our ministry will be unfruitful because we have failed to contextualize well.[11] (italics in original)

In short, contextualization means communicating the eternal truth of the gospel in a way that is *understandable*, *relevant*, and *attractive* to a particular culture, so that unbelievers in that culture will be challenged to repent and trust in Jesus Christ alone for their salvation.

Some Christians get nervous about the term *contextualization*, as it seems to suggest that the gospel is "relative" rather than "absolute" truth. This is a very legitimate concern, and contextualization has sometimes been misused in this way. Hence, it is important to be completely clear: *the gospel is absolute Truth with a capital T that transcends time, place, and culture*. But this fact does not negate the need for the unchanging truths of Scripture to be contextualized so that they can be understood in different cultural settings. As Keller points out, even the isolated act of translating the Bible into a local language requires contextualization, as the local language is necessarily reflective of the local culture.[12]

Note that contextualization is not a "necessary evil"; rather, it is at the very heart of Jesus's mission. Jesus's incarnation involved the eternal and unchanging Word of God taking on a human body, in particular, the sort of body that would have been typical of the people to whom he was trying to *communicate*: Jewish people living in Palestine in the first century. And his ministry involved translating the *universal* truths of God into words and deeds that could be understood by the people of that *particular* culture.

And just as the eternal and unchanging Word took on the flesh and cultural trappings of a *particular people* in order to reveal himself to *those people* at a particular time, so too the local church is to embody that eternal and unchanging Word in the particular cultural setting in which it finds itself. As the local church seeks to live out the new realities of the kingdom of God in its setting—in some mysterious but very real sense—it becomes the "Word made flesh" in that setting, speaking and acting like Jesus himself would speak and act if he himself had chosen to come to that particular culture at that particular point in time. And, of course, Jesus has indeed made this choice, as evidenced by the fact that his body is in that culture in the form of the local church.[13]

Missiologist Lesslie Newbigin explains that as the local church lives out the realities of the kingdom of God in its setting, it is able to demonstrate that this new kingdom life is a real possibility—i.e., is "plausible"—for the unbelievers in that setting. No longer is the gospel just something that works for other people, e.g., just for the missionaries or just for white people; rather, the local church can speak and act in such a way that local unbelievers can see that this new community and its way of life is something that is possible for them. Unbelievers are able to say, "Yes, I see. This is true for me, for my situation," so that they will want to join the church community too.[14]

According to Timothy Keller, such contextualization requires that the local congregation "reflect the demographic makeup of the surrounding community, thereby giving non-Christian neighbors attractive and challenging glimpses of what they would look like as Christians."[15]

Indeed, nobody is better able to communicate the good news of the kingdom of God to unbelieving Masai—in a way that is *understandable, relevant, attractive, and plausible*—than a community of redeemed Masai who are trying to figure out how to live out the realities of this new kingdom in their cultural setting.

In summary, the global church must engage in integral mission, but it must do so in a way that enables the local church to be what Christ has created it to be: his "body" and "fullness" in a particular setting. All of these considerations are summarized in the **Integral Mission Principle**.[16]

> ***Integral Mission Principle***
>
> The *local* church is to engage in integral mission: proclaiming and demonstrating among people who are poor the good news of the kingdom of God in a contextually appropriate way.

The Masai church's microfinance ministry is a successful example of the **Integral Mission Principle**, and therein lies part of its theological significance. As the Masai church engages in integral mission, it is communicating, imperfectly but really, something of what Jesus Christ would have sounded and acted like if he had been born into the Masai tribe instead of into the tribe of Judah. And as a result, the Great Commission is being advanced, as evidenced by the fact that unbelievers are asking to join the Masai community of believers.

It is important to note that one of the keys to the success of this story is that the microfinance ministry was designed in such a way that the members of the Masai church could undertake the ministry on their own, using their own gifts, talents, and resources. Indeed, savings and credit associations are indigenous to Kenyan culture and well within the capacity of local people to own and operate themselves. As such, this microfinance ministry is a vehicle that very poor churches can use to be the fullness of Jesus Christ in their settings.[17]

The Role of the Parachurch

None of this should be taken to mean that there is no role for parachurch organizations, including international Christian relief and development agencies. Indeed, these organizations often do profoundly important work, and they have expertise, capacities, and callings that extend well beyond those of the local congregation. For example, as will be discussed in chapter 10, microfinance institutions provide services that local congregations cannot and should not try to provide on their own. It is bad stewardship for churches to ignore the tremendous gifts that God has given to parachurch ministries, and it is simply unbiblical for a church to own and operate every institution in its society.[18]

Rich Stearns, President of World Vision US, an affiliate of the largest Christian relief and development organization in the world, puts it this way:

> Churches call in experts to help with all kinds of things: music, accounting, audiovisual support, counseling, and building construction. Shouldn't we do the same to assist us in tackling complicated problems [in the Global South]? Some of this expertise may reside within our congregations, but we will likely have to look outside as well, perhaps hiring people with the necessary skills or partnering with organizations that have experience and a long track record of success.... Even when those with specific expertise provide project leadership, there will always be some valuable places where volunteers from your church can also add value.[19]

At the same time, there is a need for the global body to reconsider the current manner in which many parachurch organizations function. As Bryant Myers, the former vice president for international program strategy at World Vision International, explains:

> The church represents a special challenge to many involved in Christian development (i.e., poverty alleviation), since much of the work in the last quarter century has been done by the so-called parachurch agencies. Made up of Christians, these agencies go directly to Christians in the pews to solicit funds and then directly to poor communities to help the poor. The local church on both ends is too frequently ignored, or worse, seen as part of the problem. This is a seriously flawed view.... The church is the bearer of the biblical story because it is Christ's body in the world. As Christians, we are part of this body, and that's the way it is. With all our warts and pimples, witnessing about Christ and doing his work within the context of the church is our mission.[20]

Designing and implementing the proper relationship between the church and the parachurch with respect to poverty alleviation is not an easy task. Indeed, as Ecuadorian theologian Rene Padilla states, "One of the greatest challenges we Christians have at the threshold of the third millennium is the articulation and practical implementation of an ecclesiology that views the local church, and particularly the church of the poor, as the primary agent of holistic mission."[21]

How can the global body—including the parachurch—function in such a way that a church comprised of materially poor people can serve as the "primary agent of holistic mission"? There is no easy answer to this question, and not all of these issues can be resolved in this book. But Newbigin provides a helpful guideline: parachurch ministries "*have power to accomplish their purpose only as they are rooted in and lead back to a believing community.*"[22]

Figure 2.1 illustrates this idea. The Bible indicates that there are some things that the local church must do *directly*: preach the Word, administer the sacraments (or ordinances), exercise discipline, engage in fellowship, and care for the poor, especially poor believers (Galatians 2:10).[23] When the church engages in these activities, it *directly* ministers holistically to the people in its midst, and it also ministers *indirectly* by equipping its members for "works of service" in two additional contexts.

FIGURE 2.1 The Church, the Parachurch, and Other Spheres of Society

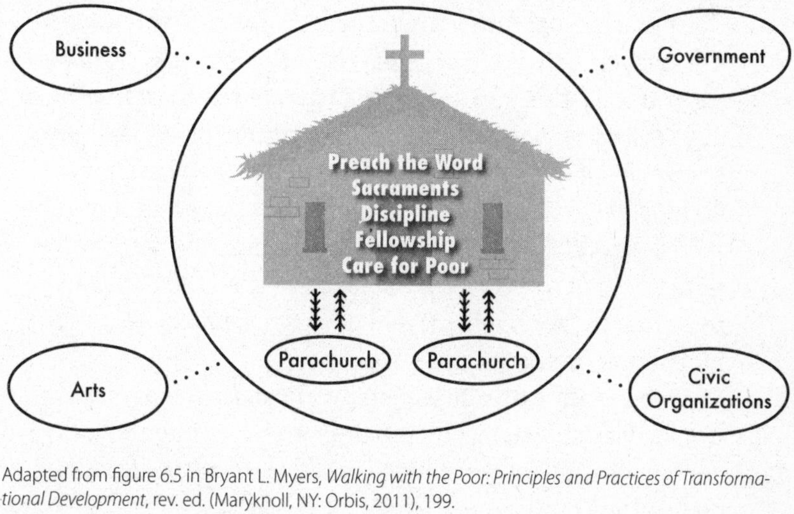

Adapted from figure 6.5 in Bryant L. Myers, *Walking with the Poor: Principles and Practices of Transformational Development*, rev. ed. (Maryknoll, NY: Orbis, 2011), 199.

First, some believers are called to be "salt and light" in institutions that are not parachurch ministries in that they are not engaged in explicitly Christian ministry, e.g., government, business, the arts, and civic organizations. Christ is the creator, sustainer, and reconciler of all things, including these institutions, so Christians must work in them as well, faithfully seeking to use words and deeds that bear witness to the present and future reign of Christ as much as possible (Matthew 5:16; Colossians 1:15–20). However, these institutions do not originate in the local church; that is, they are not "rooted in" the local church and are not expressions of the church's ministry.[24]

Second, some believers are called to be involved in parachurch ministries, which explicitly seek to help the global body of Christ to fulfill its mission. Indeed, these organizations often receive financial support and other forms of assistance from churches. Although these parachurch ministries may sometimes be national or even international in scope—e.g., some Christian relief and development agencies—they must work in such a way that the local church—not the parachurch ministry—is seen as the primary manifestation of Jesus Christ in that setting. There are several steps that can help to foster this:

1. The parachurch ministry must intentionally connect the people to whom it is ministering to the local church, so that they can be nurtured in their faith.
2. The parachurch ministry must see itself as an expression of the local church, not just as part of the global body. Amongst other things, this means that the parachurch must intentionally seek to support and advance the vision, priorities, and testimony of the local church.
3. As much as possible, parachurch ministry workers should be members of the local church(es) with which the parachurch ministry is partnering; they should see themselves as representing those church(es) and not just as employees of the parachurch ministry.
4. The local church and its leadership must see the parachurch ministry as an extension of their church and intentionally support the ministry through volunteers, prayers, finances, counsel, encouragement, and joint initiatives.

These considerations present an enormous challenge to the staff of Christian relief and development organizations and of other parachurch ministries, whose work often fails to be "rooted in and lead back to a believing community." Myers challenges these organizations and staff to reconnect to the local church:

> Our (Christian relief and development) practitioners need to recover from their pride and professionalism and find a way to become part of the Christian community on the ground and thus function as part of the local body of Christ. Agencies must figure out a way to become engaging, supporting and empowering partners of local churches, with each discovering and respecting the respective roles of the others in God's work of transformation.[25]

What happens when the parachurch fails to "be rooted in and lead back to a believing community?" At least two major problems emerge.

First, the local church is unable to use its gifts to fulfill its God-given calling. In other words, the **Integral Mission Principle** is violated. In the process, the long-term spread and impact of the gospel is undermined in the local culture, for the local congregation is the primary vehicle that God has established for evangelism, discipleship, and the spreading of the kingdom. Indeed, long after the funding for the parachurch organization has dried up, the local church will still be present in that cultural setting. Hence, it is imperative that the local church be strong and flourishing in order for the gospel to blossom in the culture over the long term.

Second, failing to connect the poor to the local church is highly detrimental to the poor. As explained in *When Helping Hurts*, material poverty is deeply rooted in the brokenness of human beings' foundational relationships with God, self, others, and the rest of creation.[26] Because Jesus Christ is the only one who can reconcile these relationships (Colossians 1:20) and because he is embodied in the local church, it is in the local church—in its words, deeds, and sacraments—that the only ultimate solution to poverty can be found. Thus, relief and development organizations that truly want to help the poor must work in such a way that poor people are incorporated into the life and worship of a local congregation; and they must work in such a way that poor people trust in Jesus Christ—not the relief and development organization—as their Savior. More about all of this will be discussed in chapters 6 and 7.

In this light, the savings and credit association of the Masai is again noteworthy, for it is actually a parachurch ministry that is deeply rooted in the life of the local church. The church does not own and operate this ministry. Rather, the church equipped its members to start this ministry on their own as an outflowing and expression of the reality of the reign of Jesus Christ in their congregational life. Both the Masai women who run the group and the larger community see the savings and credit association as an expression of the local church, even though it is technically not owned and operated by the local church. In other words, as pictured in figure 2.1, the savings and credit association is a parachurch ministry that is "rooted in and lead(s) back to a believing community."

All of these considerations are summarized in the **Church and Parachurch Principle**.

> ***Church and Parachurch Principle***
>
> Parachurch ministries must be "rooted in and lead back to" the local congregation(s) that minister in the same location.

Although this principle is sound, there are clearly all sorts of practical challenges in applying it in the real world. For example, in the case of frontier missions work, where no local congregation has yet been established, the parachurch ministry will need to be "rooted in" a sending congregation(s) from a different context until a local church is planted. In addition, there may be contexts in which established congregations are simply not preaching the Word of God faithfully, implying that they are not legitimate churches. In such instances, efforts may need to be taken to plant new churches. And there are other caveats as well, but such caveats do not undermine the general principle.

Poverty Alleviation as a Foretaste of the Coming Kingdom

As mentioned earlier, Jesus's miracles were acts of reconciliation, restoring people to what they were created to be. In these acts, Jesus gave a preview of that great day when his kingdom will come in its fullness, a day in which there will be no more blind, or lame, or lepers, because full restoration will have come to the entire cosmos.

The church is an "ambassador" of King Jesus and has been given the "ministry of reconciliation" (2 Corinthians 5:18–21). Therefore, like the King it represents, the church must pursue integral mission in a way that is restorative so that its acts will also give a preview of the coming kingdom. When working with people who are poor, such restoration involves helping the poor to be able to work and to support themselves and their families through that work, because that is part of what humans were created to do (2 Thessalonians 3:6–10; 1 Timothy 5:1–15). Indeed, being able to work and to support one's family through that work is part of what it means to be human (Genesis 1:28–30).

Unfortunately, not all approaches to poverty alleviation accomplish this; in fact, many well-meaning attempts to help the poor often cripple the poor by undermining their desire and capacity to work.[27] These considerations lead to the **Poverty-Alleviation Principle**.

The Masai church's microfinance ministry is consistent with the **Poverty-Alleviation Principle**. The women in the savings and credit association have been empowered to be very productive, using their gifts to work and to help their families to thrive. In fact, the restoration is so complete that the Masai women are becoming restorers of others. As the Masai missionary states, "I want to teach the girls living in the interior regions, so that I can empower them to be just like us."

Poverty-Alleviation Principle

Poverty alleviation is the ministry of reconciliation, seeking to restore poor people to what God created them to be. One result is that people will be able to glorify God through work and to support their families through that work.

Summary

Ironically, in an era of unprecedented wealth and rapid globalization, the local church in the Global South, a "church of the poor" with few material gifts, is on center stage in the unfolding drama of the kingdom. Hence, as the global body pursues the Great Commission, it must use strategies that strengthen the local church's ability to pursue integral mission, working in such a way that the gifts and testimony of the local church are enhanced rather than undermined. Furthermore, integral mission must be done in such a way that the poor are restored to what God created them to be: people who can work and support their families through that work. The microfinance ministries described in this book are consistent with these principles.

Application Questions

1. Are your church and its ministry partners pursuing "integral mission," or are they making the mistake of ministering only in words or only in deeds?

2. If you are working with a parachurch organization, how effectively is your work engaging, supporting, and empowering the local church? What changes could you make to do this more effectively?

3. Does your church see parachurch ministries as a blessing or a curse? What changes could you make to work with parachurch ministries more effectively?

4. Are your church's or organization's current ministries amongst the poor helping to restore them to being able to work and to support their families through that work? Or are your approaches actually undermining their capacity to work? What changes could you make to enable your ministries to be more restorative?

CHAPTER 3

INTEGRAL MISSION: AVOIDING UNHEALTHY DEPENDENCIES

> There were no needy persons among them. For from time to time those who owned land or houses sold them, brought the money from the sales and put it at the apostles' feet, and it was distributed to anyone who had need.
>
> —*Acts 4:34–35*

> When Western missionaries use their ethnocentric influence and economic affluence in ministry, they inevitably birth ministries that are carbon copies of their expensive, Western forms of Christianity. This action makes it nearly impossible for local disciples of Christ to implement effective evangelism, discipleship, worship, acts of compassion, leadership training, and church planting by mobilizing their own local resources and cultural expressions.
>
> —*Jean Johnson, missionary to Cambodia*[1]

As we saw in the previous chapter, integral mission has been part of the church since its inception;[2] however, two new realities present unique challenges and opportunities for pursing integral mission in the twenty-first century. First, the center of Christianity has shifted to the Global South, meaning that the Great Commission is largely in the hands of churches with few material resources. Second, coexisting with these materially poor churches are Christians from wealthy nations, who possess unprecedented economic, human, and technological resources. Taken together, these realities raise two practical questions for the body of Christ at the start of the twenty-first century:

1. *How can materially poor churches and indigenous missionaries in the Global South advance the Great Commission in the context of widespread poverty inside their congregations and communities?*
2. *What are the roles of financially prosperous churches, mission agencies, Christian relief and development organizations, church-equipping ministries, and donors in this process?*

Answering these two key questions requires the global body to develop new strategies and ministry models for the twenty-first century, for unfortunately, all too often the approaches being used create two unhealthy dependencies: (1) unhealthy dependencies on the part of the churches in the Global South; and (2) unhealthy dependencies on the part of poor individuals and communities to whom the global body is trying to minister. This chapter considers some of the broad principles that should shape these strategies and argues that the Masai church's microfinance ministry represents a model that is consistent with these broad principles.

From Dependence to Dignity for Churches in the Global South

There is considerable debate within the missions community about how to answer these two key questions.

For missions strategists like John Rowell, the answer lies in mobilizing the vast resources of Christians in the West, who possess greater financial wealth than any other Christians in history. Rowell argues that the biblical call to generosity requires Western churches and individual Christians to use their wealth to help needy churches to engage in ministry in the Global South.[3] He would undoubtedly have the same view of wealthy Christians in non-Western nations as well.

Other strategists, like Glenn Schwartz, strongly disagree, arguing that channeling resources from wealthy nations will create crippling dependencies in the churches in the Global South, preventing them from using their own gifts to develop effective and expanding ministries.[4] Such strategists often appeal to the venerated "three-self paradigm" developed by John Nevius in the nineteenth century, which states that new churches must be *self-governing*, *self-supporting*, and *self-propagating*. Schwartz argues that introducing outside funds, even during the early stages of a new church, will undermine that church's ability to achieve the "three selfs."

Although Rowell agrees with Schwartz that unhealthy dependencies should be avoided, he does not believe that such dependencies are inherent to the channeling of financial resources from wealthy nations to churches and ministries in the Global South. In his book *To Give or Not to Give? Rethinking Dependency, Restoring Generosity, and Redefining Sustainability*, Rowell states:

> As a premise, I am suggesting that dependency need not be a problem, even when outside funding predominates, if Western contributions are made without strings being attached and if national leaders are able to assert themselves by taking their rightful role in casting vision and initiating ministry. If national leaders are truly autonomous and if they remain free from control exercised by more well-provisioned partners, the negative realities we associate with dependency can be largely reduced without denying legitimately needed support for the poor.[5]

Schwartz strongly disagrees. In his book *When Charity Destroys Dignity: Overcoming Unhealthy Dependency in the Christian Movement*, he states:

> [Rowell's] book advocates a "Marshall Plan"[6] of mission giving to mobilize large amounts of money in western churches in support of cross-cultural church planting. It represents a massive donor-driven missiology which is characterized more by compassion for the donor's need to give, than for preserving the dignity of those who are to be helped. In that respect, it represents the tragedy of well-meaning compassion. If such an emphasis is carried out, it will increase rather than decrease the number of those affected by unhealthy dependency. And that means that overcoming such dependency will be an even greater challenge than it already is.[7]

This ongoing debate over dependency is not just an academic exercise; indeed, the forces of globalization have made the sharing of resources an issue that the global body deals with on a daily basis. Due to lower costs of travel, instantaneous global communication via the internet, and the growth of short-term missions, most individual congregations in Western nations and in other wealthy regions are now engaged in some fashion with ministry in the Global South. This engagement spans a wide range of activities: funding expatriate missionaries, sending short-term teams, constructing buildings, or paying the salaries of indigenous workers. *Indeed, churches in wealthy nations and churches in the Global South are in greater contact on a regular basis than at any time in history.*

And as they come into greater contact with one another, they immediately encounter a glaring reality: *the tremendous disparities in wealth between them*. Even the average congregation in the West possesses financial, human, and technological resources that are greater than the vast majority of the congregations throughout human history. In contrast, many of the congregations in the Global South are not just *ministering to* the poorest people on the planet: they are *comprised of* the poorest people on the planet. Simply put: coexisting within the body of Christ are people living in different worlds. And due to globalization, these two worlds are increasingly coming into contact with one another, thereby placing the issue of resource sharing—and hence the issue of dependency—on center stage daily.

In Search of Healthy Interdependency within the Global Body

So which side is right in the dependency debate: Schwartz's or Rowell's?[8]

It is beyond the purpose of this book to provide a detailed analysis of all the arguments in this debate; however, we authors have several core convictions on this issue, convictions that are shared by many—and perhaps most—mission strategists.

First, Schwartz's concerns about the dangers of unhealthy dependency within the body of Christ are entirely valid, for the history of Western missions has some very disturbing features.

On the one hand, there is no doubt that God used Western missionaries in powerful ways, many of them dying from disease or martyrdom in the process of spreading the gospel. These heroes of the faith are worthy of our highest respect and admiration.

At the same time, like all of us, Western missionaries were sinful and imperfect, and there were often some very harmful dimensions to their approach. During what some refer to as the "era of dependence" from 1793–1945,[9] Western missions in the Global South were often shaped by colonial attitudes, cultural imperialism, and the Enlightenment worldview. As a result, Western institutions and culture were often exported as though they were inherent to the gospel. The implicit goal behind many of these efforts was to make the Global South, which was "underdeveloped" and "heathen," more like the West, which was "developed" and "Christian."

The effects were devastating on many levels. Churches and individual poor people in the Global South were often crippled by feelings of inadequacy and inferiority. Moreover, they often lacked the financial and human resources to sustain the Western institutions that were exported to them—e.g., large church buildings—making them necessarily dependent on the West to sustain their ministries.[10] As a result, churches in the Global South have often been disempowered from using their own gifts—human, spiritual, cultural, and financial—to minister effectively in their own contexts, which they understand better than Westerners typically do.

Unfortunately, these problems did not cease with the end of the era of colonization. As churches in the West increasingly engage with their brothers and sisters in the Global South, they often repeat many of the same mistakes as their ancestors. For example, in describing current attempts at partnerships between churches in the West and the Global South, Ajith Fernando, a church leader from Sri Lanka, reports that non-Christians in his country believe "a new colonialism has dawned: 'First the Christians came with the Bible in one hand and the sword in the other. Now they come with the Bible in one hand and dollars in the other.' "[11] Similarly, a recent gathering of church leaders from West Africa identified "neocolonialism" as one of the problems they face in working with the Western church.[12]

Although there are many aspects to neocolonialism, unhealthy financial dependencies play such a predominant role that the Lausanne Movement recently engaged in a multiyear, global listening process that resulted in the *Lausanne Standards: Affirmations and Agreements for Giving and Receiving Money in Mission*. In describing the rationale for creating these standards, Lausanne states:

> During widespread discussions in the Lausanne movement, concerns have been expressed about problems related to international funding of mission projects, activities, and organizations. Many, though not

> all, believed these problems were seriously interfering with the goal of bringing the *whole gospel* to the *whole world*.[13]

The standards then specifically warn that the problem of "unhealthy dependency" can arise when foreign funds are used to support local ministries.[14]

In summary, Glenn Schwartz is right: "unhealthy dependency" is a major problem in the global church, and both the church in wealthy nations and the church in the Global South need to diligently search for ways to avoid this plague.

However, it is too strong a statement to say that the problem of "unhealthy dependency" implies that the vast resources of the church in wealthy nations should all remain at home.

The Bible envisions the global church as one body with no national or geographic boundaries. This one body is called to steward all of its resources—spiritual, human, technological, theological, organizational, and financial—in order to achieve the Great Commission: *together.* Indeed, one of the key concerns of the New Testament is the sharing of financial resources across congregations. Acts 11:29–30 discusses an offering taken by the church in Antioch for the needy church in Judea. And Paul writes extensively about an offering taken from congregations located in the northwest extreme of the body for a needy congregation located in the southeast extreme of the body, i.e., the church in Jerusalem (Romans 15:23–33; 1 Corinthians 16:1–4; 2 Corinthians 8–9).[15] In fact, Paul considered the delivery of this offering to be so important, that he was willing to risk his life in order to deliver the funds himself (Romans 15:30–31).

Moreover, it is clear that such transfers of financial resources were to be an ongoing part of the life of the global body. Consider Paul's explanation to the church in Corinth about the offering they were taking:

> Our desire is not that others might be relieved while you are hard pressed, but that there might be equality. At the present time your plenty will supply what they need, so that in turn their plenty will supply what you need. The goal is equality, as it is written: "The one who gathered much did not have too much, and the one who gathered little did not have too little." (2 Corinthians 8:13–15)

In other words, Paul envisioned the church—not only as a local congregation—but as a global fellowship of congregations that would be transferring resources from those which had much to those which had little. What an incredible challenge for the global body in the twenty-first century, a body that has greater economic disparities within it than at any time in its history!

Yes, unhealthy dependency is a major problem, but as Chuck Bennett, the former head of Partners International, once stated:

> To refuse to share our resources with overseas brethren because there have been abuses is like saying we should outlaw marriage because some husbands beat their wives. The problem is real, but the solution is simplistic. I'm convinced it's possible to "help without hurting."[16]

It is for these reasons that many missions strategists[17] are calling for the global body to pursue partnerships characterized by "interdependence" or "healthy dependency," which strategist Daniel Rickett defines as "the capacity to use outside resources (e.g., foreign funds) while reinforcing the qualities of autonomy, responsibility, and resourcefulness."[18] Rickett argues that in a healthy dependency, both parties:

- Maintain their independence and capacity to instruct, correct, and refuse the other.
- Honor and uphold the unique and divine calling of the other.
- Recognize their responsibilities, and work to fulfill them.
- Trust God for what they need, and make the most of the resources at hand.
- Act in a manner that safeguards the other's dignity and honors Christ.[19]

In the context of pursuing the Great Commission, the central agent that must be strengthened and honored in any partnership is the local church. Again, this is not meant to imply that there is no role for parachurch ministries or for ecclesiastical structures above the congregational level, but simply to recognize that, as discussed in the previous chapter, the local church is the primary manifestation of Jesus Christ in its community.[20] In keeping with Rickett's principles of healthy dependency, it is vital that global partnerships enable the local church to fulfill its divine calling by faithfully executing its responsibilities; in other words, the local church needs to be and do what God has created it to be and do: *the embodiment of Jesus Christ that engages in integral mission*.

And therein lies the tremendous tension in mission strategies in the twenty-first century. In a global church characterized by enormous disparities in wealth, it is immensely challenging to create strategies that allow for transfers of wealth across the global body *and* that simultaneously honor the calling and responsibility of the local church to be the embodiment of Jesus Christ in its own culture. Under an avalanche of foreign personnel, technology, and financial resources, how can the local congregation use its own gifts and resources to preach the Word and to engage in "works of service" in ways that embody Jesus Christ in its own cultural setting? How can the global body function in such a way that the local congregation can *be* the message it is called to *be*?

Although there are many unknowns about the best ways to foster healthy interdependencies in the global body in the twenty-first century, protecting the calling of the local church and its ability to fulfill its mission should be nonnegotiable.

It is in light of these considerations that the **Integral Mission Principle** incorporates the role of the global body.

> ***Integral Mission Principle***
>
> The *global* body must function in such a way that the *local* church is able to use its gifts to engage in integral mission: proclaiming and demonstrating among people who are poor the good news of the kingdom of God in a contextually appropriate way.

Practical Suggestions for Moving from Dependence to Dignity Within the Global Body

These considerations have profound implications for the global body's design and execution of strategies for integral mission, raising a number of difficult questions:

- At whose pace should initiatives proceed? At the pace of churches and organizations from wealthy nations or at the pace of local churches in the Global South?

- Will the scale of various ministries be consistent with the capacities of local churches and people or with the capacities of outsiders?
- When should outside resources be used? How?

This book cannot provide definitive answers to all of those questions. Indeed, it will take decades of experimentation for the global body to find such answers. However, a number of experts have provided some helpful guidelines that are worthy of consideration:

- In general, the role of the outsider is a backstage role: encouraging and supporting the local church, which must remain on center stage in its context.[21]
- Bring in outside resources (human, financial, technological, and organizational) only when those resources are not available locally and cannot be developed locally. Bring in outside resources in a way that complements, rather than undermines, the use of local resources.[22]
- Parachurch ministries should be designed in such a way that they mobilize the local church's resources and draw people into the life of the local church.[23] See the **Church and Parachurch Principle**.
- Because the kingdom is to spread over the entire cosmos (Isaiah 9:7), seek—from the very start—to design ministries that are *replicable, indigenous, and sustainable.*[24]

From Dependence to Dignity for Poor People

In addition to observing the **Integral Mission Principle**, it is vitally important that the **Poverty-Alleviation Principle** be maintained as well.

Clearly, it would be a terrible tragedy if churches and ministries were using approaches to poverty alleviation that undermined the dignity of the

> ***Poverty-Alleviation Principle***
>
> Poverty alleviation is the ministry of reconciliation, seeking to restore poor people to what God created them to be. One result is that people will be able to glorify God through work and to support their families through that work.

poor, trapping them in crippling dependencies that prevented them from being able to support themselves through their own work. Unfortunately, as explained in *When Helping Hurts*, well-meaning churches often have faulty assumptions about the true nature of poverty, causing them to use ministries that fail to truly empower the poor by restoring them to what God created them to be. In particular, churches tend to assume that poverty is due to a lack of material resources, which can lead churches to drown the poor in handouts that undermine, rather than build, their capacity as image bearers.

The good news is that it does not have to be this way. There are powerful options that churches can use to minister in ways that are consistent with the **Poverty-Alleviation Principle**, i.e., ministries that give a preview of the full restoration that the kingdom will one day bring.

When used properly, microfinance is one such option. Indeed, the rest of this book is dedicated to explaining how to pursue this option well in the context of integral mission in the Global South.

From Dependence to Dignity Amongst the Masai

One of the exciting features of the Masai church's microfinance ministry is that it avoids the two dependencies described in this chapter.

First, the global body has collaborated in such a way that the Masai church is not dependent in an unhealthy way on outside resources. As a result, the Masai church is able to use its own human, spiritual, and financial gifts to pursue integral mission in its own context (see the **Integral Mission Principle**). Westerners played a role in this story, providing consulting, training, and some financial resources. But all of these were offered in a nuanced, backstage, complementary, and supportive role in order to allow the Masai church to fulfill its calling and to minister in ways that no Westerner could.[25] In fact, in keeping with the guidelines mentioned above, the design of this microfinance ministry is *replicable, indigenous,* and *sustainable*. As a result, the Masai church will be able to expand this ministry on its own, with little or no additional foreign assistance.[26]

Second, the Masai church is avoiding unhealthy dependency on the part of the poor people to whom it is ministering (see the **Poverty-**

Alleviation Principle). Amazingly, the church is actually equipping poor women to use their own resources—human, financial, social, spiritual, and managerial—to minister to one another in the context of the savings and credit association, which the women own and operate themselves. And as they do so, these women are engaged in highly restorative ministry: helping one another to work in order to sustain themselves and their families.

In summary, the Masai church's microfinance ministry is an example of the type of strategy needed to advance the Great Commission in the twenty-first century: *the global body working together in such a way that materially poor churches in the Global South can pursue integral mission, using their own resources to bring restoration to the poor using ministries that are replicable, indigenous, and sustainable.*

Summary

The global body of Christ is blessed with greater financial, human, and technological resources than ever before. This presents both tremendous opportunities and challenges, for these resources need to be unleashed in such a way that they foster dignity rather than unhealthy dependency both on the part of materially poor churches in the Global South and on the part of the poor people to whom those churches are ministering. Hence, the global body needs to develop new strategies and ministry models as it seeks to use integral mission to pursue the Great Commission in the twenty-first century. The Masai church's microfinance ministry is an example of one such model. The remainder of this book is dedicated to explaining how to design and implement such microfinance ministries effectively.

Application Questions

1. If you have been blessed with financial resources, what, if any, are some ways in which you may have created unhealthy dependencies on the part of your ministry partners? What do you think are the factors that led to this? What changes could you make?

2. If you are a church or a ministry with few financial resources, what, if any, are some ways in which you are dependent in an unhealthy way on your financial supporters? What do you think are the factors that led to this? What changes could you make?

3. Think about a ministry in which you are participating that is seeking to help materially poor people. What, if any, are some ways in which this ministry is creating an unhealthy dependency on the part of the people it is trying to help? What do you think are the factors that led to this? What changes could you make?

4. Daniel Rickett, an expert on global partnerships, has a resource that can be used to evaluate cross-cultural ministry partnerships. Review the health of your ministry partnerships by evaluating them in light of Rickett's tool, *Checklist for Building Strategic Relationships,* which can be found on the website associated with this book. Also consider reading Rickett's excellent book: *Building Strategic Relationships: A Practical Guide to Partnering with Non-Western Missions* (Stern Press, 2008).

CHAPTER 4

MICROFINANCE: SO MUCH LESS . . . AND SO MUCH MORE

Because of the savings and credit associations, our husbands beat us less than they did before.

—*Poor women in church-centered microfinance ministry in Togo, West Africa*[1]

If your daughter shows a flair for guitar, you don't force her to paint instead. Just so, my evaluation leads to a prescription to help microfinance play to its strengths. Instead of using it to put capital in the hands of as many poor people as possible on the hope of launching them all into entrepreneurship and out of poverty, focus on mass-producing services to help people manage the uncertainties of being poor. To the extent practical, deemphasize pure credit, which amplifies risk, in favor of savings and insurance, which can cushion in times of trouble.

—*David Roodman, microfinance researcher*[2]

As mentioned earlier, the standard story of microfinance has become almost legendary: *Lend money to poor people so that they can start or expand microenterprises in order to earn a living. As a result, the incomes of the poor borrowers go up, lifting them and their families out of poverty. Moreover, as the loans are repaid, the money can be lent over and over to lift even more people out of poverty. If one is looking for a sustainable approach to poverty alleviation, it does not get much better than this!*

This "microcredit-for-microenterprises" story of microfinance is truly inspiring, so inspiring that for the past several decades providing loans to aspiring microentrepreneurs has been one of the leading strategies—perhaps the premier strategy—for alleviating poverty in the Global South.

In reality, microfinance is both so much less and so much more than the "microcredit-for-microenterprises" story suggests. It is *less*, because it is unlikely that the vast majority of the world's poor will achieve a substantial increase in their incomes through loans to microenterprises. It is *more*, because researchers and practitioners are discovering that poor households need a vast range of financial services—including many types of loans, savings, insurance, and money-transfer services—and they are experimenting with innovative ways to address those needs. Seen in this light, microfinance has the potential to impact poor households in more ways—albeit in more subtle ways—and on a larger scale than the simple "microcredit-for-microenterprises" story suggests.

This is a critical juncture, as there is growing disillusionment with the "microcredit-for-microenterprises" story. In contrast to the legend, a number of recent studies have found that microloans are not launching most poor microentrepreneurs on a rapid upward trajectory out of poverty. In addition, reports of unscrupulous practices by some microfinance institutions in India and Mexico have left many people wondering if lenders to the poor are more interested in lining their own pockets than in helping the needy. This disillusionment is creating some danger that donors and decision makers will abandon microfinance altogether. This would be a tragedy. For the fact that microfinance is not what many thought it was does not negate the fact that it can be a powerful tool to improve the lives of billions of poor people, albeit in different ways than many had expected.

Thus, what is needed is a new narrative, a narrative that recalibrates our expectations. This new narrative needs to expect less out of the "microcredit-for-microenterprises" approach. At the same time, this new narrative needs to open our eyes to see the incredible opportunities for microfinance as a whole. Towards that end, the first section of this chapter explains the limitations of "microcredit-for-microenterprises," while the second section introduces the vast potential of the "microfinance-for-households" approach for improving the lives of billions of poor people.

The Limits of the "Microcredit-for-Microenterprises" Strategy

Founded in 1976, the Grameen Bank of Bangladesh reports 8.6 million poor members, having lent $15.5 billion since its inception, with an average repayment rate of 97 percent![3] Grameen's success has inspired many others to use the "microcredit-for-microenterprises" strategy, including missionaries, denominations, individual churches, parachurch ministries, and Christian relief development agencies. But by far the greatest volume of such loans have been provided by microfinance institutions (MFIs), nongovernment organizations (NGOs) like Grameen that are specifically created to lend money from donors or investors to microentrepreneurs.[4] Reaching over 204 million borrowers, MFIs are the premier vehicle for the "microcredit-for-microenterprises" strategy.[5] As such, although the discussion below is relevant to all who are lending to microenterprises, MFIs' loans will be the focal point.

Why is it too much to expect that MFIs' "microcredit-for-microenterprises" strategy will lift the vast majority of the world's poor out of poverty? There are at least three reasons.

An Insufficient Number of Microentrepreneurs

First, there are simply not enough "microentrepreneurs" to enable microenterprise loans to end global poverty. Consider figure 4.1, which provides estimates of the primary sources of income for the world's poor, defined as the approximately 2.6 billion people living on less than $2 per day.[6] As this figure illustrates, of the 1.6 billion poor people who are of *working age*, only 180 million—11 percent—can be classified as "microentrepreneurs," that is, poor people whose *primary* occupation consists of operating their own small businesses. In other words, only 11 percent of the world's *working* poor—less than 7 percent of the total number of poor people in the world—could even hope to be the type of person who could get a business loan to lift themselves out of poverty. And, as will be discussed further below, receiving such a loan is no guarantee that the microenterprise will generate positive profits, much less move the owner and their family out of poverty.

Of course, one could argue that business loans to this 7 percent could have impacts on the wider economy through a "trickle-down" effect: successful microenterprises need to hire employees, creating jobs for

FIGURE 4.1 Primary Sources of Income for People Living on Less than $2 Per Day

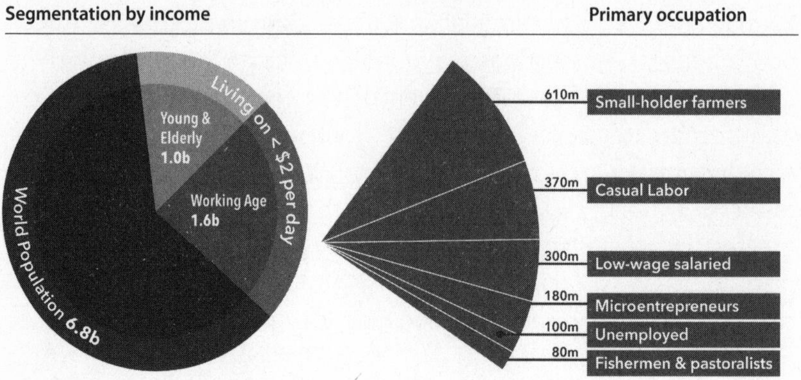

From Bill & Melinda Gates Foundation, "Financial Services for the Poor: Strategy Overview," *Global Development Program* (November 2010): 8.

those who are not entrepreneurs. Unfortunately, this "trickle-down" effect does not appear to occur. Research has found that microenterprises hire only a tiny number of workers beyond the owners' family members. Using data from thirteen Global South countries, Banerjee and Duflo find that microenterprises headed by people who are living on $2 per day or less employ between 0.10–0.25 nonfamily members, i.e., not even a half-time person.[7]

It is important to note that many microentrepreneurs that borrow from MFIs live above $2 per day. One would expect these people to have larger microenterprises and the capacity to employ more people as their businesses grow. Unfortunately, Banerjee and Duflo find that even microenterprises headed by people living on $6–$10 per day—well above the poverty line of $2 per day, only employ between 0.70–1.20 nonfamily members.[8]

MFIs' Products Are Mismatched with the Needs of Many Poor Microentrepreneurs

There is a second reason that the "microcredit-for-microenterprises" strategy is unlikely to lift the vast majority of the world's poor out of poverty: *MFIs' typical loan products are usually unable to serve many of the 180 million microentrepreneurs living on less than $2 per day*. There are at least three reasons for this:

- MFIs need to cover their costs of operations, and it is much cheaper to work in urban areas than rural ones, as greater population density lowers the transportation costs per borrower. Unfortunately, despite the rapid growth in cities' populations, as much as 75 percent of the world's poor still live in rural areas,[9] placing many of them beyond the reach of MFIs.
- It is expensive to lend very small amounts of money. As a result, most MFIs cannot afford to offer loans smaller than $40–$50, a size which is too large and too risky for the poorest people.
- In addition to being very small, the incomes of many microentrepreneurs are highly "*irregular and unpredictable*,"[10] implying that they need to be able to access loans on a very short notice and to have considerable flexibility in repaying their loans. In contrast, MFIs' standard loan products are often rigid in terms of both availability and repayment schedules, thereby making such loans inappropriate for many microentrepreneurs.

In order to illustrate the last two points and to lay a foundation for what is ahead, consider the story of Pumza from the pathbreaking book *Portfolios of the Poor: How the World's Poor Live on $2 a Day.*[11]

Pumza supports herself and her four children by selling cooked sheep intestines in a crowded urban area of Cape Town, South Africa. Her total income consists of business profits of approximately $95 per month and government-provided child support of $25 per month, meaning that this family lives on an average of $0.80 per member per day.

Pumza's microenterprise is a simple one. Every day she spends about five dollars to buy raw sheep intestines, cooks them on an open fire, and sells them to passersby. About once a month she travels to buy wood for the fire, spending between one and five dollars, depending on how much wood she decides to buy.

Pumza's microenterprise is a simple one, but it is full of drama nonetheless. For in addition to Pumza's revenues being low, her revenues are also highly *irregular and unpredictable*, as pictured in figure 4.2. If Pumza's sales are low today, she can be in real trouble, as she will not have the money she needs to buy raw sheep intestines to sell tomorrow. Why doesn't Pumza just sell today's unsold sheep intestines tomorrow? Customers prefer fresh meat, so if she tries to sell today's

FIGURE 4.2 Pumza's Business Revenues and Expenses

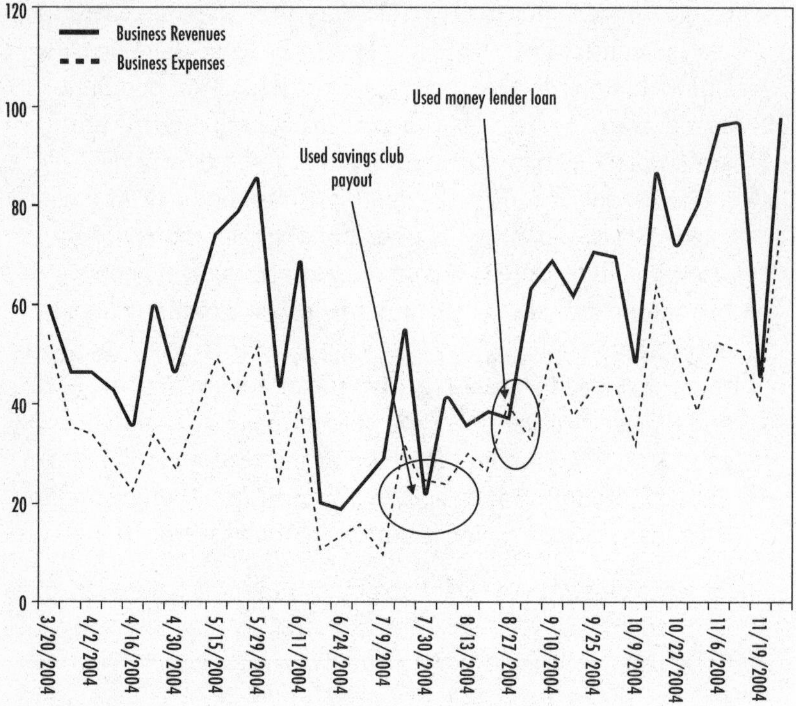

Figures are daily cash flows aggregated biweekly. U.S. dollars converted from South African rand at \$ = 6.5 rand rate are on vertical axis. Figure is from Daryl Collins, Jonathan Morduch, Stuart Rutherford, and Orlanda Ruthven, *Portfolios of the Poor: How the World's Poor Live on \$2 a Day* (Princeton, N.J.: Princeton University Press, 2009), 41.

unsold meat tomorrow, she will lose customers to other sellers. She needs cash today to buy the raw intestines so that she can earn enough to survive tomorrow.

Sometimes Pumza can solve a sales shortfall by using the child-support money she receives from the government, but when that is not available she needs immediate access to cash to enable her to buy the inventory she needs. Unfortunately, as for most poor people, Pumza does not have access to a financial system—e.g., a bank—that enables her to save and to borrow money whenever she needs it. Hence, she sometimes has to borrow from an informal money lender—whom some would call a "loan shark" or a "shylock"—who charges her 30 percent interest per month, which becomes 360 percent interest per annum.

Seeking to avoid this high interest payment, Pumza has also formed a savings and credit association with some other sheep intestine sellers. Pumza and the other group members make daily savings contributions to this association and take turns receiving a payout from the group, a payout that Pumza uses to purchase her business supplies.

As will be described in chapter 8, savings and credit associations represent an informal form of microfinance that can provide capital for microenterprises and other purposes. Although these associations are sometimes simply referred to as "savings groups," this book calls them "savings and credit associations," because these groups provide *both* savings and lending services to their members.

The oval regions in figure 4.2 illustrate the days on which Pumza has used the loans from the money lender and the payouts from the savings and credit association to finance her business so that she can keep food on her family's table.

It is crucial to note that there are MFIs operating in Cape Town that would be a potential loan source for Pumza, but she is not using them. The loan that Pumza needs to buy a day's worth of sheep intestines is too small to make her an appealing client to most MFIs.[12] Furthermore, the *irregularity and unpredictability* of her income require financial services that are available on a daily notice and have flexible repayment schedules. As summarized in *Portfolios of the Poor*, like all poor people, Pumza needs financial services that are *convenient, flexible, and reliable*.[13] Although sound MFIs provide very reliable services, their standardized procedures are often lacking when it comes to convenience and flexibility. Both the money lender and the savings and credit associations can be superior on both counts, so superior that Pumza is willing to pay high interest rates to obtain the convenience and flexibility she needs.[14]

Note that the drama in Pumza's microenterprise is not just a business drama, it is a household drama. The daily fluctuations in the profits of microentrepreneurs translate into daily fluctuations in their households' ability to feed their children, to get them medical care, to keep them in school, to have peace of mind, and to be able to think about the future. As will be discussed further below, one of the greatest impacts of microfinance may very well be reducing the fluctuations in these incomes.

The Questionable Impacts of MFIs' Loans

There is a third reason that the "microcredit-for-microenterprises" strategy is unlikely to lift the vast majority of the world's poor out of poverty: *It is not clear that MFIs' loans actually help to reduce poverty for the average borrower.* How can this be? Aren't there thousands of stories of people who have received microenterprise loans and who appear to be better off?

Yes, there are, but such stories are insufficient to prove that business loans for microenterprises are effective at reducing poverty for most borrowers. In reality, there is a continuum of outcomes from these loans. For some borrowers, the loans result in an increase in their incomes; for others, the loans have no effect at all; and for some, the loans may actually plunge them deeper into poverty. Stories of positive impact do not reveal what is happening overall, or even what is happening to the average borrower.

Of course, like any NGO, MFIs have an incentive to report successful outcomes to appeal to their constituencies. Therefore, even if the average outcome for borrowers is negative, there may still be plenty of positive stories that can be told. Moreover, if the microentrepreneurs that experience negative outcomes from their loans drop out of the program—which is likely—then the most visible clients of an MFI will be those who have been successful.[15] As a result, a casual visitor to an MFI that meets with a group of the MFI's current borrowers will generally see only those borrowers that have been helped by the program.[16]

But while they are generally less visible, borrowers who have been hurt from taking MFIs' loans really do exist. For example, in one highly publicized incident in October 2010, the government of the state of Andhra Pradesh in India virtually shut down MFIs' operations there in response to reports of suicides resulting from overindebtedness of MFI clients. It appears that profit seeking by MFIs and other lenders resulted in a highly competitive environment in which too much loan capital was chasing too few qualified borrowers. In the absence of information sharing amongst these lenders about the total amount of debt that each borrower was incurring, many borrowers took too many loans from multiple lenders, burying themselves with a debt load that they could not handle. And as these borrowers struggled to repay their loans, some lenders reportedly employed heavy-handed collection techniques, pushing a number of borrowers into despair.

Just as the Andhra Pradesh incident was raising concerns, several sophisticated studies were released that found no empirical evidence that microloans had any impact on standard measures of material poverty in the first eleven to twenty-two months.[17] Although these studies are helpful and should be taken seriously, like all research, they have some weaknesses. In particular, there is good reason to believe that many of the positive impacts of microfinance are likely to be long-term, perhaps even multigenerational. The current studies are too short-term in nature to capture these longer-term impacts. The appendix to this book describes the methodology of these studies in greater detail.

Although there is a need for much more research before it can be concluded that "microcredit-for-microenterprises" has no impact, the incidents in Andhra Pradesh and these empirical studies have combined to put the microcredit industry on the defensive and have given the entire industry some much-needed pause.[18] For example, the Microcredit Summit Campaign, which has historically been one of the leading proponents of microenterprise loans, states in its annual report for 2012 that it is time to "recover the soul of microfinance" and outlines a number of initiatives it is spearheading to protect borrowers and to improve the performance of MFIs.[19] The report also argues for expanding microfinance to include more services than simply loans for microenterprises, an issue which will be discussed in greater detail below.

The Source of Widespread Poverty Reduction

In summary, the "microcredit-for-microenterprises" story has led many to have expectations that neither the loans nor the microentrepreneurs could fulfill. It is simply too much to expect that microenterprises operated by some of the world's poorest people could be the primary engine for economic growth and for poverty alleviation, even in the limited material sense of raising people's incomes above the poverty line. There are simply too few microentrepreneurs living on less than two dollars per day, MFIs cannot serve many of them, and the loans to them appear to have too limited an impact. As Roodman states, it is time for a completely different perspective on these microenterprise owners:

> Labeling them "microentrepreneurs" romanticizes their plight and implies too much hope for their escape. ... A less fashionable view of poor entrepreneurs ... is as victims of economic systems that fail to employ them. To put this more constructively, since the Industrial Revolution, explosive job creation has powered all national economic successes. Comprehensive economic development is hard to imagine without increases in jobs. In this view, the people of whom we speak [i.e., the microenterprise owners] have not benefited from such development. They are "people without jobs" or "self-employed" ... who heroically but tenuously survive their circumstances. ... Poor people are engaged in just getting by.[20]

Indeed, even when one considers the "middle class" in the Global South, it does not appear that there are a sufficiently large number of dynamic microentrepreneurs for microenterprises to serve as the primary engine of economic growth and poverty alleviation. In their surveys from thirteen Global South countries, Banerjee and Duflo find that as a household's income rises above the poverty level of two dollars per day per person, the households typically try to obtain jobs for family members rather than expand their microenterprises. In fact, Banerjee and Duflo find that "having a regular, well-paying, salaried job may ... be the most important difference between the poor and middle class."[21]

Indeed, most economists believe that a necessary condition for widespread poverty alleviation—in the purely material sense of raising incomes above the poverty line—is rapid economic growth on a national level that is driven by increases in agricultural productivity and mass industrialization,[22] with China being the most recent example. It is through rising agricultural output and small-, medium-, and large-scale enterprises—not microenterprises—that the Global South can create enough jobs to achieve widespread reductions in poverty.

In the absence of such overall economic growth, poor people are often forced to become self-employed via their own microenterprises. But being an "entrepreneur by force" is fundamentally different from being truly gifted with the skills and resources to start and expand a business enterprise that can create jobs and become part of the engine of economic growth for the country as a whole. The poor need jobs, and creating enough jobs to eradicate poverty will take something more than business loans to microentrepreneurs. In this sense, microfinance is not the silver bullet that many have assumed.

However, as described in the next section, a broader perspective on microfinance than the simple "microcredit-for-microenterprise" story opens up a whole new world of possibilities for microfinance than most people have imagined.

The Vast Potential of "Microfinance-for-Households"

In order to understand this broader perspective, it is helpful to start by focusing on poor *households* rather than on the *microenterprises* that only a small fraction of those households own. Then we can ask: *What are the financial services needed by the 2.6 billion people living in those households?*

As *Portfolios of the Poor* illustrates, this approach opens up a whole new world of possibilities for microfinance to improve the lives of poor people. Building upon earlier studies,[23] the research team for *Portfolios of the Poor* interviewed poor households at least twice a month for a full year, enabling them to create "financial diaries" that sought to document every penny that flowed in and out of their sample of 250 households from Bangladesh, India, and South Africa.

The picture that emerges in *Portfolios of the Poor* is of poor households that are intensely engaged—every day—in using a wide range of activities to enable them to manage their money. The financial tools these households use to accomplish this day-to-day financial management comprise their "portfolios," just as stocks, bonds, and mutual funds comprise the portfolios used by wealthier people around the world. *Portfolios of the Poor* argues that despite their very low incomes—indeed *because* they have very low incomes—poor people living on less than two dollars per day are more *actively* engaged in day-to-day financial management than the rest of the world. This finding provides the opportunity for microfinance to address far more issues than the "microcredit-for-microenterprise" story has led the world to believe.

Portfolio Management for Vulnerable Households

To illustrate, consider the lives of Subir, age thirty-seven, his wife, Mumtaz, age twenty-nine, and their children, ranging in age from a newborn to fourteen years old.[24] The family lives rent-free on a small plot of government-owned land in Dhaka, the capital city of Bangladesh. More than a decade earlier, Subir and Mumtaz moved to Dhaka after the Ganges River washed away their tiny parcel of land in central Bangladesh. With almost no money, Subir and Mumtaz settled in an area known as the "fire slum," because it burned down so often. There they built a hut with timber and bamboo walls and corrugated tin sheets for the roof.

Subir and Mumtaz have access to a free public water pump and a free public toilet, both of which they share with the others in the slum. Their only monthly utility bill is the few pennies they pay for the electricity to operate the single lightbulb in their hut.

In contrast to the image of a microentrepreneur, the family patches together its income from a variety of sources:

- Subir pedals a rickshaw owned by a local transportation business, usually working no more than four days per week due to the very physical demands of this job. On occasion, he is given the opportunity to drive a motorized rickshaw. On a good day, Subir earns $2.50, but his earnings fluctuate dramatically, depending on "weather, political strife, harassment by the police, and simple good and bad luck."[25]
- Following the birth of their fifth child, Mumtaz returns to working as a maid, earning approximately $10 per month.
- Iqbal, the fourteen-year-old son, earns some money picking scrap metal and does not attend school regularly. Toward the end of the year of the financial diaries, he gets a job in a garment factory earning $27 per month.
- Salauddin, the ten-year-old son, picks rags, earning $6 in a good month.

The total income from all of these sources results in an average income of only $0.27–$0.45 per family member per day, placing them in the category of "extreme poor," i.e., people living on less than $1.25 per day.

But, as in the case of Pumza, focusing solely on the family's low level of income misses two other central features of that income: it is *irregular and highly unpredictable*. For a family teetering on the edge, these income fluctuations—which are small in absolute terms but huge in percentage terms—represent significant threats to their daily existence. Indeed, when a family's daily income falls below the "vulnerability line" in figure 4.3, the family faces significant stresses and risks that typically include the following:

- *malnutrition*, which exposes all of them—but especially infants—to physical, psychological, and social trauma that can have lifelong effects;
- *untreated illnesses*, which can lead to lasting physical and cognitive impairment and even death;
- *removing children from school*, which undermines the family's long-run financial future;
- *family strife*, which can include physical and emotional abuse of women and children.[26]

Seeking to avoid these pitfalls, Subir and Mumtaz manage their finances *continuously* in order to smooth their daily consumption, saving on good days and borrowing on bad days in order to make sure

FIGURE 4.3 Consumption Smoothing

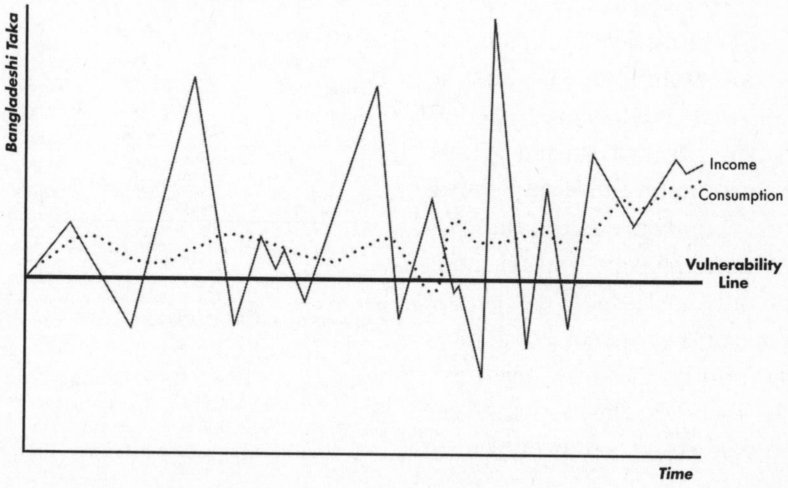

their daily needs are met. By using a variety of financial tools that enable them to save and borrow, Subir and Mumtaz seek to smooth their income into a "consumption curve" that is less variable and that stays above the "vulnerability line."

How do the poor do this? Figure 4.4 illustrates Subir and Mumtaz's closing balance and flows of assets and liabilities for the year in which they were part of the *Portfolios of the Poor* study (1999–2000). Note that while their overall balances are small, the annual turnover—i.e., the total amount of money flowing into and out of the household in each category—is quite large. Moreover, they are using a total of nine financial tools to manage their cash flows. Taken together, these two facts illustrate the point made earlier: *the poorest people in the world are very actively managing financial portfolios in order to smooth their consumption*. Remarkably, these financial transactions are being conducted by people who are poorly educated or illiterate. When asked how they can keep track of so many financial details, one poor woman explained, "We talk about it all the time, and that fixes it in our memories." Another added, "These things are important—they keep you awake at night."[27]

There are several other points to note from figure 4.4. First, in contrast to what many people believe, the poor can and do save. Even though Subir and Mumtaz's family are in the category of "Extreme Poor" and are living on only $0.27–$0.45 per person per day, they are not living "hand to mouth." Despite their meager incomes, they are still able to save money on good days. In

FIGURE 4.4 Portfolio Summary for Subir and Mumtaz Over the Research Year

	Closing balance	*Turnover*
Financial assets		
Microfinance savings	10.20	49.40
Private loans out	30.00	117.00
Home savings	5.00	18.00
Subtotal	$45.20	$184.40
Financial liabilities		
Microfinance loan	30.00	47.00
Interest-free loan	14.00	84.00
Private loan	15.00	105.00
Pawn loan	0	10.00
Moneyguarding	2.00	66.00
Shop credit	4.00	50.00
Subtotal	$65.00	362.00
Financial net worth	-$19.80	
Total turnover		$546.40

Note: US$ converted from Bangladesh takas at $=50 takas, market rate.

From table 2.2 in Daryl Collins, Jonathan Morduch, Stuart Rutherford, and Orlanda Ruthven, *Portfolios of the Poor: How the World's Poor Live on $2 a Day* (Princeton, N.J.: Princeton University Press, 2009), 34.

fact, it is this very ability to save that keeps them alive on bad days. Unfortunately, the historical focus of the microfinance industry on "microcredit-for-microenterprise" often overlooked the fact that poor people, who are highly vulnerable, would often prefer to save than borrow, as saving is less risky for them.[28]

Savings Principle

Poor people can and do save, but they need more effective systems for doing so.

Second, without access to formal financial service providers such as banks, Subir and Mumtaz are forced to rely on a portfolio of informal services to meet their consumption-smoothing needs, including saving under their mattress, borrowing from and lending to friends and relatives, obtaining loans from local shops and pawn stores, and "moneyguarding" by placing money on "deposit" with another family or holding such "deposits" for others. Although this informal finance system is vital, the households in the *Portfolios of the Poor* study regularly complained that these informal tools were far from satisfactory, lacking reliability, privacy, and transparency,[29] and thereby creating the opportunity for a microfinance ministry to improve the lives of the poor.

Third, note that loans from MFIs represent only a very small fraction of the total financial services being used by Subir and Mumtaz. Indeed, in the households in the *Portfolios of the Poor* sample, MFIs account for only 15 percent of all cash turnover, 13 percent of all assets, and 21 percent of all debt.[30] Again, the "microcredit-for-microenterprises" story misses a vast world of opportunities for addressing the financial service needs of poor households.

As discussed earlier, MFIs are typically unable to provide loans that are sufficiently small to serve the extreme poor like Subir and Mumtaz. Hence, it is somewhat surprising to see that Subir and Mumtaz have a loan from an MFI. Indeed, Subir and Mumtaz explain that they were originally not interested in MFIs, because they wanted to save, not borrow, and most MFIs focus on providing loans. Like many poor people, Subir and Mumtaz consider borrowing to be too risky, given their highly vulnerable situation. But over time, Subir and Mumtaz were able to find an MFI that provided savings services, enabling them to open an account that they used primarily for consumption smoothing. As Subir and Mumtaz grew more comfortable with this MFI, they eventually decided to take out a small loan; however, they did not use the money to buy a rickshaw for Subir so that he could be self-employed in his own microenterprise. Given that they had no safe place to park a rickshaw at night, they feared this strategy would be too risky. Rather, they used the loan to buy rice and a wooden cupboard and to make a loan of $20 to a fellow rickshaw driver.

Many observers fret when they see MFIs' loans being used for non-business purposes, as such diversions seems to be counter to the goal of "microcredit-for-microenterprises." Rather than fretting over this, the world should see such diversions as indicative of the vast range of financial services needed by poor households and should seek to develop a full range of microfinance services to meet those needs. In particular, the church has the opportunity to develop holistic microfinance ministries in far more ways than was previously understood.

The Vast Universe of Microfinance Needs

While most, if not all, households are engaged in consumption smoothing, poor households have a host of additional needs for *convenient, flexible, and reliable financial services.*[31] In the past several decades, microfinance researchers have been able to summarize these financial service needs into the following categories:[32]

1. **Consumption Smoothing:** As demonstrated by Subir and Mumtaz, poor households are engaged in continuous financial management, saving and borrowing to ensure they can meet their daily consumption needs in the face of incomes that are *small, irregular, and unpredictable*.
2. **Business Investments:** Due to few employment opportunities, many poor households are forced to operate their own microenterprises or to farm small plots of land. They need financial services to provide capital for start-up, day-to-day operations, and business expansion.
3. **Household Investments:** Poor households need financial services to enable them to save or borrow for relatively large expenditures such as repairing a leaky roof, buying a cooking pot, or paying school fees for their children. Although these

expenditures may sound less exciting than business investment, they are crucial for the family's health and long-term survival. In particular, keeping children in school is absolutely essential for the family's long-run economic health.

4. **Life-Cycle Needs:** Weddings, funerals, and other significant milestones can consume a very high percentage of a family's annual income. Savings and loan services can help to pay for these events, as can insurance products such as life insurance and burial insurance.
5. **Emergencies:** Unexpected events can put an enormous strain on poor families. In particular, health emergencies are one of the leading reasons that families fall into a financial crisis.[33] Thus, in addition to being able to save and borrow, multiple forms of insurance to help with emergencies are vitally needed throughout the Global South.

Note that within each of these five categories, a vast range of financial services need to be developed. For example, just in the category of emergencies, there is a need for many forms of insurance including medical, crop, accident, unemployment, property, disability, and so on. And each of these products needs different pay-in and payout structures for people living at different levels of poverty. The possibilities are virtually endless.

Unfortunately, while the world's financial systems largely address the financial service needs for people who are not poor, current systems are not properly designed to meet the particular circumstances of poor households. In other words, the existing banks, credit unions, and insurance companies do not have products that are attuned to the needs of poor households, whose incomes are low, unreliable, and unpredictable. The authors of *Portfolios of the Poor* summarize the situation as follows:

> As we watched all this [research] unfold, we were struck by two thoughts that changed our perspective on world poverty, and on the potential for markets to respond to the needs of poor households. First, we came to see that money management is, for the poor, a fundamental and well-understood part of everyday life. It is a key factor in determining the level of success that poor households enjoy in improving their own

> lives. Managing money well is not necessarily more important than being healthy or well educated or wealthy, but it is often fundamental to achieving those broader aims. Second, we saw that at almost every turn poor households are frustrated by the poor quality—above all the low reliability—of the instruments that they use to manage their meager incomes. This made us realize that if poor households enjoyed assured access to a handful of better financial tools, their chances of improving their lives would surely be much higher.[34]

And this is where the opportunities for microfinance ministry are nearly limitless. The poorest people on the planet have a felt need that is "fundamental to achieving ... broader aims," a felt need that the "microcredit-for-microenterprise" strategy has only begun to address, a felt need that some of the poorest churches on the planet are already addressing in profound ways. These considerations are summarized in the **Microfinance for Households Principle**.

Microfinance for Households Principle

Poor households need convenient, flexible, and reliable financial services for:

1. Consumption Smoothing
2. Business Investments
3. Household Investments
4. Lifecycle Needs
5. Emergencies

Shifting Paradigms

The new narrative of microfinance requires shifting our expectations for the impact on poor households' consumption from the upper dotted curve to the lower dotted curve in figure 4.5. The "microcredit-for-microenterprises" story led the world to believe that loans to poor microentrepreneurs would quickly raise their incomes, lifting them out of poverty as shown in the upper dotted curve. For a small fraction of the world's poor, this may be true. But for most people, the "microfinance-for-households" strategy will likely yield the lower dotted curve, reducing the overall fluctuations in their consumption so that life becomes a bit more stable, providing the possibility that, over a long period of time, the family may experience an increase in its income, if not in this generation then in the next.

Although stabilizing a family's consumption seems less exciting

FIGURE 4.5 Revised Expectations of Impacts of Microfinance

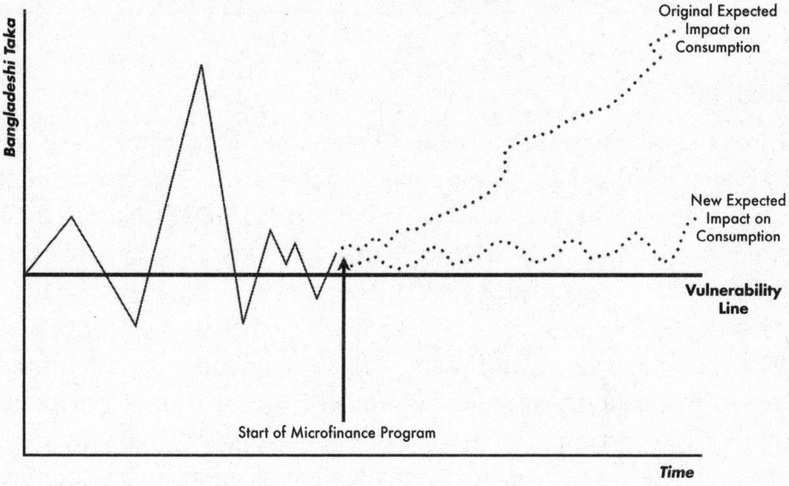

than increasing it, the effects may be more profound than first meets the eye. For when a household is brought back from the edge of a cliff—the vulnerability line—the effects can be dramatic. With death less imminent, it becomes possible for the household to catch its breath a little, to have a bit more peace of mind, to dare to think about the future, and maybe even to acquire a small dose of one of the most powerful antidotes to human suffering: hope.

Moreover, the methodologies employed in microfinance ministries allow for even more powerful effects. As will be discussed further in chapter 5, poverty can be conceived of as brokenness in people's foundational relationships with God, self, others, and the rest of creation. By intentionally incorporating evangelism and discipleship, church-centered microfinance ministries are able to address all four of these relationships, thereby having more profound effects than immediately meets the eye. Although much more research needs to be done to determine the exact causes, magnitudes, extent, and longevity of the impacts being reported from the frontlines, the numerous testimonies from poor people are too powerful to ignore: God is clearly using microfinance ministries to bear witness to the transformative power of his kingdom all over the Global South.

Summary

The standard "microcredit-for-microenterprises" story of microfinance has been overhyped: the vast majority of the world's poor will not achieve substantial increases in their incomes through loans to their small businesses; however, this realization does not negate the fact that microfinance can have powerful impacts in far broader ways than most people ever imagined. The world simply needs to recalibrate its expectations to see the different—albeit profound—impacts of the "microfinance-for-households" approach. Through a variety of loans, savings, insurance, and money-transfer services, this broader approach can stabilize the household, dramatically reducing its vulnerability and setting the stage for long-run improvements in overall well-being. Moreover, when combined with evangelism and discipleship activities, microfinance ministries can have dramatic impacts on people's deepest spiritual needs.

Application Questions

1. Think of a time in your life in which your overall well-being improved even though your income did not go up. What caused your life to be better?

2. Suppose you were told that there was a low-cost ministry that could save the lives of poor children, keep them in school, improve their parents' marriage, and lead their entire family into a deeper relationship with Jesus Christ; however, you were also told that this ministry would be unlikely to dramatically increase the family's income, at least not in the short run. Do you think that this ministry would be worth supporting? Why or why not?

3. List all of the financial services you use. Try to imagine not having access to any of them. How would you need to adjust your life?

PART 2

ALLEVIATING POVERTY

CHAPTER 5

WHAT IS POVERTY? THE TRUE NATURE OF THE PROBLEM

> [Poor] people tended to equate poverty with powerlessness and impotence, and to relate wellbeing to security and a sense of control of their lives. ... [One poor woman] argued, "The rich one is someone who says, 'I am going to do it,' and does it." The poor, in contrast, do not fulfill their wishes or develop their capacities.
>
> —*Research team studying poverty in Brazil*[1]

> We were poor on the outside, but also on the inside, because poverty starts in the heart.
>
> —*Celestin, member of church-centered savings and credit association of HOPE International in Rwanda*[2]

What is poverty? This is not just an academic question, for the way that we diagnose the problem of poverty determines the solutions that we use to alleviate poverty. If we get the diagnosis wrong or if we treat symptoms rather than underlying causes, we won't help poor people to get better. Indeed, we could even make their situation worse. We have to get the diagnosis right. Good intentions are not enough.[3]

And of course, a sound diagnosis is not sufficient, for we must also find a way to cure the disease once we know what it is. We need what many researchers and practitioners call a "theory of change," an articulation both of what the goal is and of how to get there.

Drawing on the pioneering work of Bryant Myers,[4] a leading Christian development thinker, the book *When Helping Hurts* analyzes the problem of poverty and its solution in the context of the grand drama of Scripture: creation, fall, redemption, and consummation.[5] This chapter and the next expand on this framework, delving deeper into the nature of the Triune God and of the world he created. Some of this material is a bit abstract, but bear with it, for as we shall see in chapter 7, these concepts have profound implications for the design of microfinance ministries.

Poverty as a Web of Deprivation

One of the biggest mistakes in poverty alleviation is oversimplifying the problem, and thus oversimplifying the solution. We see people who are hungry, holding out their hands asking for food, so we give them food. There are some situations in which this is a good thing to do, but even in those situations we are usually simply addressing the symptoms rather than the underlying causes, which are far more complex.

Ibu Emptat's Story

To illustrate, consider the following summary of an interview conducted by Abhijit Banerjee and Esther Duflo, two of the world's leading researchers on poverty:

> In a village in Indonesia we met Ibu Emptat, the wife of a basket weaver. A few years before our first meeting (in summer 2008), her husband was having trouble with his vision and could no longer work. She had no choice but to borrow money from the local moneylender—100,000 rupiah [$18.75 US] to pay for medicine so her husband could work again, and 300,000 rupiah [$56 US] for food for the period when her husband was recovering and could not work (three of her seven children were still living with them). They had to pay 10 percent per month in interest on the loan. However, they fell behind on their interest payments and by the time we met, her debt had ballooned to 1 million rupiah [$187 US]; the moneylender was threatening to take everything they had. To make matters worse, one of her younger sons had recently been diagnosed with severe asthma. Because the family was already mired in debt, she couldn't afford the medicine needed to treat his condition. He sat with us throughout our visit, coughing every few minutes; he was no longer able to attend school regularly. The family seemed to be caught in a classic poverty trap—the father's illness made them poor, which is why the child stayed sick, and because he was too sick to get a proper education, poverty loomed in his future.[6]

The family is trapped: Sickness causes poverty, which causes sickness, which causes poverty, which causes a loss of property to the moneylender, which causes more poverty, which causes sickness, which causes . . .

Note that there is no single solution to the entrapment. Health insurance could have helped to cushion the blow of the father's illness, but such insurance is often unavailable in poor countries; and even if it existed, it is unlikely that the family could have afforded it anyway.[7] Moreover, even if they had insurance, there is the additional problem of inadequate healthcare services to provide the necessary medical care. The problems are multifaceted, and the solutions must be as well.

The Web of Deprivation

The complexity of the situation becomes even more apparent when we consider that the story above captures only a snapshot of just one facet of Ibu Emptat's family's plight: an illness leading to unemployment leading to more illness. In reality, Ibu Emptat's family is likely to be facing a far more complex set of obstacles, which are interconnected and which work together to ensnare Ibu Emptat's family. Based on numerous interviews of poor people across the Global South, Robert Chambers, a leading development expert, has identified five "clusters of disadvantage," which commonly interact to form a web that traps poor households in a life of deprivation.[8]

As pictured in figure 5.1, the five clusters are as follows:

- *Material Poverty*: The household does not own sufficient income-producing assets: land, livestock, machinery, housing, and education.
- *Physical Weakness*: There is a high ratio of nonworking people—elderly, children, sick, and infirmed—to income-earning people. Malnutrition and a range of diseases weaken the family members and undermine their ability to work.
- *Isolation*: The family is geographically, socially, and economically isolated from the mainstream institutions of society, including: markets, financial systems, social services, educational opportunities, political processes, and information.

FIGURE 5.1 Web of Deprivation

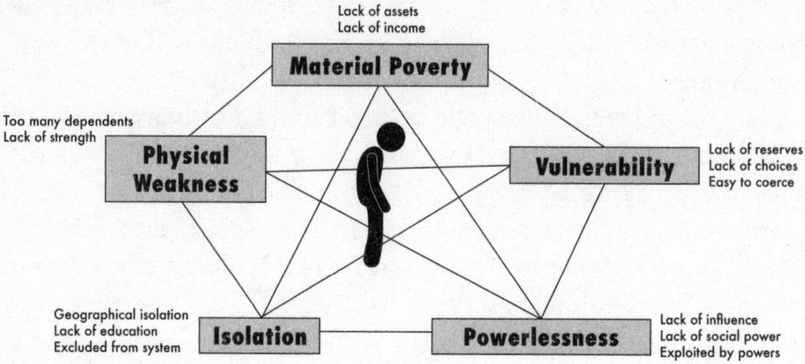

Adapted from Bryant L. Myers, *Walking with the Poor: Principles and Practices of Transformational Development*, rev. ed. (Maryknoll, NY: Orbis Books, 2011), 116, Figure 4-2; originally adapted from Robert Chambers, *Rural Development: Putting the Last First* (London, UK: Longman Group, 1983), 112, Figure 5.1.

- *Powerlessness*: The family feels it has no voice and is unable to influence the world around them. They are subject to exploitation by those with greater power, including police, landlords, moneylenders, government officials, merchants, and employers.
- *Vulnerability*: The family does not have the financial resources to withstand shocks coming from illness, bad weather, fires, accidents, or expensive social customs such as funerals or weddings.

It is possible to see this web at work in Ibu Emptat's story. The family is in *material poverty*, because her husband is struggling to support the family on the meager income of a basket weaver. Because the family is *vulnerable*, it is unable to withstand the shock caused by the husband's illness and loss of work. Due to their *isolation* from mainstream insurance and financial systems, the family is forced to borrow from an informal moneylender, who is able to exploit the family because of their *powerlessness*. Furthermore, the family's inability to purchase medicine is making one of their dependent sons *physically weak*, thereby undermining his ability to get an education. This lack of education will contribute to the son's *material poverty* in the future, making it very likely that the web of deprivation will ensnare this family across generations.

Chambers's web of deprivation is an excellent summary of how poor people describe their experience with poverty. As such, it provides practitioners with a powerful framework for understanding the lives of poor people and their "felt needs." Hence, as practitioners consider the design of various poverty-alleviation ministries—including microfinance ministries—they should seek to address as many aspects of this web as possible.

However, like all frameworks, Chambers's web has a few weaknesses. First, it is primarily focused on symptoms rather than underlying causes. We need to know why each of the clusters of disadvantage exists in the first place if we are going to get at the root causes of the web of deprivation. Second, and related to the previous point, Chambers's framework fails to articulate the spiritual nature of human beings and of reality in general. We need to dig deeper to unearth a biblical understanding of the root causes of poverty and of poverty alleviation. Therefore, in the remainder of this chapter and the next, we shall analyze the problem of poverty and its solution in the context of the grand drama of Scripture: creation, fall, redemption, and consummation. Chapter 7 then applies the concepts to the design of microfinance ministries.

Poverty and the Image of God

Let us begin here by examining the overall narrative of the creation and the Fall.

Creation

The Triune God Creates Image Bearers

Poverty alleviation is fundamentally about people. In particular, it is about helping people like Ibu Emptat and her family to have better lives. This naturally leads to the following question: what is the "good life"? In other words, what constitutes "human flourishing" for them?

The answer to this question is not arbitrary. God has designed human beings in a particular way and for specific purposes. When humans live out and experience God's design, they experience *human flourishing*, i.e., the good life for which we are all longing. Hence, we need to understand what the human being is created to be and do in order to understand the goal of poverty alleviation.

The Bible does not present a systematic description of the exact nature of the human being.[9] But a number of theologians have found it consistent with the overall biblical narrative to summarize the "substance" of the human creature as consisting of a mind, heart, actions (or will), and body, all of which are integrally connected to one another.[10] Indeed, there is considerable support for the mind-heart-actions-body combination amongst philosophers, educators, social scientists, and natural scientists.[11] For the purposes of this book, we shall define these terms as follows:

- The *mind* is the cognitive center that rationally processes words, pictures, ideas, sounds, smells, and other data received through the senses.
- The *heart* is the locus of human beings' deepest loves, affections, and commitments. As such it is the driving force behind the rest of the creature. For this reason the heart is pictured a bit bigger than the other components of the human being in the figures that follow.[12]
- The *actions (or will)* are the things that humans attempt to say and do as they carry out their daily existence.
- The *body* consists of the organs, nerves, cells, blood, bones, skin, etc., that interact with the mind, heart, and actions and with the rest of the world.

Now what is this human being, this mind-heart-actions-body combination, supposed to do? For what purpose are we created? The Bible teaches that humans are made in the "image of God" (Genesis 1:26–28).[13] Nowhere does the Bible give a precise definition of the term "image of God," but the fundamental idea is that human beings serve as God's representatives and agents, reflecting his qualities in the world.[14]

In particular, many theologians are emphasizing that human beings represent the relational nature of the Triune God.[15] Indeed, God is inherently a relational being; from all eternity, the three persons of the Trinity—the Father, Son, and Holy Ghost—have existed in loving, intimate relationship with one another, a love that overflows when this Triune God creates and cares for both humans and for the creation in general.[16] Note that each person of the Trinity has four key relationships: (1) relationship with the other persons in the Godhead; (2) relationship with self; (3) relationship with human beings; and (4) relationship with the rest of creation.

As those who bear the image of this Triune God, representing him to the world, human beings are created to enjoy the same four key relationships, albeit in qualitatively different ways: relationships with God, self, others, and the rest of creation (Deuteronomy 6:4–6; Genesis 1:26–28).[17] Note that human life is not arbitrary. God designed humans to be a certain thing and to operate in a certain way in all of these relationships:

- *Relationship with God*: This is humans' primary relationship, the other three relationships flowing out of this one. Indeed, human beings' primary purpose is "to glorify God and to enjoy him forever."[18] This is our *calling*, the ultimate reason for which we were created. We were created to serve and give praise to our Creator through our thoughts, words, and actions. When we do this, we experience the presence of God as our heavenly Father and live in a joyful, intimate relationship with him as his children.
- *Relationship with self*: People are uniquely created in the image of God and thus have inherent dignity and worth. While we must remember that we are not God, we have the high *calling* of reflecting God's being, making us superior to the rest of creation.
- *Relationship with others*: God created us to live in loving relationship with one another. We are not islands! We are made to know one another, to love one another, and to encourage one another to use the gifts God has given to each of us to fulfill our *callings*.
- *Relationship with the rest of creation*: The "cultural mandate" of Genesis 1:28–30 teaches that God created us to be stewards, people who understand, protect, subdue, and manage the world that God has created in order to preserve it and to produce bounty. Note that while God made the world "perfect," he

> left it "incomplete." This means that while the world was created to be without defect, God *called* humans to interact with creation, to make possibilities into realities, and to be able to sustain ourselves via the fruits of our stewardship.

In summary, when our entire substance—mind, heart, actions, and body—is living in right relationship to God, self, others, and the rest of creation, we experience *human flourishing*. This is what humans are created to be. It is the good life for which we are longing. It is the goal of poverty alleviation for Ibu Emptat and her family.

No analogy is perfect, but the human being can be summarized by the tire depicted in figure 5.2. The substantive dimension of the creature—the mind, heart, actions, and body—is represented by the hub, and the relational dimension of the creature—God, self, others, and the rest of creation—is represented by the spokes. When the hub is properly aligned with the spokes, the tire is well-formed and can function properly, delivering a smooth ride as it travels down the road. Similarly, when human beings are able to use their entire substance to live in right relationship with God, self, others, and the rest of creation, we are well-formed and can function properly, thereby enjoying human flourishing as God intended. This is what we should be striving for as we try to bring poverty alleviation to Ibu Emptat and her family.

The tire is meant to communicate wholeness and interconnectedness. Every part of the tire—the hub and each of the four spokes—must be properly aligned in order for the tire to be well-formed and to function properly. If even one of the spokes gets bent or broken, the entire tire—i.e., the whole person—will get distorted, as we shall see further below.

Created for Communion with God

It is impossible to overstate the importance of the first relationship: human beings are wired for communion with God, that is, the first spoke in the tire.[19] This wiring is as much a part of the creature called a "human being" as are this creature's arms, legs, kidneys, nerves, and blood vessels. Adam and Eve enjoyed this communion daily. Indeed, walking in fellowship with God was as much a part of their experience as other aspects of their humanness: breathing, eating, speaking,

FIGURE 5.2 The Human Being as Image Bearer

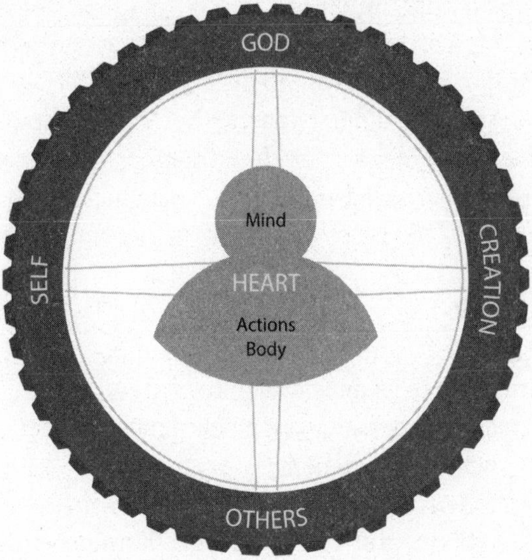

thinking, working, etc. In fact, their relationship to God was *the most* important part of their experience, shaping all other aspects of their being. As theologian J. Todd Billings explains:

> To be human is to be in communion with God.[20]

This statement is true for all human beings, not just for Adam and Eve. Humans are created to have a relationship—not just a legal arrangement but a real and vibrant intimacy—with the Father, Son, and Holy Spirit. The implications of this for poverty-alleviation strategies are manifold, given the integral connection between each dimension of a human being, as represented by the tire.

Unfortunately, due to the Enlightenment thinking of the seventeenth and eighteenth centuries, the centrality of communion with God to personhood has been virtually lost in the Western world, even within the Western church. The Enlightenment taught the West to rely on human reason and the scientific process to control the material world. Religious "superstitions" about spiritual affairs were often seen as obstacles to the mastery of the universe. When applied to the concept of human beings, Enlightenment thinking has been particularly devastating, often conceiving of human beings as solely material in nature, and denying their spiritual dimension.

Although Christians in the West acknowledge both the spiritual and material aspects of the human being, they tend to act as though these two aspects can be compartmentalized from each other. For example, when a Christian in the West becomes sick, both the diagnosis and the treatment of the illness tend to proceed along purely biological lines, with little or no attention paid to the possibility of either spiritual causes or solutions.

This compartmentalization has profoundly shaped the design of many poverty-alleviation strategies from the West, including some of the approaches used by Christian relief and development organizations. Far too often, attention is paid to addressing the physical needs of poor people without addressing their very human need for communion with God, as though these components of a human being were somehow unrelated to one another. But because all the aspects of a human being are intimately and inextricably connected to one another, an intimate relationship with God relates to all aspects of humanness, including even the physical. In terms of the tire, if the spoke relating to God is broken, problems will radiate throughout the rest of the tire, damaging the other three spokes and the hub.

This truth has dramatic implications for all aspects of poverty-alleviation ministries, including their design, execution, funding, marketing, pace, scale, and evaluation. *Poverty-alleviation ministries need to be designed in light of the fact that communion with God is central—not tangential—and that such communion is not separable from the other dimensions of human existence.*

The Goal of Poverty Alleviation

As we have already seen, the creation narrative provides us with very important insights about the very definition of full human flourishing. Stated differently, the creation narrative provides us with the goal of poverty alleviation, enabling us to update the **Poverty-Alleviation Principle** as shown on the next page.

This goal is fundamentally different from becoming rich or from becoming like the West. You see, once the West defined human beings

> ***Poverty-Alleviation Principle***
>
> Poverty alleviation is the ministry of reconciliation, seeking to restore people to living in right relationship with God, self, others, and the rest of creation.

as being fundamentally material in nature, the goal for the West became clear: pursue greater consumption of material goods and material comforts. And the West found a way to achieve its goal by accumulating capital—especially factories and machinery—and inventing new technologies.[21] The results have been nothing less than staggering, resulting in unprecedented levels of material prosperity.

But the evidence of profound brokenness and despair in the West and other materially wealthy nations is steadily mounting, for human beings are wired for something more. To give just one example, there has been an explosion of serious mental illness among American youth. Indeed, between 1950–1999, the rate of suicide of people under the age of twenty-four increased by 137 percent.[22] Seeking to uncover the root causes of the rising rates of mental illness, an expert team gathered at Dartmouth Medical School to examine the leading empirical evidence, mostly from the field of neuroscience, and concluded:

> ... the human child is "hardwired to connect." We are hardwired for other people and for moral meaning and openness to the transcendent. Meeting these basic needs for connection is essential to health and human flourishing. Because in recent decades we as a society have not been doing a good job of meeting these essential needs, large and growing numbers of our children are failing to flourish.[23]

In other words, human beings are wired for relationship, and even neuroscience is discovering that a breakdown in relationships with God and with others is undermining human flourishing in America's youth.

Indeed, the biblical vision of the good life is fundamentally different from simply producing and consuming more material things. *In this light, the goal of poverty alleviation is not to turn the poor nations into the wealthy nations, but rather for both the poor nations and the wealthy nations to look more like the New Jerusalem*. As we shall see in the next two chapters, achieving this goal requires different tools than the ones the wealthy nations have used to achieve their goals. In other words, we need a different "theory of change" than the one employed by the wealthy nations of the world.

Cultural Systems in a Sinless World

God gave human beings the task of developing his creation, i.e., of creating culture (Genesis 1:26–28). We shall summarize culture as the economic, political, religious, and social systems that humans create, systems that include all of the following:

- *Formal institutions* such as government, banks, businesses, churches, and schools
- *Informal associations* such as Bible study groups or knitting circles
- *Cultural norms* such as acceptable morals, manners, dress, and speech

As depicted by the arrow from humans to systems in figure 5.3, human beings bring themselves into this task, implying that the way that humans create cultural systems reflects their foundational relationships to God, self, others, and the rest of creation. For example, because William Wilberforce loved "others" regardless of the color of their skin, he devoted his life as a politician to banning the slave trade in England at the start of the nineteenth century. Wilberforce shaped the political system in a way that reflected his fundamental belief

FIGURE 5.3 A World without Sin

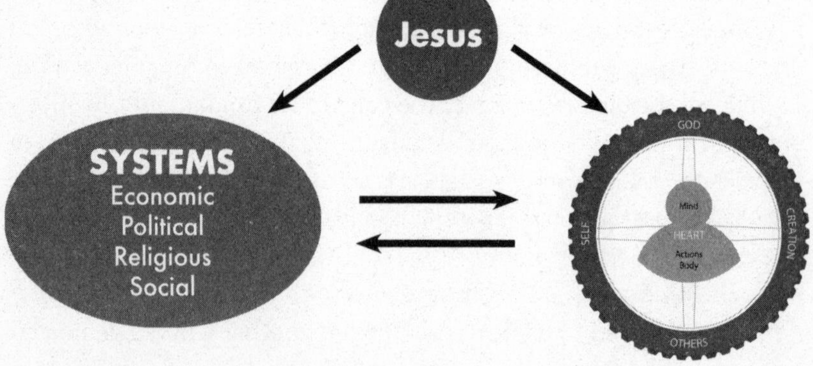

that Africans—that is, "others"—were fully human and deserved to be treated as such.[24]

Note also the arrow in figure 5.3 that flows from systems to individuals. The systems of a society dramatically affect individuals' experience of the four key relationships and have impacts that pierce deep into human beings' substance: mind, hearts, actions, and bodies. We do not live in vacuums. Human beings are profoundly shaped by the cultures in which we live. To continue with our analogy, think of the cultural systems as the road on which the tire travels. The condition of the road dramatically impacts the ride and even affects the very shape of the tire, impacting both the spokes and the hub. Similarly, cultural systems partly determine the extent to which people experience human flourishing, shaping both people's relationships and substance.

It takes *both* a well-formed tire and a good road to experience a smooth trip.

In summary: *People affect systems, and systems affect people.* In a world without sin, the individuals and systems would interact in such a way that they would support human flourishing in the way that God intended.

The Role of Jesus in the Creation

It is extremely important to note that Jesus has been actively engaged in the entire creation since its inception (see figure 5.3). Consider Colossians 1:16–17:

> For in him [Jesus] *all things* were created: things in heaven and on earth, visible and invisible, whether thrones or powers or rulers or authorities; *all things* have been created through him and for him. He is before *all things*, and in him *all things* hold together. (italics added)

Note in this passage that Jesus is described as the creator and sustainer of *all things*. He holds the atoms in place; governments, schools, families, and even restaurants cannot rise or fall without his permission; he has every hair on our heads numbered. In other words, Jesus is engaged with and has power over every aspect of the cosmos: the material world; people; cultural systems (economic, political, religious, and social); and spiritual beings.

The description of Jesus in Colossians 1 is far different from many Western understandings of God. As pictured in the top left panel of figure 5.4, God is connected to the cosmos, sustaining it in the palm of his hand. In contrast, under the influence of the Enlightenment, deists of the seventeenth century taught that God created the world to operate on its own, winding it up like a clock and then letting it run according to "laws of nature," apart from his sustaining hand. The "modern worldview" of Western secularism took deism one step further, questioning God's very existence and arguing that the universe started and functions on its own.

Development thinker Darrow Miller argues that Western Christians have syncretized biblical theism with deism, resulting in what he calls "evangelical gnosticism," a sacred-secular divide in which God is Lord of the spiritual realm—Sunday worship, devotions, evangelism—but is irrelevant to the rest of life: the material world, business, sports, science, and poverty alleviation.[25]

The Jesus described in Colossians 1 is far more present and far more connected to everyday life than most Western Christians realize. Indeed, although many would articulate the biblical theism of the top left panel, many Western Christians actually live as "functional deists," trusting God to save souls but not seeing him as particularly relevant to daily life. This faulty worldview distorts many things, including Western Christians' approach to poverty alleviation, with devastating consequences. Let us consider just two examples of this problem.

First, too often material resources (money, machines, food) and technology (agricultural techniques, health practices) are used to address poverty without narrating that Jesus is ultimately the creator and sustainer of those resources and technology. This can result in the program staff and the materially poor worshiping either the resources and technology themselves or the false gods whom they think provided them. This is not just some esoteric problem that will only surface in the next life, if at all. As we shall see further below, because every aspect of the human being is interconnected—as represented by the tire—a broken relationship with God will ripple through the whole person, impacting every aspect of that person, including their material well-being in the here and now of the "real world."

FIGURE 5.4 Biblical Theism Versus Western Worldviews

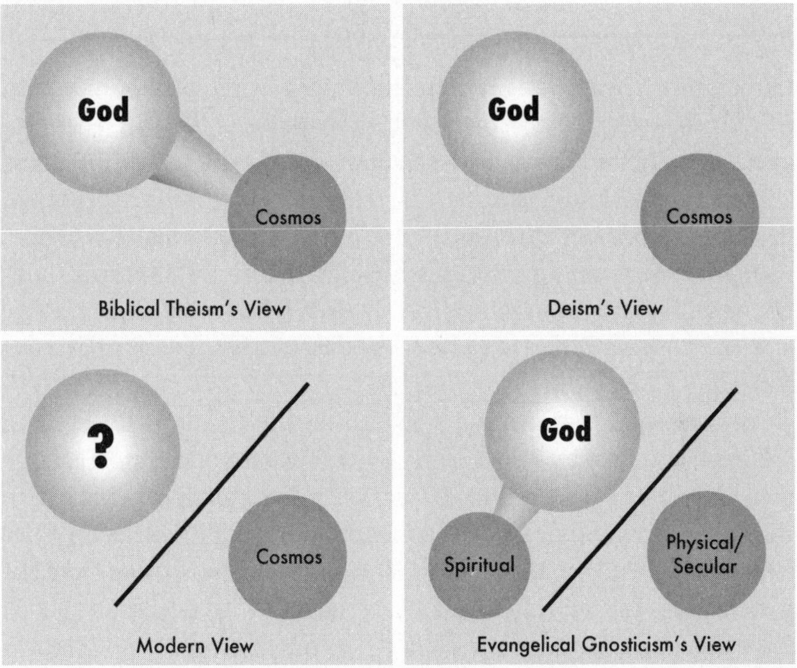

Figure 3.1 from Steve Corbett and Brian Fikkert, *When Helping Hurts: How to Alleviate Poverty Without Hurting the Poor . . . and Yourself*, 2nd ed. (Chicago: Moody, 2012), 88. Originally adapted from Darrow L. Miller with Stan Guthrie, *Discipling the Nations: The Power of Truth to Transform Cultures* (Seattle: YWAM, 2001), 43–44, figures 1.7–1.10.

Second, functional deism limits our understanding of what God can do in the world. In addition to creating and sustaining the regular functioning of the cosmos—that is, the "laws of nature"—God can and does intervene in the functioning of the world. We can pray to him, asking him to take actions, and he does act. If we really believed this, perhaps our ministries would spend as much money hiring prayer departments as we do on hiring fundraising and marketing departments. And if we really believed this, perhaps we would spend more time asking God to change materially poor communities, and maybe just a little less time planning how we were going to change them. The way we spend our money and time is a reflection of our basic understanding of the cosmos, and for many of us that understanding is closer to functional deism than it is to biblical theism.

The Fall

Broken Communion with God Undermines Human Flourishing

Unfortunately, Adam and Eve sinned, which severed communion with God for all human beings. In the Fall, humans become God's "enemies" and are "alienated" from him, becoming "objects of wrath" (Romans 5:10; Ephesians 2:3; Colossians 1:21). The Western, evangelical church has often emphasized the "legal" problem of this separation from God: Humans have sinned against a holy God and deserve his eternal punishment. *This is absolutely true. Fallen human beings really do have a legal problem. We have all sinned and are deserving of God's eternal punishment (Romans 3:23; 6:23).*

But the legal problem is not the fullness of the problem. Human beings are created for relationship, their most important relationship being communion with God. Hence, when this relationship is lost in the Fall, human beings lose the most important dimension of their *creatureliness*. And because this dimension cannot be isolated from the rest of the creature, the loss of a relationship with God sends shock waves throughout the entire being.

As figure 5.5 illustrates, this severed relationship with God has an effect on human beings that is something like removing a spoke from the tire. The removal of the spoke puts pressure on all the other spokes. They can't hold up under the strain; they start to collapse; and the hub gets damaged as well. Indeed, the entire tire—the whole person—starts to cave in on itself and gets distorted in every dimension. In other words, broken communion with God results in broken relationships with self, others, and the rest of creation. And the damage does not end there, for the Fall also impacts human beings' very substance: minds, hearts, actions, and bodies.

This process can be observed all the way back in Genesis 3. Adam and Eve's sin against God rippled through their other three relationships: their relationship with self was marred, as they developed a sense of shame about their humanness and covered their nakedness; their relationship with others was broken, as Adam quickly blamed Eve for their sin; and their relationship with the rest of creation became distorted, as thorns would now infest the ground and women would

FIGURE 5.5 The Distortion of the Human Being

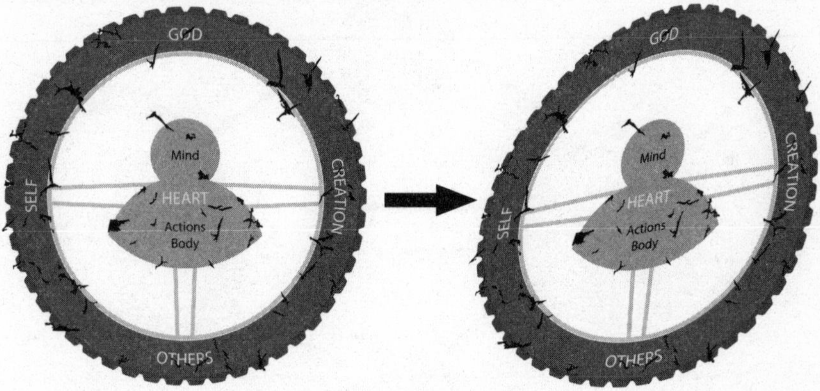

have pain in childbearing. And the damage does not end there, for the impacts of the Fall drive deep down into people's substance, affecting our minds, hearts, actions, and bodies (Psalm 38; Romans 1:18–32).

As mentioned earlier, the failure to understand communion with God as central to the very nature of human beings has had devastating impacts on the design and execution of poverty-alleviation strategies. Too often technical interventions—microfinance, clean water, improved agricultural techniques, malaria nets, etc.—are introduced apart from any efforts to restore people's communion with God. Such approaches amount to trying to repair the hub or to strengthen a broken spoke in figure 5.5 without doing the most important thing: replacing the spoke that is missing altogether, i.e., the relationship with the Triune God that can help to make the tire whole again.

Chapter 7 will discuss more fully the implications of these ideas for the design of microfinance ministries. *But for now, note that poverty is partly rooted in the effects of the Fall on both the substantive and relational dimensions of human beings, so poverty-alleviation efforts must address both of those dimensions as well.*

Cultural Systems in a Fallen World

As figure 5.6 illustrates, because culture is a manifestation of human activity, the corruption of human beings' natures is necessarily manifested in brokenness in the economic, social, religious, and political

FIGURE 5.6 A Fallen World

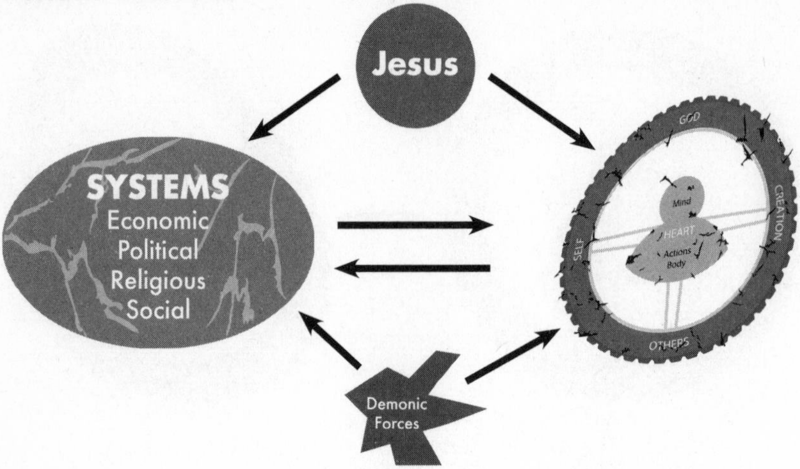

systems that humans create. As a result, systems that God intended to support and to express human flourishing, do so imperfectly at best. And at their worst, they inflict oppression and harm on God's image bearers. The road—that is, the systems—on which the tire rolls is full of potholes, which do damage to the tire. *Broken people create broken systems, and broken systems create broken people.*

Of course, most aspects of the systems develop over very long periods of time, implying that most individuals are unable to effect much change in the systems that are impacting their lives. In particular, as Chambers's web of poverty emphasizes, poor people often feel *powerless* to effect change in the world around them. Indeed, poor people are often oppressed by systems that have been formed over thousands of years, that are national or even global in scope, and that they have no ability to change.

The systems dramatically impact humans' relational dimension. For example, even if a person in the Global South attempts to relate properly to creation by working, it is extremely difficult for them to do so. The economy often does not create enough jobs, and the financial system makes it difficult to start microenterprises. No matter how hard the person is willing to work, it is extremely difficult for them to find work that enables them to earn a living. The broken systems simply do not permit them to experience a proper relationship to creation or to experience human flourishing in its fullest sense.

In addition, researchers are discovering that the impact of broken systems drives deep into the very substance of human beings, shaping minds, hearts, actions, and bodies in profound ways. Philosopher James K. A. Smith reviews both the philosophical and scientific literature, suggesting that cultural systems shape an individual's actions, creating habits that the person often does not consciously choose. Over time, these habitual actions imprint on both the individual's heart and mind in ways that are often subconscious. This subconscious self then automatically takes actions that are consistent with the way that the systems have conditioned it to act, creating even deeper imprints on the person's heart and mind.[26]

Given that materially poor people in the Global South have been profoundly victimized by systemic brokenness and injustice for generations, we should expect there to be deep imprinting of this brokenness and injustice on their minds, hearts, actions, and bodies. And indeed, recent research suggests that this is the case. For example, there is evidence that colonization or systemic racism rewires the brains of those being victimized, the result being that the oppressed internalize the racist lies of their oppressors and start to *automatically* think, feel, and act in ways that are consistent with those lies. In particular, the oppressed start to unconsciously believe that they really are an inferior race or class of people and that the oppressors really are inherently superior. The resulting self-loathing is very difficult to reverse.[27]

More about the implications of these ideas for ministry design will be discussed in chapter 7. *But for now, note that poverty is partly caused by broken systems that undermine both the substantive and relational dimensions of human beings, so poverty-alleviation strategies need to address these broken systems as well.*

The Role of Demonic Forces

In the section on creation, we saw that Western Christians have often underestimated the extent to which Jesus Christ is actively involved in the world, often acting as though the world largely operates on its own. The blindness of many Western Christians to spiritual forces is even greater when it comes to the role of demonic forces. But the Bible is quite clear that such forces are quite active in human affairs:

> Finally, be strong in the Lord and in his mighty power. Put on the full armor of God, so that you can take your stand against the devil's schemes. For our struggle is not against flesh and blood, but against the rulers, against the authorities, against the powers of this dark world and against the spiritual forces of evil in the heavenly realms. Therefore put on the full armor of God, so that when the day of evil comes, you may be able to stand your ground, and after you have done everything, to stand. (Ephesians 6:10–13)

Satan and his legions are at war with God, which put them at war with human beings, who bear God's image. These demonic forces attack people directly through various diseases, calamities, and temptations, and indirectly through oppressive systems that work to enslave them.

Note that the primary defense against Satan and his legions are not material resources or technology—the tools of Western civilization—but spiritual power coming from God. Indeed, the weapons described in the rest of the passage are not malaria nets, clean water, and high-yielding varieties of plants—all of which have their role—but rather truth, righteousness, the gospel, faith, salvation, the Bible, and prayer (Ephesians 6:14–18).

More about the implications of these ideas for ministry design will be discussed in chapter 7. *But for now, note that poverty is partly caused by demonic forces that undermine both the substantive and relational dimensions of human beings, so poverty-alleviation strategies need to address the issue of demonic forces as well.*

A Sound Diagnosis of the Disease of Poverty

This chapter began by arguing that properly treating the disease of poverty requires a sound diagnosis of its underlying causes. By examining the overall narrative of the creation and Fall, we have been able to discern something about the underlying causes of poverty, which are summarized in the **Nature of Poverty Principle**[28] (see next page).

Readers might be feeling a bit overwhelmed at this point, thinking: *The problem of poverty is too big and too complex. It would take a miracle to solve all of this*. That is true: poverty alleviation does require a miracle. As the next chapter explains, the good news is that the Triune God is unleashing this miracle right now in the cosmos as a whole and in the lives of individual people. But first, let's return to Ibu Emptat.

> ***Nature of Poverty Principle***
>
> Poverty is the inability for a human being to live in right relationship with God, self, others, and the rest of creation. This poverty is due to broken individuals, broken systems, and demonic forces.

The Underlying Causes of the Web of Deprivation

Ibu and her family are trapped in Chambers's "web of deprivation." This chapter has argued that this web is symptomatic of something deeper: human's inability to live in right relationship with God, self, others, and the rest of creation as a result of three things: (1) broken individuals, (2) broken systems, and (3) demonic forces. An important implication of this perspective is that poverty-alleviation efforts should not focus just on the symptoms of poverty—i.e., on the "web of deprivation"—but rather on the underlying causes.

To illustrate, let us consider just one of the clusters of Chambers's web: *material poverty*. Too often poverty-alleviation efforts have only treated the symptom of *material poverty* by giving handouts of material things, like food, clothes, or money. As discussed in *When Helping Hurts*, although this approach deadens the pain, it can actually exacerbate the underlying causes of the *material poverty* and create crippling dependencies.

Of course, addressing the underlying causes of *material poverty* is easier said than done, for individuals, systems, and demonic forces are complex, and they interact with one another in complicated ways that we are not even close to understanding fully. But in order to illustrate just a bit of how this works, this section gives just a few examples of the ways in which broken individuals, broken systems, and demonic forces lead to brokenness in the four key relationships for people in the Global South like Ibu Emptat. In addition, the section illustrates a few ways how this relational brokenness can contribute to *material poverty*. The discussion is not meant to be comprehensive but rather to show

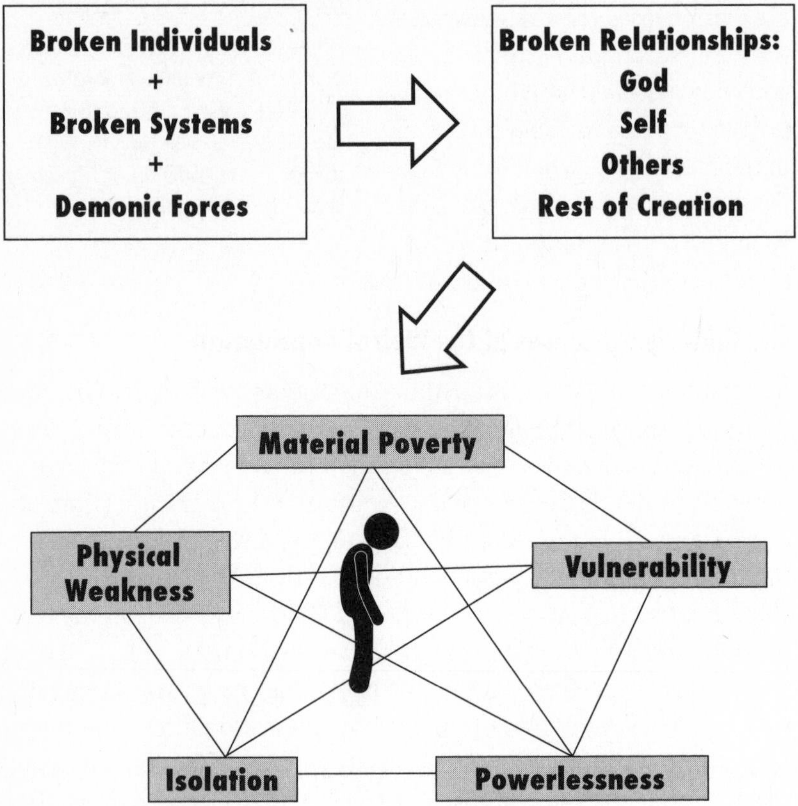

FIGURE 5.7 The Underlying Causes of Chambers's Web of Deprivation

the ideas in figure 5.7 for just one of the clusters in Chambers's web of deprivation. A similar exercise could be conducted for the other clusters.

Broken Relationship with God

Traditional religion commonly appears in a variety of forms in the Global South.[29] Generally speaking, traditional religionists believe there is a creator-god of the world, who is inaccessible to humans. However, they also believe there are many personal spiritual beings and impersonal spiritual forces that control the material world. Because traditional religionists believe that these spirits regularly take actions to either harm or to help people, a significant amount of time, energy, and money are often devoted to trying to appease or manipulate these spirits. For example, a poor household might spend a small fortune to purchase a bull to offer as a sacrifice, a behavior that would contribute to that household's *material poverty*.

Note that simply handing out material resources to this person—i.e., treating the symptom of *material poverty*—will not bring healing to their broken *relationship with God*. Indeed, there are examples in which increases in such material resources lead people to spend more on sacrifices, fetishes, witchdoctors, and shamans, thereby sinking them deeper into idolatry.[30]

Unfortunately, the effects of traditional religion on material poverty are far more comprehensive than just the monetary costs of sacrifices to appease or manipulate the spirits. Dabbling in the occult invites demonic forces into one's life, forces that wreak havoc on people's minds, hearts, actions, and bodies. Moreover, traditional religionists' broken *relationship with God* spreads like a cancer into the other three relationships, because the various dimensions of human beings are interconnected, as represented by the tire.

Broken Relationship with Self

Traditional religionists believe that there is no fundamental difference between humans, animals, and plants, as all of them are subject to the control of the spirits. This core conviction often leads to the following views about self:

- Lack of inherent dignity and worth as an image bearer
- Little sense of either personal agency or responsibility
- Feelings of being victimized by the spiritual powers
- Fatalistic tendencies about one's lot in life

And *broken systems* have further crushed the self-image of these *broken individuals*. As mentioned earlier, researchers are finding that the lies of the oppressors about their superiority can become emblazoned into the minds of the oppressed. Centuries of colonialism, neocolonialism, and internal oppression by powerful elites have confirmed the loss of dignity that is inherent to the traditional worldview.[31]

The effects of the broken *relationship with self* on *material poverty* are manifold. For example, there is evidence that people with low levels of self-esteem, of human agency, and of personal responsibility tend to:

- Drop out of school earlier
- Engage in destructive lifestyles, including sexual promiscuity and abuse of drugs and alcohol
- Struggle to be assertive in the labor force or entrepreneurial in business[32]

Clearly, all of these behaviors have negative impacts on one's income, thereby contributing to *material poverty.*

Note again that simply addressing the symptom of *material poverty* through handouts of material resources may very well make the underlying cause of that *material poverty* worse. The prolonged use of handouts can further lower people's self-esteem and sense of personal responsibility, thereby causing crippling dependencies. Treating symptoms rather than underlying causes can be deadly.[33]

Broken Relationship with Others

Traditional religionists have very strong allegiance to their own family, tribe, and deceased ancestors, but they often view people from other tribes as inferior or as potentially exploitable. Once again, this *individual brokenness* was exacerbated by *systemic brokenness*, as the colonizers regularly encouraged intertribal conflict, often pitting one tribe against another in attempts to divide and control the people they were seeking to dominate.

The intertribal conflict has often been a major contributor to *material poverty.*[34] As just one example, the Rwandan civil war of 1994, in which an estimated 800,000 people were killed in only three months, resulted in a 40 percent decrease in gross domestic product in the year of the conflict and higher poverty rates in the subsequent years.[35]

Once again, simply pouring in material resources in such a situation can sometimes make matters worse. For example, government officials sometimes use foreign aid for personal gain or to provide favors to their own tribe. Such actions further undermine trust in the political process and "justify" the other tribe engaging in similar behaviors when its people are in power.[36]

Broken Relationship with the Rest of Creation

God placed human beings as stewards over creation, which includes both preserving the world and working to unpack its potential. One of the results of this preserving and unpacking was that humanity would be able to support itself (Genesis 1:28–29).

Unfortunately, *broken systems* at global, national, and local levels damage the environment, undermining the ability of both current and future generations to support themselves. Pollution of air and water, deforestation, overfishing, and soil degradation contribute to poor health, reduced yields, and natural disasters, all of which increase *material poverty*.[37]

In addition, *broken systems* create economies in the Global South that do not create sufficient employment opportunities. There are a multitude of causes for this, including unjust trade policies in wealthy countries, disruptive flows of financial capital, inadequate property rights, and corrupt and ineffective governments. The lack of jobs forces many in the Global South to become self-employed as "microentrepreneurs," where they then encounter a broken financial system that makes it difficult to either save or borrow the capital they need to start their own microenterprises. Clearly, if people cannot find jobs or start their own businesses, *material poverty* will be just around the corner.

In addition, the worldview of traditional religion has resulted in *broken individuals* who are often unaware that God has given them dominion over creation. The idea that humans have the capacity to effect profound change in the world around them is largely absent in the traditional worldview, resulting in self-imposed limits on the possibilities for creativity, innovation, entrepreneurship, problem solving, and progress.[38] Indeed, several leading economists are now arguing that the primary factor needed to launch modern economic growth is a shift from a traditional worldview to a worldview in which human-led innovation and progress are seen as possible.[39] Robert Lucas, Nobel Laureate in Economics, explains:

> For income growth to occur in a society, a large fraction of people must experience changes in the possible lives they imagine for themselves and their children, and these new visions of possible futures must have enough force to lead them to change the way they behave....

> In a successfully developing society, new options continually present themselves and everyone sees examples of people who have responded creatively to them.... The people who respond to the new possibilities that development creates are also the ones who make sustained development possible. Their decisions to take new risks and obtain new skills make new possibilities available for those around them.[40]

Once again, in such a context, simply providing handouts of material resources can do more harm than good. Repeatedly giving poor people things does not increase their sense that they are image bearers with God-given capacity to effect changes in their environment. Rather, such handouts may very well further ingrain the idea that outside forces—in this case, the wealthy people giving the handouts—need to change the world, because the poor cannot.

Summary

The first step in successfully addressing the problem of poverty is to correctly diagnose the cause of the problem. Poor people are caught in a "web of deprivation" that includes material poverty, physical weakness, isolation, powerlessness, and vulnerability. This web is ultimately rooted in the brokenness in human beings' relationships with God, self, others, and the rest of creation, a brokenness which is due to broken individuals, broken systems, and demonic forces. Building on these ideas, the next two chapters will introduce a "theory of change," an articulation both of what the goal is and of how microfinance ministries can help to get there.

Application Questions

1. Reflect on your relationships to God, self, others, and the rest of creation. What evidence is there of brokenness? What have been the consequences of this brokenness? What could you do to improve those four relationships in your life? Be specific.

2. If your church or ministry provides handouts of material resources to individuals or communities, how are those handouts helping or hindering the people you are trying to help?

3. Reflect on the materially poor people you are trying to help. What evidence is there of brokenness in their relationships to God, self, others, and the rest of creation? Through research and speaking with them, try to discern how broken individuals, broken systems, and demonic forces may be contributing factors.

4. Using your answer to question #3, how might you begin to work with the materially poor to address the five clusters in Chambers's web of deprivation?

CHAPTER 6

A TRINITARIAN THEORY OF CHANGE

> Some [members of the savings and credit association did] not come to church regularly. However ... they now come to church every week. Now we see their life changing.
>
> —*Facilitator of a church-centered savings and credit association in Togo, West Africa*[1]

> If you want to judge how well a person understands Christianity, find out how much he makes of the thought of being God's child and having God as his Father. If this is not the thought that prompts and controls his worship and prayers and his whole outlook on life, it means he does not understand Christianity very well at all.
>
> —*J. I. Packer*[2]

Microfinance is about providing financial services, which is very important, especially for extremely poor people. But *microfinance ministries* are about far more than money. Consider the following quotes from members of church-centered savings and credit associations in West Africa:

> Because of the savings group and through the teaching we are receiving, I have accepted Jesus as my Lord and Savior. And he has changed my life.
>
> The teaching [in my savings and credit association] has revealed many things to us. We learned that money comes from God. We are custodians. This teaching has brought revolution to my home. My mindset has changed. My wife and my children too. In my home, poverty is no longer an issue.... The way we face financial problems and needs and how we start a business [is different now]. Not all problems are gone but there is hope. With God's help the problems go away.

> My husband said, "Where did you get this teaching from? This is new and what we need." Now there is change in my relationships with my husband and my children.
>
> When I came back home I used to not greet my family members before going to bed. That brought me some trouble with my wife. Because of that training I [received in my savings and credit association], I changed my way of behaving to my wife.
>
> There is a union within the [savings and credit association] ... and you can tell that when you pray about something, it is different than when you don't.
>
> Before the savings group, the members did not understand how to apply the Bible to their lives. Now, I am seeing slow but steady changes in their behavior.[3]

As these quotes illustrate, microfinance ministries are about far more than money. Indeed, churches in the Global South often report that participants in their microfinance ministries experience significant changes in their lives: church attendance improves, husbands stop drinking, marriages are restored, hope and joy increase, enemies are reconciled, and women have dignity and voice. Microfinance ministries are not magic, and like all ministries, progress is often slow. But as the above quotes illustrate, there is clearly more going on in microfinance ministries than simply creating lump sums of money, as important as those lump sums are.

How is this happening? What is causing these changes?

This chapter and the next attempt to answer these questions by articulating a "theory of change," i.e., a statement of how the various features of a microfinance ministry can help people to move out of poverty. We will do this in two stages. First, this chapter explores the Triune God's "theory of change," that is, his overall plan for bringing change to the cosmos and to the lives of individual people. Understanding what God is doing and how he is doing it helps us to "get on board" with his work. Indeed, things go better when we flow with the purposes and plans of God. Second, the next chapter will then apply God's change process to the design of microfinance programs in the hope of creating more effective ministries.

God's Change Process

In order to understand God's change process in the context of poverty alleviation, it is helpful to remember the ultimate goal, as is articulated in the **Poverty-Alleviation Principle**.

This goal is fundamentally different—and far more grand—than simply increasing people's material prosperity.

In addition, it is important to remember the problem that needs to be solved, as articulated in the **Nature of Poverty Principle**.

> ***Poverty-Alleviation Principle***
>
> Poverty alleviation is the ministry of reconciliation, seeking to restore people to living in right relationship with God, self, others, and the rest of creation.
>
> ***Nature of Poverty Principle***
>
> Poverty is the inability for a human being to live in right relationship with God, self, others, and the rest of creation. This poverty is due to broken individuals, broken systems, and demonic forces.

In particular, note that poverty is due to broken relationships caused by three things: (1) broken individuals, (2) broken systems, and (3) demonic forces. Hence, our theory of change for microfinance ministries will need to address all three of these causes as much as possible. The good news is that God has a plan for doing just that!

Redemption and Consummation

The story of God's work in the world has four main parts: creation, fall, redemption, and consummation. The previous chapter discussed creation and the Fall. We saw that Colossians 1:16–17 teaches that Jesus is the *creator* and *sustainer* of the entire cosmos. As we now look at the final two stages in God's story—redemption and consummation—we see that Jesus Christ is the *reconciler* as well. Continuing with Colossians 1:18–20, we read:

> And he [Jesus] is the head of the body, the church; he is the beginning and the firstborn from among the dead, so that in everything he might have the supremacy. For God was pleased to have all his fullness dwell in him, and through him to *reconcile to himself all things*, whether things on earth or things in heaven, by making peace through his blood, shed on the cross. (italics added)

As we saw in chapter 2, Jesus's mission was to declare the good news that he is ushering in the kingdom of God. And in this passage we see that King Jesus is using his reign to reconcile "all things." To reconcile means to put into right relationship again, and King Jesus is doing this to "all things," including the broken relationships that are at the very heart of poverty. King Jesus is truly good news for the poor!

Of course, it is important to remember that this comprehensive reconciliation is both "now" and "not yet." It is "now," because King Jesus already reigns over the entire cosmos (Matthew 28:18; Ephesians 4:8–10). It is "not yet," because the consummation of Christ's kingdom will not happen until he comes again (Romans 8:18–25).

How does Christ's reconciling work address the *broken individuals, broken systems, and demonic forces* that cause the broken relationships that are at the heart of poverty?

King Jesus Restores Broken Individuals

Union with Christ Makes a New Creature

As pictured in figure 6.1, the Trinity is on a mission. The Father sends the Son and the Holy Spirit to save broken individuals. The Spirit moves in unbelievers' hearts, pointing them to the crucified Son. Through repentance and faith in the Son alone, fallen sinners are saved from the punishment they deserve and are declared righteous before a holy God. Commonly called "justification," this process solves the "legal" problem *for those who repent and believe*. It is truly good news!

But there is so much more to this redemption than solving our legal problem! Consider the following verse:

> Therefore, if anyone is in Christ, the new creation has come: The old has gone, the new is here! (2 Corinthians 5:17)

Note in this passage that believers are described as being "in Christ." Indeed, theologians are rediscovering "union with Christ" to be the central idea of salvation for human beings, for throughout the New Testament, believers are described as being "in Christ" and Christ is described as being "in believers."[4] There is certainly a profound mystery in all of this, but it would be a mistake to simply spiritualize

FIGURE 6.1 Trinitarian Redemption

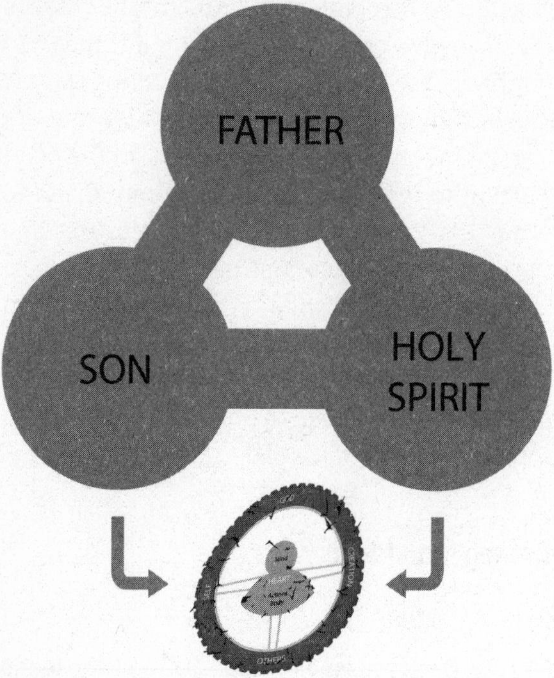

Adapted from Fred Sanders, *The Deep Things of God: How the Trinity Changes Everything* (Wheaton, Ill.: Crossway, 2010), 158.

this mystery as though it had no implications for the "real world." As theologian Marcus Peter Johnson explains, this union is "personal," "intimate," "vital," and "organic" in the sense that the entirety of the new creature is connected—*right now*—in a living and breathing way to the very person of Jesus Christ.[5] Just as the finger is connected to the hand, so too is the believer connected to Christ in the here and now of the "real world." This union with Christ provides believers with many benefits, including the one mentioned in this passage: Believers become *new creatures*, a new type of *being* from what they were as unbelievers.

It is quite common for those working to alleviate poverty to use the word "transformation" to talk about their work. Terms such as "social transformation," "transformational development," "structural transformation," "agricultural transformation," and "community transformation" are common parts of the conversation, and indeed all of these are important ideas. But let us not miss the fact that union with Christ provides the most dramatic and profound transformation a human being can possibly experience! Union with the person of Jesus Christ literally makes a new creature that is distinctly different—not just legally but in its creaturely essence—from the old one.

And what is the difference between these old and new creatures? The Bible describes the person not united to Christ as being "dead," due to their alienation from God (Ephesians 2:1–3; Colossians 1:21). This strong language is not surprising, given what we have already discussed about the nature of human beings. Since the human being is designed for relationship with God, those without such a relationship are necessarily experiencing an existence that is less than fully alive. In contrast, the new creature is alive and is in the process of becoming even more alive:

> And we all, who with unveiled faces contemplate the Lord's glory, are being transformed into his [Jesus's] image with ever-increasing glory, which comes from the Lord, who is the Spirit. (2 Corinthians 3:18)
>
> Do not lie to each other, since you have taken off your old self with its practices and have put on the new self, which is being renewed in knowledge in the image of its Creator. (Colossians 3:9–10)

Humans beings are created to be image bearers. The Fall distorts every dimension of the human being, making humans very imperfect image bearers. But as these passages indicate, the new creature is being restored to what Jesus Christ already is: the perfect image bearer of the Triune God (Colossians 1:15).[6] *In Christ, an individual's substance (mind, heart, actions, and body) is being restored in its ability to relate properly to God, self, others, and the rest of creation; in Christ, the tire is being made whole again.*

Of course, this renewed image bearer must necessarily be in communion with God, for such a relationship is inherent to the very nature of human beings, as depicted in the first spoke of the tire. Indeed, the Bible indicates that this is indeed the case for the new creature in Christ:

> But when the set time had fully come, God sent his Son, born of a woman, born under the law, to redeem those under the law, that we might receive adoption to sonship. Because you are his sons, God sent the Spirit of his Son into our hearts, the Spirit who calls out, "*Abba*, Father." So

> you are no longer a slave, but God's child; and since you are his child, God has made you also an heir. (Galatians 4:4–7)

By being united to the Son of God, a believer is adopted as a child of the heavenly Father and gets to refer to him by the endearing term, "Abba." In Christ, the believer stands in the same intimate relationship to the Father and to the Holy Spirit as the Son does. In Christ, the believer is brought into the very fellowship of the Trinity (John 17:20–26; Ephesians 2:6; 2 Peter 1:3–4).

Figure 6.2 pictures this process. In Christ, the missing spoke in the tire is restored, which creates both the possibility and the power for the other spokes to be restored as well. As a result, the tire is well-formed again. And though remaining fully human and never divine, this restored image bearer is brought—via union with Christ—into the intimate fellowship of the Trinity.

Theologian J. Todd Billings puts it so beautifully:

> Since we were not created to be autonomous, self-made people but were created to be in communion with God, when the Spirit leads us back into communion with God in Christ, we do not lose our true selves. We regain them. Our new self in Christ, which comes forth from the future, is our true self.[7]

Note in particular the last sentence in this quote. While the entire creation is groaning for the kingdom to fully come (Romans 8:18–22), those who are in Christ experience the kingdom *now*. Believers are new creatures in Christ—*now*—and this new creature is who the believer will be—in an even more glorified form—when the kingdom is fully consummated. Moreover, if you are a believer, this new creature is not somebody foreign to you. It is you! The real you! It is who you were really created to be. *It is you, restored.*

Of course, there is also a "not yet" of the kingdom for believers, a point that will be unpacked further below. In particular, believers still have their old natures clinging to them, and some of those old natures are pretty rotten. But that truth notwithstanding, by God's grace alone, believers are new creatures *now*, and unbelievers are *not* those new creatures *now*. And this new creature is fundamentally different—in both its substantive and relational dimensions—from the old creature, right *now*.

FIGURE 6.2 Trinitarian Adoption and Restoration

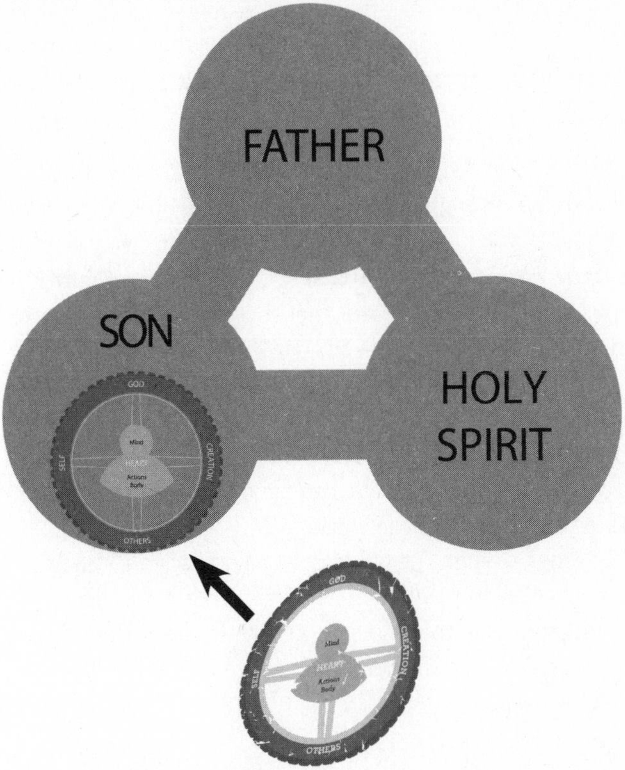

In light of the **Nature of Poverty Principle** and the **Poverty-Alleviation Principle**, these are incredibly powerful truths for the entire poverty-alleviation movement to consider, for believers have a *capacity* to experience increased human flourishing—to experience true poverty alleviation—in the present in a way that is simply impossible for unbelievers, who are not new creatures. This should give Christians who are working in poverty alleviation—including microfinance—an incredible passion to help poor people to be united to Christ, for this union provides the greatest hope for all people, including the poor.

Union with Christ Means Union with the Church

It is truly remarkable to consider what was on Jesus's mind as he knelt to pray in the Garden of Gethsemane, just before he was arrested.

Jesus was in extreme anguish, for he knew that he was about to be tortured, and he knew that he was about to be forsaken by his Father. What was on Jesus's mind at the moment? What was his primary concern? The last recorded words of Jesus before he was arrested are in the following prayer:

> "My prayer is not for them [the disciples] alone. I pray also for those who will believe in me through their message, that all of them may be one, Father, just as you are in me and I am in you. May they also be in us so that the world may believe that you have sent me. I have given them the glory that you gave me, that they may be one as we are one—I in them and you in me—so that they may be brought to complete unity. Then the world will know that you sent me and have loved them even as you have loved me.
>
> "Father, I want those you have given me to be with me where I am, and to see my glory, the glory you have given me because you loved me before the creation of the world.
>
> "Righteous Father, though the world does not know you, I know you, and they know that you have sent me. I have made you known to them, and will continue to make you known in order that the love you have for me may be in them and that I myself may be in them." (John 17:20–26)

Moments before his arrest, Jesus's primary concern was this: "*That all of them may be one, Father, just as you are in me and I am in you. May they also be in us . . .*"

Yes, King Jesus restores *individuals*, but he does not restore them to *individualism*; rather, he restores them to community, community with the Trinity and community with one another. As figure 6.3 illustrates, believers are not united to Christ as individuals; rather, believers are united to Christ along with the entire church, which is the very body of Jesus Christ. *To be united to Christ is to be united to his church.* This church includes believers throughout all ages, but it is also made manifest in the local assembly in which the believer participates (1 Corinthians 12:12–31; Ephesians 4:11–13). Individuals *and* the church participate in the intimate fellowship of the Trinity *together.*

Union with Christ means the entirety of the new creature is connected—*right now*—in a living and breathing way to the very person

FIGURE 6.3 Restoration of Broken Individuals Via Union with Christ and His Church

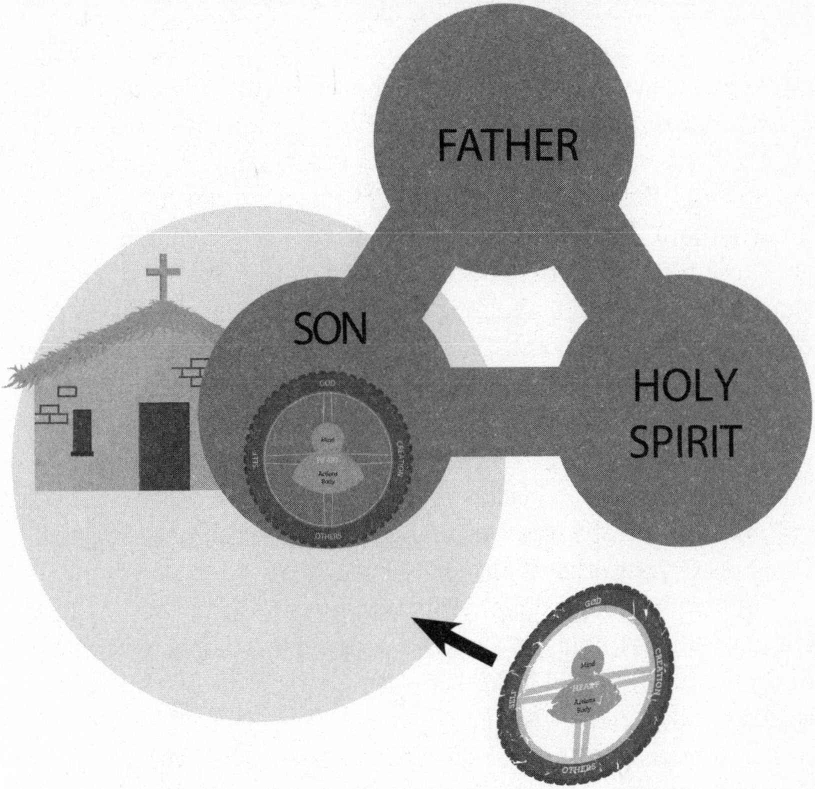

of Jesus Christ. And since the church is the very body of Jesus Christ, union with Christ means that the new creature is connected—*right now*—in a living and breathing way to the church. *Christ, individual believers, and the church are all organically connected—right now—into one living and breathing organism.*

I Love Jesus But I Hate the Church

About a dozen years ago, the authors of this book attended a small conference in Washington, DC, with the leaders and staff from most of the major Christian organizations that were using microfinance as a poverty-alleviation strategy. The goal of the conference was to explore ways to maintain a Christ-centered approach in microfinance programs. During one of the presentations, the speaker asked the participants, "What do you think of the local church?"

For the next twenty minutes, the attendees expressed their exasperation with local churches: "We can't work with the church"; "The church has no vision for helping people"; "Church members are the worst borrowers"; "The church is bureaucratic"; "Churches are all about grace, which undermines accountability for loan repayment"; "Churches are irrelevant"; "We love Jesus, but we do not like the church."

These responses are not unusual, for many people who are passionate for Jesus and for helping poor people often have a particular disdain for the local church. Indeed, there are many legitimate reasons for such frustrations. Too often the church cares only for people's spiritual needs without having a concern for their physical needs. Too often the church empowers hypocrites to abuse hurting people. Too often the church is full of bickering bureaucrats who are only bent on maintaining their own power. And too often the church seems to be about everything other than, well, Jesus.

But perhaps there is another reason for this disdain for the local church. Perhaps this disdain is actually rooted in a flawed understanding of the fundamental nature of what a human being is and of how God is working in the world.

As mentioned in the previous chapter, although Christians in the West acknowledge both the spiritual and material aspects of the human being, they tend to act as though these two aspects can be compartmentalized from each other. Hence, a person who is passionate about poverty alleviation might tend to focus on things that clearly address physical needs: malaria nets, clean water, microfinance loans, etc. And indeed, those are good things to be concerned about. But because the various dimensions of a human being are intimately and inextricably connected to one another, as depicted in the tire, people's relationship with God—the first spoke in the tire—relates to all aspects of humanness, including the physical. *In other words, if one is concerned about the physical well-being of poor people, they should also be concerned about their spiritual well-being, because every aspect of a human being is interconnected.*

What does the local church—with all of its warts and failures—bring to the table in poverty alleviation? A lot more than is apparent at

Why Bother Working with the Local Church?

Although most microfinance organizations avoid the local church, a number of Christian organizations very intentionally design their microfinance programs to work with local churches. In particular, there are increased efforts to help churches to promote various forms of savings and credit associations (see chapter 12). We asked the leaders of some of these church-centered microfinance programs why they bothered working with the local church:

"We believe that working in partnership with the local church builds their capacity to go beyond the church walls to serve their communities. While it is often a longer process, over time the foundation is stronger through mission compatibility and stability. The local staff is motivated by their faith, which the local church strengthens and encourages."

Suzanne Schultz-Middleton, program director, Five Talents International

"It's not a bother, it's a privilege! The analogy of a bride and her bridesmaids immediately comes to mind. HOPE's commitment to the church really is a matter of mission and calling aligning with the mission and calling of the church, the bride of Christ. Using that analogy, what a privilege to act as a bridesmaid serving the bride! We believe that the local church is uniquely equipped and, in fact, called to engage the physical and spiritual needs of its community. As the bridesmaid, we're privileged to be used by God in equipping the local church to create and sustain holistic, church-centered savings group ministries."

Phil Smith, director of savings and credit associations, HOPE International

"We believe the local church is God's instrument for change and justice. Our work is more sustainable through the church that has been around for over two thousand years. The church's extensive presence helps us assist remote and hard-to-reach communities."

Donald Mavunduse, head of east and southern Africa Team, Tearfund

"We fully believe that the church is God's vehicle for lasting change in our world. We like to say that the church has the largest participation, the fastest proliferation, the longest continuation, the strongest authorization, the highest motivation, and the widest distribution. Therefore, sustainable holistic development has to include the church."

Courtney O'Connell, Savings for Life senior technical advisor, World Relief

first sight, particularly when the eyes have been blinded by a Western understanding of the world, which does not see the spiritual as "really real" or as connected to the material. The compartmentalization of Western Christians necessarily leads to an underappreciation of what the local church contributes to poverty alleviation. Because Westerners think the spiritual and physical are unrelated, and because so much of the church's activities seem focused on the spiritual, the local church seems irrelevant to poverty alleviation, including microfinance.

But because poverty is rooted in brokenness in the four key relationships, poverty alleviation is necessarily about reconciling those four key relationships. (See the **Nature of Poverty Principle** and the **Poverty-Alleviation Principle.**) Hence, since King Jesus is the reconciler of all things, only he—and he alone—can truly alleviate poverty. And he is embodied in the local church. If you love Jesus, you must love the church. If you love poor people, you must love the church. There is no other option. In the next chapter, we shall see that all of this has profound implications for the design of our microfinance ministries, but this is a good time to be reminded of the **Church and Parachurch Principle**.

> ***Church and Parachurch Principle***
>
> Parachurch ministries must be "rooted in and lead back to" the local congregation(s) that minister in the same location.

In summary, union with King Jesus—and his body, the church—is God's theory of change for restoring broken individuals.

King Jesus Mends Broken Systems

Union with Christ is the foundation for restoring broken individuals to having the capacity to live in right relationship with God, self, others, and the rest of creation. But as we saw in the previous chapter, such restoration is not sufficient to enable humans to fully experience human flourishing, for the cultures in which humans live—i.e., the economic, political, religious, and social systems—dramatically impact every aspect of human existence, even going so far as to impact the minds, hearts, actions, and bodies of the oppressed. In other words, the road on which the tire travels needs to be sound in order for the tire to have a smooth ride. Indeed, the **Nature of Poverty Principle** reminds us that broken systems are one cause of poverty.

The good news is that King Jesus is reconciling "all things." He is changing the systems of this world, ushering in a new heavens and a new earth in which the systems will be completely supportive of human flourishing (Revelation 21:1–7). Christians disagree about how much of this change happens "now" and how much is "not yet" until Christ returns. But three things are clear.

First, Christ reigns over the entire cosmos right now, so positive change is possible right now. There is no external force that can prevent Christ from accomplishing his purposes.

Second, Christians are called to faithfully seek to change oppressive systems, realizing that the ultimate success of such efforts depends on Christ himself (Isaiah 58:1–12; Matthew 6:33). Indeed, microfinance is one example of this, as it seeks to change oppressive financial systems that undermine human flourishing for poor people.

Third, although both believers and unbelievers currently benefit from Christ's work in the cosmos, when the kingdom comes in its fullness, only believers will enjoy the benefits of Christ's reconciliation of all things, while unbelievers will face judgment (Revelation 21:6–8). Again, this should give Christians incredible passion to share the good news of the gospel with unbelievers so that they too can become united to Christ and can fully partake of Christ's overturning of oppressive systems.

Moreover, this passion should be further enhanced when we consider the fact that believers have a profound way of experiencing Christ's reconciliation of broken systems *right now*. As mentioned earlier, believers are not united to Christ as individuals; rather, believers are united to Christ along with the entire church. The Bible teaches that the church is a "holy nation," a nation that is set apart from all the other nations of the earth (1 Peter 2:9). And this new nation—despite all her failings and weaknesses—is the primary manifestation of the kingdom of God in the present age.[8] Indeed, in the church people get a foretaste of what the kingdom will be like when it is fully consummated.

It is important to recognize that this kingdom—this "holy nation"—has cultural systems with laws, norms, procedures, rituals, and messages that are radically different from those in the culture at large. For example, in a world in which colonialism, neocolonialism, and cultural elites have oppressed people based on their tribe, color, gender, or caste—imprinting lies on the very brains of the oppressed[9]—the local church provides a new cultural system in which all members have equal dignity as renewed image bearers and can enjoy celebrating the wonder of their God-given diversity. In the local church, believers get to experience—right now—a bit of what it will be like when Christ completely mends the broken systems of the world.

In summary, union with King Jesus—and his body, the church—is God's theory of change for combating broken systems.

King Jesus Defeats Demonic Forces

Demonic forces wage war on people, including Christians (Ephesians 6:10–12). They sometimes do this by taking direct actions against people, such as inflicting diseases, but they can also work indirectly through oppressive cultural systems.[10] The good news is that King Jesus's death has conquered these spiritual forces, so that when Jesus comes again, the demons will be prevented from inflicting any more harm on people or on the cosmos in general (Colossians 2:15; Revelation 20:10).

Until that great day, those who are in Christ can use his power to resist Satan's attacks, for King Jesus is more powerful than these demonic forces (Luke 10:17–19; John 10:27–30; Ephesians 6:10–18; 1 John 4:4). Indeed, believers are given spiritual tools—the "whole armor of God"—to fight against demonic forces, and as we do so, we can rest in this wonderful promise: "Resist the devil, and he will flee from you" (Ephesians 6:10–18; James 4:7).

Union with King Jesus—and his body, the church—is God's theory of change for defeating demonic forces.

In summary, we can now introduce the **Union with Christ Principle**.

> ***Union with Christ Principle***
>
> Being united to King Jesus—and his body, the church—is God's theory of change for addressing the broken individuals, broken systems, and demonic forces that cause poverty.

Living Between the Times

Those who are united to King Jesus get to experience his reign over individuals, systems, and demonic forces, allowing them to once again live in right relationship with God, self, others, and the rest of creation. However, although believers are presently united to Christ and do experience some of the benefits of this union right now, they will not experience the full benefits of this union until Christ returns.

Indeed, as figure 6.4 illustrates, there are several things hindering the believer from experiencing complete poverty alleviation—i.e., full image bearing—in this life.

First, although believers are new creatures, the old nature is still present, meaning that believers relate imperfectly to God, self, others, and the rest of creation. This old nature often dies very slowly; in fact, sometimes the old nature is actually much more prominent than the new nature. Being united to Christ creates a new direction for the believer, but for many of us, the initial starting point in this process is an old nature that is quite ugly and quite powerful.

Second, our new nature is currently connected to a body that is decaying (not pictured in this diagram because it is already complicated enough!). We are lacking the new body—an imperishable body—that awaits us at the final resurrection from the dead (1 Corinthians 15:35–58).

FIGURE 6.4 Life Before the Final Coming of the Kingdom

Third, the cultural systems are still broken, creating an environment that is still hostile to image bearing. Remember, a well-formed tire is insufficient for a smooth ride. There needs to be a good road as well.

And finally, demonic forces continue to wage war against all of humanity, including believers. These forces can create a very bumpy ride for even a well-formed tire.

Hence, for all of these reasons, although union with Christ gives assurance of complete and full alleviation of poverty for believers, there are no guarantees of an easy life prior to the final consummation of the kingdom.

Beware of the Prosperity Gospel

Unfortunately, a prominent heresy in the church has missed this last point. The "prosperity gospel," sometimes called the "health and wealth gospel," has become widely popular in both the United States and in many places in the Global South. Succinctly put, the prosperity gospel teaches that God promises to bless Christians with increasing wealth and physical health in this life. Moreover, it is often taught that such blessings can be increased if the believer has more faith, puts more money in the offering plate, or increases in sanctification.

The global gathering of the Lausanne Movement in Cape Town, South Africa, in 2010 took a firm stand against the prosperity gospel:

> We gladly and strongly affirm every initiative in Christ's name that seeks to bring healing to the sick, or lasting deliverance from poverty and suffering. The prosperity gospel offers no lasting solution to poverty, and can deflect people from the true message and means of eternal salvation. For these reasons it can be soberly described as a *false gospel* (italics added).[11]

Space does not permit a complete refutation of this "false gospel," so readers are strongly encouraged to study its heresies in greater detail elsewhere.[12]

However, it is important to caution readers that some of the teachings in this book could be misunderstood and could lead to some of the same errors that are found in the prosperity gospel. For example, in the previous chapter we argued that brokenness in individuals is one contributor to material poverty, and in this chapter we argued that union with Christ through faith restores individuals from their brokenness. Taken together, it seems like becoming a Christian will result in greater material prosperity. That sure sounds like the prosperity gospel!

Yes, but that is *not* what we are saying. Here is the key. *All else being equal*, a person who is saved from alcoholism or laziness will likely experience an improvement in their financial situation, as both of these sins tend to contribute to material poverty (Proverbs 23:20–21).

But all else is not equal. A Christian could be very strong in their relationship to Jesus Christ and remain very poor because broken systems or demonic forces are oppressing them (see the **Nature of Poverty Principle**). Again, it is not just the tire that needs to be well-formed in order to have a smooth ride. The road must be smooth as well.

Indeed, there are many examples in the Bible of very godly people whose earthly existence was not one of wealth and prosperity. For example, consider the apostle Paul, the author of much of the New Testament. It would be hard to find a more sanctified Christian, yet he was shipwrecked, flogged, imprisoned, stoned, hungry, cold, naked, and finally executed. It is entirely possible to be a very sanctified person and to be lacking in both material prosperity and physical health in this life. Indeed, churches in the Global South are full of such godly people.

Yes, growing in sanctification can help to overcome material poverty, but the Bible does not teach that either becoming a Christian or growing in sanctification will guarantee either wealth or physical health in this life. Those who are propagating such lies are creating false expectations and doing incredible harm to poor people across the Global South. Run from the prosperity gospel. Run fast!

What about Unbelievers?

The discussion has emphasized the radical difference between being a new creation and not being a new creation, i.e., between believers and unbelievers, both in this life and the next. This emphasis is consistent with the Bible's teaching, and it needs to be stressed lest we underestimate the power of being united to Christ in overcoming poverty.

However, this emphasis must be balanced with three related additional truths.

First, as mentioned earlier, believers still have their old natures hanging around, and for some of us that old nature is very ugly and very powerful. Therefore, it is quite common to find unbelievers who do all sorts of good things and who are even a whole lot nicer people than many believers. Indeed, many unbelievers work very hard to improve the lives of people who are poor, and those contributions should be recognized and celebrated.

Second, the message of Christianity is *not* that believers are inherently better people than unbelievers. On the contrary, the Bible teaches that all humans are fundamentally broken. Believers are simply on a superior trajectory into the future, not because we are so great, but because we are being rescued by the only one who is truly great: King Jesus.

Third, being a new creation provides no reason for boasting on the part of believers, for our new creatureliness is completely a free gift from God and not something that we deserve or have accomplished on our own (Ephesians 2:8–9). A true understanding of the gospel always leads to humility and an attitude of grace and concern for others, not a sense of superiority.

Summary

Being united to King Jesus through saving faith is God's theory of change for addressing the broken individuals, broken systems, and demonic forces that cause poverty. Believers experience this union right now, making salvation absolutely essential to poverty alleviation; however, the full benefits of this union will not be experienced until Christ fully consummates his kingdom. The primary place in which believers experience the benefits of their union with Christ in the present age is in their participation in the life of the local church. The next chapter explores the implications of these considerations for the design of microfinance ministries.

Application Questions

1. Are there any ways in which you have limited salvation to its legal dimension instead of looking to Jesus Christ to restore your entire personhood as a new creature?

2. In your own words, what does it mean to you that you are united to the very person of Jesus Christ and that you are an adopted child of the Father? How could you make these truths more real in your life?

3. In what ways may you be limiting the scope of impact that King Jesus can have in your life, in your church, in your community, and in your country?

4. How has your church helped you to become a new creation and to grow more and more as a restored image bearer in your relationships with God, self, others, and the rest of creation? Where could your church improve in this regard?

5. What can you do to strengthen your church's ministry both to believers and to unbelievers?

CHAPTER 7

RESTORING BROKEN PEOPLE: TRANSFORMATIVE MINISTRY

> We are always witnesses to something. The only question is to what or to whom? . . . We want people to observe and say, "Theirs must be a living God!"
>
> —*Bryant Myers*[1]

> When the crowd saw what Paul had done, they shouted in the Lycaonian language, "The gods have come down to us in human form!" Barnabas they called Zeus, and Paul they called Hermes because he was the chief speaker. The priest of Zeus, whose temple was just outside the city, brought bulls and wreaths to the city gates because he and the crowd wanted to offer sacrifices to them.
>
> —*Acts 14:11–13*

King Jesus really is doing something in the world—right now. He is in the process of reconciling all things; for people, this means restoring them to full human flourishing as image bearers of the Triune God. As we saw in the previous chapter, the way that God accomplishes this is by uniting people to the very person of King Jesus, who restores broken individuals, mends broken systems, and defeats demonic forces for those who are united to him. This is poverty alleviation in its fullest sense. King Jesus is the answer for all of us, including the materially poor.

But what are the implications of all of this for our efforts to help the materially poor? In particular, how can God's change process help us to design microfinance ministries that address the brokenness in people's relationships with God, self, others, and the rest of creation? In other words, what is our "theory of change" for microfinance ministries?

This chapter seeks to answer these questions by looking at how various components and features of a microfinance ministry can bring the reconciling work of King Jesus to bear on broken individuals, broken systems, and demonic forces. However, as we do so, it is important to remember that God is not bound by any formulas. Hence, what follows is not some magic recipe that, if followed perfectly, will result in the transformation we long to see. God does whatever he pleases, so he cannot simply be "programmed in." That having been said, the Bible does reveal some of the ways that God usually works. We shall draw on that revelation, along with the latest research and best practices, to inform the design of our microfinance ministries.

Restoring Broken Individuals

Both the substantive and relational dimensions of human beings have been damaged by the Fall. What can microfinance ministries do to address this brokenness at the individual level?

As we saw in the previous chapter, organic union with the person of Jesus Christ provides believers with a restored nature, unites them to his body (the church), adopts them into the fellowship of the Trinity, and provides the power to increasingly destroy the old nature and to live according to the new nature. See figure 7.1. Are there any tools at our disposal to initiate and nurture this union?

Ministry Component #1: Connect People to the Local Church and the "Ordinary Means of Grace"

The "Ordinary Means of Grace" and Poverty Alleviation

Although salvation is ultimately dependent upon the Holy Spirit's working in people's hearts to give them a new set of affections, Christians throughout the ages have recognized that God has also ordained several tools for the church to use as part of his process of bringing people to saving faith in Christ and to nurture them in their union with him. These "ordinary means of grace" are:

- Preaching and teaching of the Word of God
- Sacraments (or ordinances) of baptism and the Lord's Supper

FIGURE 7.1 **Restoration of Broken Individuals Via Union with Christ and His Church**

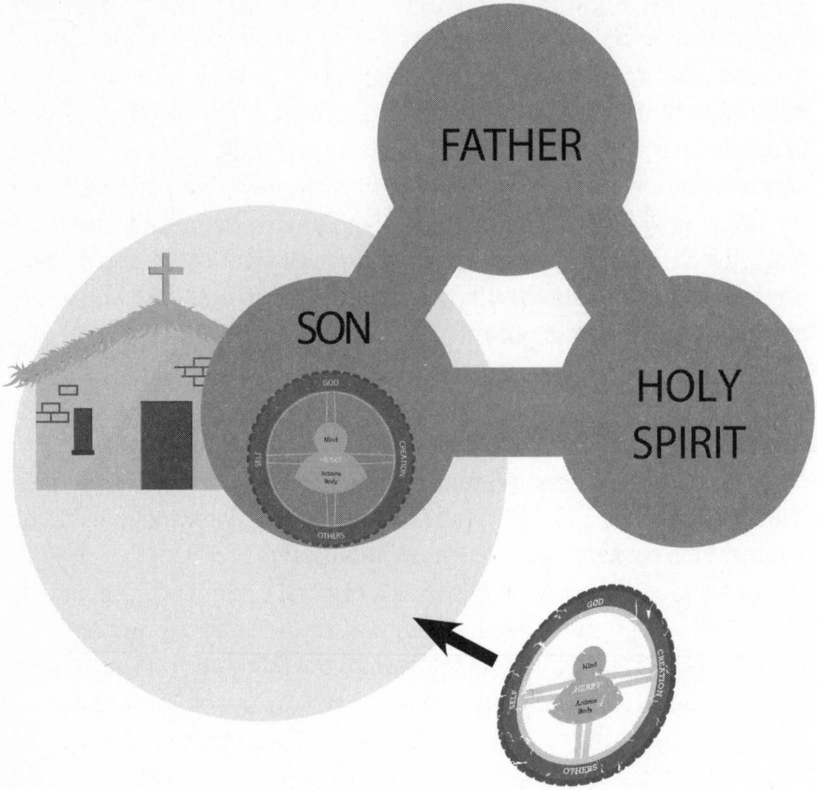

- Prayer[2]

Indeed, as the early church gathered to engage in these practices, "the Lord added to their number daily those who were being saved" (Acts 2: 47). The idea is not that these practices are powerful in and of themselves, but simply that these are the tools that God has established to unite people to Christ and to nurture them in that union.

It may seem like the ordinary means of grace are rather mundane compared to distributing malaria nets, drilling wells, stopping human trafficking, or making microfinance loans. But, as important as those things are, none of them are the means that God has ordained to effect the most incredible transformation of all: making new creatures out of old creatures through organic union with the person of Jesus Christ. It sounds strange at first, but *the ordinary means of grace are essential tools in poverty alleviation*. Thus, we can update the **Union with Christ Principle** (see box on right).

> ***Union with Christ Principle***
>
> Being united to King Jesus—and his body, the church—is God's theory of change for addressing the broken individuals, broken systems, and demonic forces that cause poverty. This union is received and nurtured through faith as the Holy Spirit applies the church's "ordinary means of grace" to people's lives.

As we saw back in chapter 2, designing and implementing the proper relationship between the church and parachurch ministries is not an easy task. Indeed, churches and microfinance ministries have often wanted very little to do with one another! But it is simply impossible to alleviate poverty apart from the local church. Poverty is rooted in broken relationships that only Jesus Christ can restore, and Christ is embodied in and offered by the local church as it administers the ordinary means of grace.

Recall the statement of theologian Rene Padilla from chapter 2: "One of the greatest challenges we Christians have at the threshold of the third millennium is the articulation and practical implementation of an ecclesiology that views the local church, and particularly the church of the poor, as the primary agent of holistic mission."[3] How can "churches of the poor"—which appear to have so few resources—be the primary agents of holistic mission? If one conceives of human beings and of poverty in solely material terms, such churches have virtually nothing to offer. But once we understand poverty as being rooted in broken relationships, King Jesus is the only hope, and he is actually present—in a real and living way—in the assembly of materially poor churches. In this light, these churches have much more to offer than first meets the eye: King Jesus!

Worship and Poverty Alleviation

In addition, there is another aspect of the church's role in poverty alleviation that is rarely considered. As we have seen, a relationship with God—one of the spokes in the tire—is central to human flourishing, and one of the most important aspects of this relationship is worship.

This reality necessarily informs the design of microfinance ministries, for as Jayakumar Christian, national director of World Vision India, notes: at the end of any poverty-alleviation initiative, people will be worshiping something.[4] The challenge is to make sure that people end up worshiping the right thing: King Jesus. This is easier said than done, for when outside organizations bring assistance to a materially poor community, it is very common for them to become the object of worship. After all, they are the ones who are bringing the malaria nets, drilling the wells, and dispensing the penicillin. As Bryant Myers explains:

> If the development agency and its expertise and resources are the central feature of the program, the agency will become the object of worship. In one case in India it was discovered that World Vision had been added to a tribal community's list of gurus—those who have answers the community does not have—and prayers and sacrifices had been instituted to ensure that this new guru (i.e., World Vision!) kept helping the community. . . . What we put at the center of our program is our witness. We must always ask if we are a dependent people, looking to God for every good thing. We want people to observe and say, "Theirs must be a living God!"[5]

Church and Parachurch Principle

Parachurch ministries must be "rooted in and lead back to" the local congregation(s) that minister in the same location.

The Church and Parachurch Revisited

It is for all of these reasons that the **Church and Parachurch Principle** is so vital in poverty alleviation.

We pictured this principle in figure 2.1, which is replicated in figure 7.2.

Yes, there is a role for the parachurch, a profoundly important role. Oftentimes the parachurch does things that the local church simply does not have the capacity to do. But the parachurch needs to step back a bit and allow the local church—churches that are often comprised of very poor people—to be on center stage, not because these churches are so great but because the King whom they embody is so great! When the parachurch is "rooted in and leads back to a believing community," people are drawn into the fellowship of the local church where they can encounter the very presence of King Jesus in the preaching of

FIGURE 7.2 The Church, the Parachurch, and Other Spheres of Society

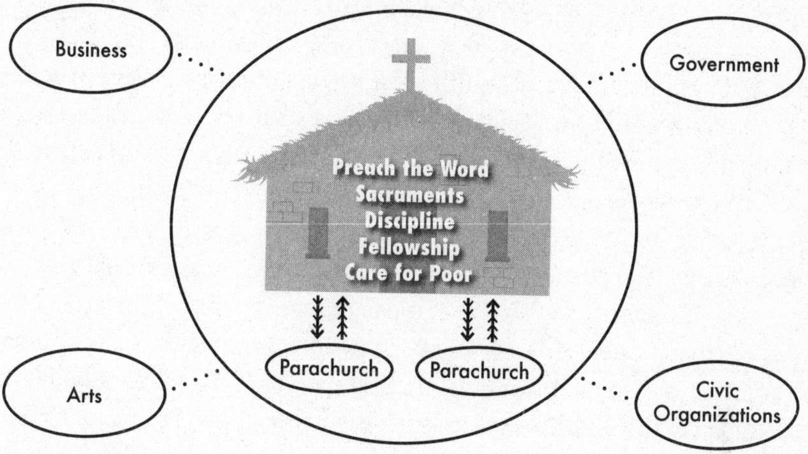

Adapted from figure 6.5 in Bryant L. Myers, *Walking with the Poor: Principles and Practices of Transformational Development*, rev. ed. (Maryknoll, NY: Orbis, 2011), 199.

the Word, the administration of the Lord's Supper and baptism, and prayer. And as they do so, and as the Holy Spirit works in their lives, they will fall down and worship him and him alone, the only one who can truly alleviate their poverty. Part IV of this book provides models of microfinance ministries that are consistent with the **Church and Parachurch Principle**.

Getting the Word Right

The preaching and teaching of the Word of God is absolutely essential for people to be united to Christ, for "faith comes from hearing" (Romans 10:14–17). Unfortunately, not all churches preach the Word of God accurately, making pastoral education absolutely critical to poverty alleviation. In particular, there are at least three common errors when it comes to the preaching and teaching in materially poor churches in the Global South.

First, some churches erroneously teach that Christianity is about being a good person and living a good life. In contrast, the gospel teaches that nobody can measure up to God's standards, which is the reason that the Father sent his only Son, Jesus Christ, to pay the penalty for our sins on the cross. By putting our faith in Christ alone, our sins are forgiven, we become new creatures, we are adopted as sons and daughters, and we can look forward to a new heaven and a new earth. Although this gospel is universally true, there are some particular challenges to communicating it to those influenced by traditional religion, requiring some nuances in the presentation of the message.[6]

Second, as discussed in chapter 6, many churches are erroneously propagating the "health and wealth" or "prosperity" gospel, which falsely teaches that God promises to bless Christians with physical health and material prosperity in this life. It is easy to see why this "false gospel" has been so appealing to many poor people, but it sets them up for tremendous disappointment when God does not give them what was promised in this life. There is an extremely urgent need to correct this growing heresy in the global church.

Third, under the influence of Western missionaries, many churches in the Global South erroneously communicate "evangelical gnosticism." As discussed in chapter 6, Western Christians have tended to syncretize biblical theism with the "modern" worldview, resulting in a sacred-secular divide in which God is perceived as being concerned with getting people's souls to heaven but as being largely irrelevant to the rest of life. Unfortunately, Western missionaries have often exported this evangelical gnosticism to the Global South, with very negative results.

As illustrated in figure 7.3, traditional religionists believe that spiritual forces control the material world. The highest spiritual force is the Creator God, who is holy, distant, and unapproachable. In addition, a variety of lesser spirits—demons, ancestral spirits, and impersonal spiritual forces—control the material world. Because these spirits are believed to be selfish and somewhat unpredictable, the traditional religionist has an overwhelming desire to be protected from them and to manipulate them in order to improve their highly vulnerable lives. Hence, those who are thought to have an insight into the spiritual world—shamans, witchdoctors, and diviners—are regularly consulted to determine the best ways to appease or influence the spirits through sacrifices, charms, curses, and amulets.

FIGURE 7.3 Modern and Traditional Worldviews

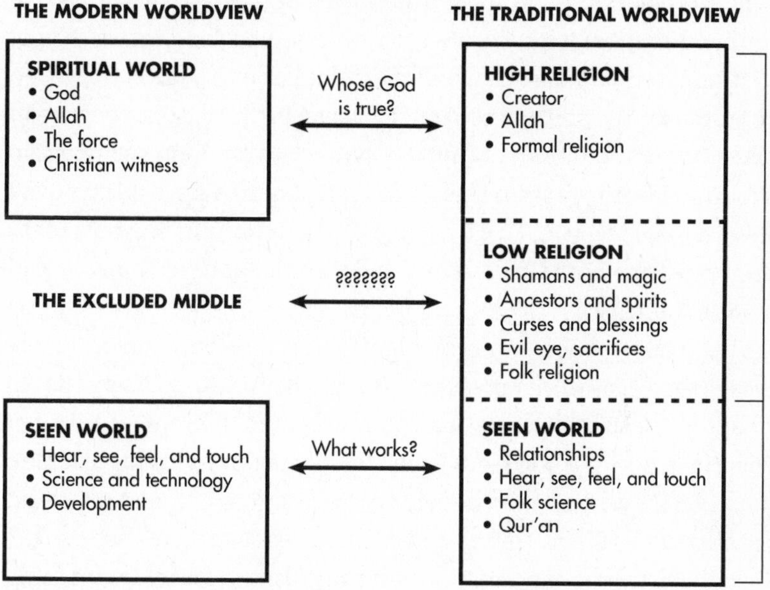

From Bryant L. Myers, *Walking with the Poor: Principles and Practices of Transformational Development*, rev. ed. (Maryknoll, NY: Orbis, 2011), 8, Figure 1.2; originally adapted from Paul G. Hiebert, "The Flaw of the Excluded Middle," *Missiology* 10, no. 1 (January 1982): 35–47.

As missiologist Paul Hiebert explains, when the evangelical gnosticism of the West collides with traditional religion, the results are far from ideal. Evangelical gnosticism focuses on "high religion," asking ultimate questions about the nature of God and of ultimate truth. But at the level of the material world, evangelical gnosticism acts as though God is mostly unnecessary, reverting to science and technology to deal with the struggles of everyday life: food, water, shelter, and health. Unfortunately, evangelical gnosticism's lack of connection between the spiritual and material realms—the "excluded middle"—provides no answer for the primary question that plagues the traditional religionist: how do I deal with the spiritual forces that are wreaking havoc with my life?

History has shown that traditional religionists respond in one of four ways to evangelical gnosticism. First, some simply remain in traditional religion, since the witch doctors seem to have a better answer for their problems than Christianity does. Second, some syncretize traditional religion with Christianity, worshiping the Creator-God of Christianity on Sunday but using the practices of traditional religion to manipulate the spirits the rest of the week. Third, some engage in surface accommodation, taking the symbols from high religion and attributing meanings from traditional religion to them, e.g., using the Bible as a magic charm. Finally, some put their hope in Western technology, rejecting both Christianity and traditional religion in favor of secular modernism.[7]

What is the solution to this problem? The solution is to return to the message that Jesus Christ preached: the kingdom of God.[8] As discussed in chapter 2, Jesus's message was that he is King of Kings and Lord of Lords. He is not "gnostic Jesus," who is only good for saving people's souls when they die. Rather, he is King Jesus, the creator, sustainer, and reconciler of all things. He has power over every aspect of the cosmos; indeed, he is far more powerful than the spiritual forces tormenting traditional religionists. Moreover, he is present, personal, and active, using his infinite power to accomplish good for those united to him. We can pray to him; he hears us; he cares; and he acts on our behalf (Romans 8:28).

Where There Is No Church

There are at least two instances in which it may not be possible to link people to a local church.

First, missionaries, who are sent out as agents of the church to spread the gospel, may be working in frontier regions where there is not yet an established church. Microfinance can sometimes be used very effectively as a means to pursue integral mission in such settings. And the goal should be to eventually plant a church as the Lord draws people into saving faith.

Second, there are contexts in which the churches' preaching is so heretical or their practices are so unbiblical that there are, in effect, no real churches. In such cases, it would be very detrimental to link people to one of these false churches. Efforts should be made to call these false churches to repentance or to plant new churches that are faithful to the gospel.

Ministry Component #2: Foster Whole-Person Discipleship in King Jesus Using Adult Education Principles

Adult Education and Discipleship

As we have seen, the substance of a human being is an interconnected mind, heart, actions, and body. One of the implications of this is that human transformation must address all aspects of the human creature. The human being cannot be transformed by simply downloading information into the brain in the same way that a computer can download a file from the internet. Rather, human beings are wired to learn through *actively* and *repeatedly* engaging the whole person across time in ways that are mutually reinforcing.[9]

There are numerous places in which this can be seen in Scripture, but perhaps there is no better illustration than the commands given to the Israelites about how to order their daily lives:

> Hear, O Israel: The LORD our God, the LORD is one. Love the LORD your God with all your heart and with all your soul and with all your strength. These commandments that I give you today are to be on your hearts. Impress them on your children. Talk about them when you sit at home and when you walk along the road, when you lie down and when you get up. Tie them as symbols on your hands and bind them on your foreheads. Write them on the doorframes of your houses and on your gates. (Deuteronomy 6:4–9)

The idea was not simply to go to worship every Sabbath to "download" the sermon. Rather, the idea was that God's Word would be applied throughout every moment of every day, narrating and affecting their minds, hearts, actions, and bodies throughout the week, *actively and repeatedly engaging the whole person across time.*

Indeed, there is a growing consensus amongst theologians, philosophers, educators, social scientists, and natural scientists that the mind, heart, actions, and body are interconnected in highly complex ways, and that this interconnectedness has profound implications for the process of discipleship.[10] For example, in his book *The Art of*

Changing the Brain: Enriching the Practice of Teaching by Exploring the Biology of Learning, scientist James Zull explains how recent brain imaging techniques (see figure 7.4) are confirming what a number of leading educators have argued for many years: transformative learning comes from a repeated, four-part cycle:

1. Concrete, real-life experience of the learner
2. Reflecting on that experience and on what could be different
3. Forming an "abstract hypothesis" about what could make life better
4. Active testing of the "abstract hypothesis"

FIGURE 7.4 The Human Brain and the Learning Cycle

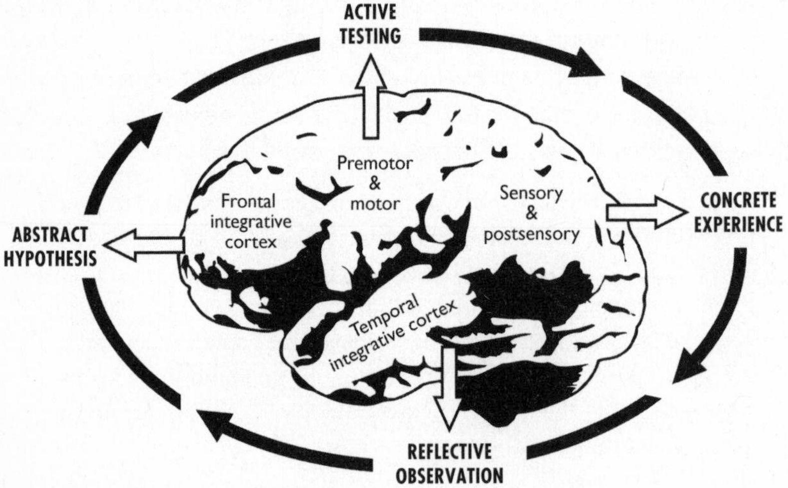

From James E. Zull, *The Art of Changing the Brain: Enriching the Practice of Teaching by Exploring the Biology of Learning* (Sterling, VA: Stylus Publishing LLC, 2002), 18.

Zull goes on to show that this cycle necessarily involves all aspects of the human being's substance: the brain, the affections (heart), the actions, and the body.[11]

The field of adult education seeks to design training and curricula in ways that are consistent with how adults actually learn.[12] In particular, adult education expert Jane Vella and the organization she founded, Global Learning Partners, have developed "dialogue education," a set of principles and techniques that attempt to operationalize the Learning Cycle in figure 7.4.[13] For example, when the members of a microfinance group meet to save and borrow their money, a lesson on a topic that is relevant to the group can be facilitated. Both the curriculum and the facilitation of the lesson can utilize the "Four As" of dialogue education, each of which corresponds to the four stages of the Learning Cycle:

1. *Anchor*: connect the topic to a relevant experience in the lives of the participants.
2. *Add*: supply new information, e.g., technical content, and invite participants to think about the implications of this information for their relevant experience.
3. *Apply*: provide an opportunity for participants to hypothesize what they could do with the new information to improve their life experience.
4. *Away*: ask participants to commit to taking specific actions to change their life experience, i.e., to "test" or "try" the hypothesis.[14]

Discipleship in King Jesus

Consider what this "experience-reflection-abstraction-testing" Learning Cycle means in the context of the church and the process of discipleship. A person should gather with a congregation on Sunday and encounter the embodiment of Jesus Christ in all of the elements of the worship service: the preaching and singing of the Word, the Lord's Supper and baptism, and prayer. It is very important that all aspects of this worship service point people to King Jesus—not to "evangelical gnostic Jesus" or to "prosperity gospel Jesus." Those in attendance should be encouraged to *reflect* on biblical truths and to consider the application of these truths to their lives—that is, to move into the formulation of an *abstract hypothesis* of the actions they will take in light of these truths. They then need to *actively test*—i.e., apply—these truths in the context of their daily lives throughout the week. Of course, it is crucial that what they actually test is consistent with the message that initiated the process: King Jesus.

And therein lies the rub in poverty-alleviation work. Churches often fail to communicate King Jesus on Sunday. And even when they do so, the current design of most poverty-alleviation strategies undermines the message of King Jesus from Monday through Saturday: Secular programs communicate the "modern worldview"—that is, material resources and technology are the answer; and many Christian organizations communicate "evangelical gnosticism," failing to show that Jesus Christ is relevant to every moment and every aspect of life. Indeed, the government funding that is used by many Christian relief and development organizations necessitates a separation of "spiritual" matters from other aspects of the program, thereby undermining the very message that Christians should be proclaiming and demonstrating: the good news of King Jesus (see the **Integral Mission Principle**).

What is needed are poverty-alleviation ministries that consistently communicate—in their words and deeds—that King Jesus is the creator, sustainer, and reconciler of all things. He has absolute power over broken individuals, broken systems, and demonic forces. Participants in these ministries need to *actively and repeatedly* engage their minds, hearts, actions, and bodies in the cycle of "experience-reflection-abstraction-testing" about the person of King Jesus and about what he means for all aspects of their lives. This is the whole-person, whole-life method of discipleship established in Deuteronomy 6, a method that neuroscience is confirming.

Ministry Component #3: Use Technical Training on Microfinance that Is Integrated with a King Jesus Worldview

One opportunity to contribute to this whole-person, whole-life discipleship occurs in the training that is necessary to be able to access the financial services in a microfinance ministry. As we shall see later, there is a range of methodologies for delivering microfinance services, and different methodologies require different types of training. But at a minimum, participants will need to understand the basic features of the financial services they are accessing, e.g., principal, interest, savings requirements, repayment schedules, etc.; in addition, in some delivery methodologies the participants will need to have a basic understanding of what makes a group-based financial system work, including such things as trust, discipline, transparency, leadership, and financial sustainability. As will be discussed further below, all of these technical topics can be taught from a biblical worldview that demonstrates the lordship and relevance of Jesus Christ to every aspect of his creation and the participants' need to put their ultimate hope in him.

Ministry Component #4: Use Complementary Technical Training that Is Integrated with a King Jesus Worldview

Many organizations are complementing their microfinance services with very simple technical training on a wide range of topics relevant to poor households: numeracy and literacy, business, health, family, agriculture, education, and rights advocacy. This complementary technical training provides an opportunity for greater impact but also introduces some new risks. For example, introducing business training into a savings and credit association in which only half the members are operating microenterprises could alienate the other half of the members, thereby undermining the solidarity of the group and perhaps causing the group to fall apart. Readers interested in learning more about introducing additional technical training are encouraged to do additional reading to understand both the possibilities and potential pitfalls.[15]

Both the technical training on microfinance in Ministry Component #3 and the complementary technical training in Ministry Component #4 provide another opportunity to communicate King Jesus and his relevance to every aspect of people's lives. Carefully integrating relevant biblical truths into the technical messages can be part of overcoming the shortcomings of "evangelical gnosticism" and the "excluded middle" described earlier.

Toward that end, the Chalmers Center for Economic Development at Covenant College (hereafter, the "Chalmers Center") has developed a portfolio of training, curricula, and tools for microfinance ministries that are available on the website associated with this book. These resources include technical content on microfinance and on a range of complementary topics related to business, home, and health. Current titles include:

- *Restore: Savings*
- *Handbook for Partnering with Microfinance Institutions*
- *Foundations for Business, Home, and Health*

- *Plan for a Better Business*
- *Manage Your Business Money*
- *Increase Your Sales*
- *Using Wisdom in Saving*
- *Plan for Better Health*
- *Using Health Care Services*
- *Preventing HIV/AIDS—It Is Our Choice*
- *Diarrhea—Its Management and Prevention*
- *Confronting Malaria in Our Community*

There are four features of these curricula:

1. *Technical Assistance*: The curricula are centered on best-practice, technical content that is highly relevant to people's lives, giving them very practical information to help them understand how to operate a microfinance group, increase their business profits, manage their finances, and improve their health. All of these provide participants with knowledge, attitudes, and practices to improve their relationships with God, self, others, and the rest of creation.

2. *Biblical Worldview*: The curricula very intentionally integrate the hope of King Jesus into the technical material and help people to apply this hope to their lives. No longer is God separated from his world, as in "evangelical gnosticism." Rather, King Jesus is presented as highly relevant to all aspects of life, addressing all three levels of the box on the right side of figure 7.3. In particular, as illustrated in figure 7.5, relevant examples are used to help people to rest in the good news of King Jesus, to forsake traditional religion and its practices, and to live as new creatures in Christ with respect to God, self, others, and the rest of creation.

3. *Adult Education Techniques*: Both the Chalmers Center's curricula and its training processes incorporate best-practice adult education principles and techniques, seeking to engage the entire substance of human beings—head, heart, actions, and bodies—in a transformative learning process.

4. *Asset-Based, Participatory-Development Philosophy*: Both the content and design of the curricula intentionally incorporate an asset-based,

FIGURE 7.5 Excerpt from Facilitator's Guide to "Plan a Better Business"

Today we are going to talk about *Step 5: Find Help for Your Business.*

Use a story to identify ways to find help to improve your business — 12 minutes

When you want to improve or expand your business, sometimes you need extra help to know how to make the proper changes.

Neema's Search for Help with Her Business

Neema wants to make more profit. She fears that her business will not provide enough for school clothes and fees in the coming year. She plans to grow her business by selling stew, kedjenou, and attiéké, plus another product. She begins to look for help to expand her business. She asks a local diviner for help to make the best decision. The man gives her an amulet to hang in her shop and a powder to sprinkle outside the door of her competitor's business.

TURN TO A PARTNER AND DISCUSS:

- **What similar practices occur in our community?**

Give 2 or 3 participants an opportunity to share. Thank and praise participants.

Troubles certainly come to us all, and we feel desperate and afraid of failure. In these times, God may seem distant, and we are tempted to trust only in our own abilities, or to ask the diviners or spirits for help with our business. However, the Bible says: [Open the Scriptures and read Deuteronomy 18:10 – 13]:

> "Let no one be found among you who sacrifices their son or daughter in the fire, who practices divination or sorcery, interprets omens, engages in witchcraft, or casts spells, or who is a medium or spiritist or who consults the dead. Anyone who does these things is detestable to the LORD. . . . You must be blameless before the LORD your God."

- **What does this mean for us when we seek help for our businesses?**

Give 2 or 3 participants an opportunity to share. Thank and praise participants.

As the people of God, we are not to consult diviners or follow their advice. When we are part of God's family, we can ask him in faith to help us. He gives us the power and strength that we need to persevere through difficulties.

Open the Scriptures to 1 John 5:14. The Bible says:

> This is the confidence we have in approaching God: that if we ask anything according to his will, he hears us.

- **Why does God hear us when we pray to him?**

When Jesus died on the cross, he gave us this access to God. He conquered all other powers (Colossians 2:15). He died to forgive our mistakes — all of them — even when we look to other sources for help instead of looking to him.

- **What questions or comments do you have?**

participatory-development perspective, which is briefly explained here; readers are encouraged to go deeper by reading *When Helping Hurts*.[16]

Asset-Based Approaches

As we saw in chapter 5, many materially poor people, especially those influenced by traditional religion, often suffer from feelings of inferiority (relationship with self) and often have little understanding that they can impact the world around them (relationship with the rest of creation). Thus, a central part of restoring people to image bearing is helping them to recover their sense of dignity and their ability to effect change. In this light, approaches that are *asset based*—which help people to discover and utilize the gifts, resources, and abilities they already have—are preferred to those that are *needs based*—which focus on what people are lacking and on what outsiders can do to fix them. The key task of an asset-based approach is to identify, mobilize, and connect the resources that are already in a low-income household or community, only bringing in outside resources when they complement the resources that are already present.

Participatory Approaches

Similarly, *participatory* approaches—which include materially poor people in the design, planning, execution, and evaluation of the ministry—are generally preferred to *blueprint* approaches—which impose predetermined programs on participants, thereby undermining their dignity as image bearers who have valuable insights to share and who are called to be stewards over their own gifts and resources.

For example, the Chalmers Center's curricula guide the group members through a process of discovering their own assets, including their ability to save rather than just borrow. Similarly, the curricula asks the group to decide the amounts for weekly savings, loans, and interest rates, rather than imposing a blueprint on them by telling them how much they will save and borrow and at what rates.

There is one important caveat to using participatory approaches in the context of microfinance: not all features of every microfinance intervention can or should be developed by materially poor people. For example, mobile phones are increasingly being used to enable people to conduct saving and loan transactions. It would be a bit silly to ask poor people to have to invent the mobile phones themselves! Similarly, some prepackaged insurance services being offered to materially poor people are designed by sophisticated actuaries and financial experts. Only a very small fraction of even the most educated people in the world have the expertise to create and deliver these services.

Hence, it takes wisdom, judgment, and some trial and error to determine which features of the microfinance ministry should be prepackaged, and which should be left in the hands of the participants. But we should always have a posture which recognizes that having voice and choice is essential to image bearing, so participation should be utilized as much as is feasible, taking into consideration the capacities, contexts, and constraints of the participants.

Developmental Approaches

Simply handing out material resources—i.e., providing *relief*—is the appropriate intervention in contexts in which people are in a crisis and are incapable of helping themselves. In contrast, *development* involves walking with households and communities across time, asking them to contribute whatever they can to their own improvement. *Relief* is done "to" or "for" people, while *development* is done "with" people. Arguably the biggest problem in poverty alleviation is that *relief* is being used in contexts that call for *development*, thereby undermining people's dignity and capacity for stewardship and creating crippling dependencies.

> ***Asset-Based, Participatory-Development Principle***
>
> Focus on local *assets* not just on *needs*; as much as possible, use *participatory* rather than *blueprint* approaches; do not use *relief* when the context calls for *development.*

In summary, we can now introduce the **Asset-Based, Participatory-Development Principle**.

Asset-based, participatory development helps to restore human beings to image bearing, which is the goal of poverty alleviation, as summarized in the **Poverty-Alleviation Principle**. Both the content and design of the Chalmers Center's curricula are consistent with the **Asset-Based, Participatory-Development Principle**.

Ministry Components #1–#4 are parts of microfinance ministries that seek to bring the power of being united to King Jesus to bear on broken individuals by addressing both their substantive and relational aspects. In other words, these Ministry Components seek to make the tire well-formed, capable of experiencing wholeness again. It is important to reemphasize that none of this is automatic, as God does as he pleases. Nevertheless, table 7.1 at the end of this chapter summarizes the various ways that these Ministry Components seek to enable people to properly experience their relationships with God, self, others, and the rest of creation, which is the goal of poverty alleviation (see the **Poverty-Alleviation Principle**).

Mending Broken Systems

As discussed earlier, a sound tire is necessary but not sufficient for a smooth ride. The roads on which the tire travels—the systems—need to be working well in order for people to actually experience human flourishing in the way that God intended. For example, imagine that Ministry Components #1–#4 help Thomas, a poor individual, to better understand his relationship to creation and to take new actions to find sustaining work. These new actions will do little good if broken economic and financial systems make it impossible for Thomas to find a job or to be self-employed.

Moreover, as discussed in chapter 5, this systemic brokenness is likely to have profound impacts on individuals, driving all the way into their substance: mind, heart, actions, and bodies. For example, if the systems do not allow Thomas to find sustaining work, they will undermine the Learning Cycle pictured in figure 7.4. As Thomas "tests" the hypothesis that he can have greater dominion over creation, he will conclude that the hypothesis is wrong, if the systems provide evidence that the hypothesis is, in fact, false. In other words, Thomas is likely to get discouraged and to quit trying if his efforts to find sustaining work fail.

How can microfinance ministries bring the power of King Jesus to bear on broken systems? Ultimately, all progress on systemic change depends upon Jesus Christ; however, he often works through people to change systems, and there are four ways that this can happen in the context of microfinance ministry.

Ministry Component #5: Connect People to the Ecosystem of the Church Family

As mentioned in the previous chapter, the local church provides an opportunity for its members to experience something of Christ's fixing of broken systems right now. In a world in which colonialism, neocolonialism, and cultural elites have created oppressive cultural systems that have imprinted lies on the very brains of the oppressed,[17] the local church operates as a holy nation, with a different ecosystem and a different set of messages than that of the world.

What are the key features of the church's ecosystem? One of the primary biblical images of the church is that it is a "family" consisting of "brothers" and "sisters" who have all been adopted by their heavenly Father.[18] As a "family," the church environment is characterized by love, safety, acceptance, support, encouragement, nurture, discipline, and accountability. As a result, believers immersed in this family are able to live in an ecosystem that nurtures their entire personhood, enabling them to grow up from being infants into mature adults, "attaining to the whole measure of the fullness of Christ," who is the image of the Triune God (Ephesians 4:1–13; Colossians 1:15). *In other words, the church family is God's primary ecosystem for nurturing believers' minds, hearts, actions, and bodies to live in right relationship with God, self, others, and the rest of creation, which is the goal of poverty alleviation* (see the **Poverty-Alleviation Principle**). Once again, the **Church and Parachurch Principle** is so crucial: microfinance ministries must be "rooted in and lead back to" a local congregation.

Ministry Component #6: Use Supportive Group Structures for Delivery of Microfinance Services

Another supportive ecosystem can be fostered in the regular meetings of the ministry's microfinance group. When the members come together to save and borrow their money, certain features of the group combine to create an environment that is supportive of restoration to human flourishing as image bearers:

- Worship through prayer, singing, and dance
- Laughter
- Fellowship

- Support and encouragement
- Development of leadership skills from running the group
- Accountability with respect to financial matters and to life in general

In other words, like the church, the group can be a place in which a new culture emerges that is distinctly different from the culture in the world around it. In a world full of racism, sexism, and classism, the group can be a nurturing oasis where members are encouraged to live out the reality of being new creatures in relationship to God, self, others, and the rest of creation.

It is important to note that this new culture is likely to provide a degree of *peer pressure*, which recent research is finding to be a very important ingredient in fostering behavioral changes. One of the most nagging aspects of poverty alleviation is that people often fail to engage in simple behaviors that could significantly improve their lives. For example, diarrhea causes 20 percent of the nine million deaths per annum for children under the age of five.[19] It is very simple to prevent most diarrhea by adding chlorine to drinking water. What is so exasperating is that even though many poor people understand the benefits of chlorine and even though it is very cheap, most people in the Global South fail to add it to their drinking water.[20]

Why? The emerging field of behavioral economics, which incorporates insights from psychology into economic analysis, is finding considerable evidence that poor people—like all of us—are often governed by impulses and emotions that place a heavy value on immediate gratification. Humans tend to avoid even minor inconveniences—like adding chlorine to water—even when those minor annoyances could yield large benefits in the future. In other words, people procrastinate, over and over again.[21]

Through the use of experiments, behavioral economists are finding that peer pressure can often help to overcome human weaknesses on a wide range of matters related to poverty alleviation. For example, researchers found that by placing a chlorine dispenser next to public water spigots in Kenyan villages, people could observe whether or not their neighbors were adding chlorine to their water. This public exposure created peer pressure that induced an increase in chlorine usage from less than 15 percent of households to 61 percent.[22]

By design, microfinance groups use peer pressure to encourage savings contributions and loan repayments. In addition, it is very likely that the groups in a microfinance ministry provide peer pressure that promotes positive behaviors with respect to God, self, others, and the rest of creation as well.

Although there is a need for more research about the effects of groups in microfinance, a recent review of the existing evidence concludes that groups in secular programs yield important psychological and social benefits, including:

- Group solidarity
- Leadership development
- Increased self-confidence
- Greater decision-making power in the household[23]

These considerations have important implications for the design of microfinance ministries. In order to reduce the time that people have to spend in meetings, a number of microfinance programs have dispensed with groups and deliver their savings and loan services directly to individuals. At first glance this approach looks more efficient for the client, but the growing evidence about the power of groups should give microfinance programs some pause before dispensing with group-based services.

Ministry Component #7: Encourage Group Members to Address Broken Systems

As the group develops greater solidarity and as members gain increased confidence, they can be encouraged to initiate community projects and even to tackle broken systems in their community. For example, the WORTH programs in Ethiopia and Nepal intentionally encourage microfinance groups to address community-wide issues. The groups have responded by undertaking community-wide projects such as constructing community buildings, clinics, schools, libraries, wells, and bridges, often using their own funds but sometimes attracting additional money from local governments or other organizations. In addition, the groups have addressed pressing community issues such as harmful cultural practices, HIV/AIDs, gender-based violence, and human trafficking through rallies, demonstrations, door-to-door campaigns, and street dramas.[24]

Ministry Component #8: Use Microfinance to Create Financial Services

As stated in the **Microfinance for Households Principle**, the financial systems in the Global South are broken, making it very difficult for poor people to manage their cash flows to meet a wide range of household needs. Microfinance seeks to combat this problem by establishing financial systems, sustainable mechanisms that provide savings, loans, insurance, and money-transfer services for poor people.

> ***Microfinance for Households Principle***
>
> Poor households need convenient, flexible, and reliable financial services for:
>
> 1. Consumption Smoothing
> 2. Business Investments
> 3. Household Investments
> 4. Lifecycle Needs
> 5. Emergencies

As discussed in chapter 4, for most poor households the impacts of microfinance will be to stabilize consumption rather than to dramatically increase it. In other words, as illustrated in figure 7.6, most households will experience the lower dotted curve rather than the upper dotted curve. What are the overall implications of this stabilization on poverty?

Again, there is a need for more research. But a recent review of results from studies using a variety of research methodologies concludes that savings and credit associations often yield the following benefits:

- Increased asset accumulation
- Superior risk management
- Greater investment in income-generating activities such as microenterprises
- Improved management of finances
- Increased in savings
- Enhanced food security
- Increased access to healthcare*

FIGURE 7.6 Revised Expectations of Impacts of Microfinance

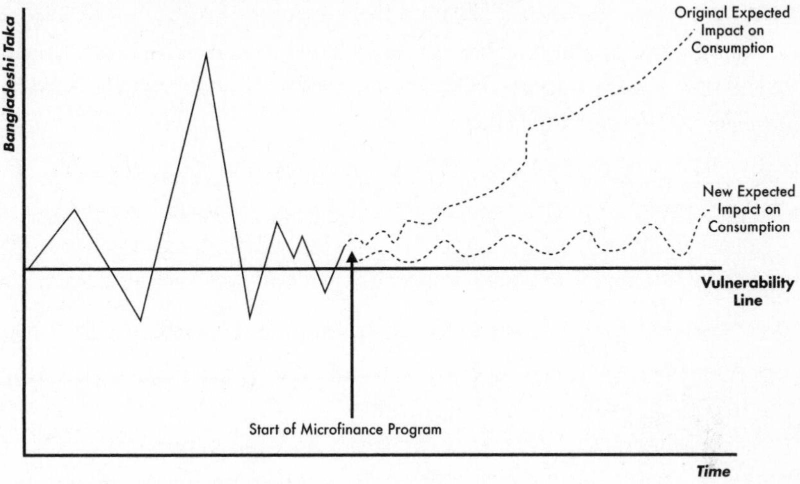

- Payments for school fees*[25]

The asterisks for the last two items are added because although participants in savings and credit associations often report that the group has enabled them to access more healthcare and to pay for school fees, the existing evidence is inconclusive as to whether or not their overall expenditures on health and education are actually increasing.

As will be discussed in chapter 8, savings and credit associations are just one type of financial system, so there is a need to explore the impacts of other sorts of systems as well, e.g., MFIs. Space does not allow for such a complete exploration. But given that the impacts just mentioned are likely to be the dominant story for most people from the emerging "microfinance-for-households" approach, we will use it as the basis in the discussion that follows.

Overall, the impacts listed above can be summarized as follows: *the "microfinance-for-households" approach creates financial systems that enable very poor families to reduce their vulnerability*, which is one of the key nodes in Chambers's "web of deprivation" (see chapter 5). This is not a small accomplishment. Creating a sustainable intervention that stabilizes life above the "vulnerability line"—and that grassroots churches in poor communities can implement—is a major achievement.

How major? Consider this: The *Human Development Report*, the annual publication of the United Nations Development Program, chooses a pressing topic to emphasize each year. The focus for 2014 is captured in the title: *Sustaining Human Progress: Reducing Vulnerabilities and Building Resilience.* The report explains:

> While globalization has brought benefits to many, it has also given rise to new concerns, manifest at times as local reaction to the spillover effects of events far away. Preparing citizens for a less vulnerable future means strengthening the intrinsic resilience of communities and countries.[26]

Helping churches on the front lines of poverty to use the "microfinance-for-households" approach is consistent with "strengthening the intrinsic resilience of communities."

Similarly, the *World Development Report*, the annual publication of the World Bank, focuses on managing risk and devotes an entire chapter to the importance of developing financial systems that can enable poor households to reduce their vulnerabilities.[27]

The development community's focus on vulnerability is relatively new, so there is a need for considerably more research about the benefits of reducing it; however, recent research suggests that the benefits could be quite large, for vulnerability appears to delve into the very substance of human beings. Eldar Shafir of Princeton University and Sendhil Mullainathan of Harvard University find that environments characterized by extreme vulnerability have profound impacts on the mind, resulting in a "psychology of scarcity" characterized by:

- *Tunneling*: People focus on managing the current or imminent crisis or need, neglecting other important issues that are more long-term.
- *Borrowing*: People will borrow money at very high interest rates to deal with the present crisis, even if this will hurt them in the long run.
- *Distraction*: People under stress are cognitively impaired, resulting in decision making that may be less than optimal.[28]

As a result, Shafir argues that if microfinance can make people just a little less vulnerable, the multifaceted impacts on poverty could be quite large.[29]

Combating Demonic Forces

Union with Christ provides believers with the power to overcome demonic forces, because "the one who is in you is greater than the one who is in the world" (1 John 4:4b).

How can believers put this power into effect?

Ministry Component #9: Teach People to Forsake the Practices of Traditional Religion and to Put on the Whole Armor of God

Many poor people in the Global South engage in the practices of traditional religion, including some professing Christians. There is a need for biblical instruction about the need to forsake such practices and to "put on the full armor of God": truth, righteousness, the gospel, faith, salvation, the Bible, and prayer (Ephesians 6:11–18).

As pictured in figure 7.3, it is extremely important that such instruction move from abstraction into very practical applications. People need to see that King Jesus has more power than the demonic forces and be shown how to live out that reality in their lives. This is where the Chalmers Center's business, home, and health curricula described in Ministry Component #4 and exhibit 7.5 can be helpful, for they bring King Jesus to bear on the practices of traditional religion in the context of people's daily lives and behaviors.

Ministry Component #10: Immerse the Entire Ministry in Ongoing Prayer

Fundamentally, integral mission is about declaring that Jesus is King, which is a declaration of his victory over demonic forces and over the effects of sin on the entire cosmos. But demonic forces, oppressive systems, and the old human nature don't go down without a fight, so it is profoundly important for everybody involved in the ministry to regularly petition the Triune God to unleash his power to crush Satan, end oppression, and transform broken people.

Summary

This chapter outlined what we shall call a "holistic theory of change for microfinance ministries," seeking to bring the reconciling work of

TABLE 7.1 Summary of Holistic Theory of Change for Microfinance Ministries

MINISTRY COMPONENT #1: Connect People to the Local Church and the "Ordinary Means of Grace"	■ Initiates and nurtures a new creature that has the capacity to relate properly to G, S, O, C. ■ New creature in Christ gets to experience full benefits of Christ's overturning of oppressive systems that contribute to broken relationships with G, S, O, C. ■ New creature in Christ is protected from demonic forces that contribute to broken relationships with G, S, O, C.
MINISTRY COMPONENT #2: Foster Whole-Person Discipleship in King Jesus Using Adult Education Principles	■ Repeated application of "Learning Cycle" — with continual narration about the comprehensive implications of King Jesus — nurtures the new creature to relate properly to G, S, O, C. ■ Unbelievers are challenged to embrace King Jesus.
MINISTRY COMPONENT #3: Use Technical Training on Microfinance that Is Integrated with a King Jesus Worldview	■ Technical content provides practical information about ways to relate better to G, S, O, C. ■ Repeated narration about the comprehensive implications of King Jesus nurtures the new creature to relate properly to G, S, O, C. ■ Unbelievers are challenged to embrace King Jesus.
MINISTRY COMPONENT #4: Use Complementary Technical Training that Is Integrated with a King Jesus Worldview	■ Technical content provides practical information about ways to relate better to G, S, O, C. ■ Repeated narration about the comprehensive implications of King Jesus nurtures the new creature to relate properly to G, S, O, C. ■ Unbelievers are challenged to embrace King Jesus.
MINISTRY COMPONENT #5: Connect People to the Ecosystem of the Church Family	■ Culture of family provides support, encouragement, and accountability that nurtures the new creature to mature in relationship to G, S, O, C. ■ Unbelievers experience some benefits of this culture, helping them relate better to S, O, C. ■ Unbelievers are challenged to embrace King Jesus.
MINISTRY COMPONENT #6: Use Supportive Group Structures for Delivery of Microfinance Services	■ Culture of group provides support, encouragement, and accountability that nurtures the new creature in relationship to G, S, O, C. ■ Unbelievers experience some benefits of this culture, helping them relate better to S, O, C. ■ Unbelievers are challenged to embrace "Colossians 1 Jesus."
MINISTRY COMPONENT #7: Encourage Group Members to Address Broken Systems	■ New creatures get to exercise proper relationship to G, S, O, C. ■ Unbelievers in the group get to experience some aspects of relating properly to S, O, C. ■ Unbelievers in group are challenged to embrace King Jesus. ■ Broken systems in community are mended, creating greater opportunity for all people to experience improved relationships with G, S, O, C. ■ Community is attracted to the God of these people who care for their community.

MINISTRY COMPONENT #8: **Use Microfinance to Create Financial Services**	■ Ability to smooth consumption above vulnerability line: • Increases sense of dignity: S • Lowers stress in family: O • Allows people to better support themselves through work: C • Reduces "psychology of scarcity" which improves decision making, improving S, O, C ■ Increased investment in income-generating activities: • Increases people's ability to support themselves through work: C • Improves people's sense of dignity from work: S ■ Enhanced food security improves health: • Increases ability to support themselves through work (C), which increases dignity (S) • Increases ability to perform in school (C), which increases dignity (S), ability to participate in society (O), and future earning capacity (C) ■ Increased access to health services improves health: • Increases ability to support themselves through work (C), which increases dignity (S) • Increases ability to perform in school (C), which increases dignity (S), ability to participate in society (O), and future earning capacity (C) ■ Increased ability to pay school fees has potential to increase education (C), which increases dignity (S), ability to participate in society (O), and future earning capacity (C)
MINISTRY COMPONENT #9: **Teach People to Forsake the Practices of Traditional Religion and to Put on the Whole Armor of God**	■ Turning away from the occult to King Jesus affects every aspect of personhood: G, S, O, C.
MINISTRY COMPONENT #10: **Immerse the Entire Ministry in Ongoing Prayer**	■ As the Triune God applies the victory of Christ's death and resurrection to demonic forces, broken systems, and broken individuals, it affects every aspect of personhood: G, S, O, C.

G = relationship with God; **S** = relationship with self; **O** = relationship with others; **C** = relationship with rest of creation

King Jesus to bear on broken individuals, broken systems, and demonic forces. Table 7.1 summarizes the potential impacts of ten Ministry Components of microfinance ministries on people's relationships with God, self, others, and the rest of creation. These components are not some magic recipe that, if followed perfectly, will necessarily result in the transformation that we long to see. However, they provide helpful guidance as we faithfully seek to create more transformative ministries, trusting in God to determine the final impacts. In practice, organizational constraints and realities on the ground will make it difficult for some ministries to implement all of these components. The good news is that King Jesus is able to overcome our imperfections, achieving his goals despite our failures and shortcomings.

Application Exercise

If you are thinking of launching a microfinance ministry, prayerfully consider the steps you might take to incorporate Ministry Components #1–#10. If you are already involved in a microfinance program, evaluate your program in light of the ten Ministry Components. What positive changes can you make to improve your program? Ask God for wisdom and strength as you seek to declare the good news of his kingdom, and then rest in the good news of Colossians 1: King Jesus is making all things new, despite our failures and weaknesses.

PART 3

UNDERSTANDING MICROFINANCE

CHAPTER 8

ROSCAs, ASCAs, AND MFIs: A PRIMER ON MICROFINANCE

> The central problem in the theory of economic growth is to understand the process by which a community is converted from being a 5 percent to a 12 percent saver—with all the changes in attitudes, in institutions, and in techniques which accompany this conversion.
>
> —*Arthur Lewis, Nobel Laureate in Economics*[1]

> It is more profitable [for microfinance providers] to put poor people into debt than it is to take care of their savings.
>
> —*David Roodman, microfinance researcher*[2]

The "microfinance-for-households" approach opens up unlimited possibilities for holistic ministry. In fact, there are so many options that it can all be overwhelming. How can a church, a missionary, or a ministry actually get started in providing financial services to poor people?

The good news is that in the world of microfinance, there are really only three basic strategies for churches, missionaries, and ministries to consider: two good ones and one that is often problematic. All of the other ministry possibilities are simply variations of those basic strategies. Part IV of this book will describe those strategies in some detail.

However, before we can do that, we need to understand some key terms in order to lay a proper foundation for the remainder of the book. This chapter introduces some of those terms, starting with a consideration of the financial portfolio of Prudence, a poor woman in Kenya.

Prudence's Portfolio

Prudence retails household goods out of her stall in the bustling marketplace of Karatina, a small town in central Kenya.[3] Like all business owners around the world, whenever Prudence's inventory runs low, she needs a "lump sum" of cash in order to buy the inventory to restock her shelves. Because this lump sum is greater than the disposable money Prudence has in her pocket, Prudence either needs to save or borrow lump sums in order to purchase the inventory she needs.

Most of the readers of this book could use a bank to acquire a lump sum of money for business purposes. We could either borrow a lump sum from a bank at a reasonable interest rate or save up for a lump sum by making regular bank deposits, earning interest in the process. Although we often take them for granted, banks play an extremely important role in facilitating the financial exchanges that characterize a thriving economy.

Unfortunately, there simply are no banks in most poor communities in the Global South. And even when banks do exist, they usually cannot afford to offer the financial services that poor people desire. There are various levels of poverty and different types of economic activities, making it difficult to generalize. However, poor people in the Global South typically need small loans in the range of $4 to $400 US, depending on their income levels and economic activities. Unfortunately, such small loans do not generate sufficient interest to cover the banks' costs of administering these loans. Hence, banks typically do not offer loans to poor people. Similarly, the amounts that poor people want to save are too small to meet the minimum balance requirements of most banks.

Prudence needs to borrow or to save in order to acquire lump sums of money to restock her shelves. But in the absence of banking services, how can she do this?

Prudence might be able to get a loan from a local moneylender, a person who is often called a "loan shark." But obtaining such a loan would be an expensive and risky proposition, as these moneylenders typically charge interest ranging from 240 percent to 360 percent on an annual percentage rate (APR), and rates can go as high as 20 percent per day (7200 percent APR) for small, high-risk loans. Moreover, these moneylenders can be quite harsh in dealing with delinquent borrowers.

> ***Microfinance for Households Principle***
>
> Poor households need convenient, flexible, and reliable financial services for:
>
> 1. Consumption Smoothing
> 2. Business Investments
> 3. Household Investments
> 4. Lifecycle Needs
> 5. Emergencies

Similarly, if Prudence chooses to save up for a lump sum, she might be able to put her money on deposit with an informal savings agent, a trusted person from her community who will store Prudence's money in a "safe" place. But this option is not cheap either. Researchers have found savers paying 30 percent APR to the savings agent in a town in India and an astounding 80 percent APR to the savings agents in Nigeria![4]

Clearly, in the absence of standard banking services, it is very difficult for poor people to acquire the lump sums of money they need in order to operate their small businesses. But as we saw in the **Microfinance for Households Principle**, poor households need lump sums of money for far more than just businesses. Indeed, it is not an exaggeration to say that lump sums can be a matter of life and death. When a child gets sick with malaria, it is a lump sum that will enable the parents to purchase the lifesaving medicine. And when the husband loses his job, it is a lump sum that will enable the family to buy enough food to avoid starvation.

In order to survive, Prudence creatively packages together a portfolio of strategies to enable her to save and borrow the lump sums she needs for a variety of purposes:

- Prudence belongs to several rotating savings and credit associations (ROSCAs), which are typically called "merry-go-rounds" in Kenya. Each member of a ROSCA makes a contribution of a fixed amount to the group's pot at their regularly scheduled meetings. The members then take turns getting the pot, with one member getting the entire pot at each meeting. Prudence uses several different ROSCAs for different purposes. One has a monthly payout that she uses to pay for her grandchildren's school fees now that their parents have died from AIDS; another ROSCA pays out weekly, which she uses to restock her market stall.

- Prudence belongs to an accumulating savings and credit association (ASCA) in which she can take out small, short-term loans periodically. The ASCA functions as a simple credit union that is owned and operated by the poor members themselves. In addition to being able to get loans from the ASCA, Prudence earns interest on her savings deposits into the ASCA. Last year she was able to withdraw her savings and interest just before Christmas, providing her with $109 to use for holiday expenses.
- Prudence belongs to an informal, funeral insurance group. When Prudence dies, the group will distribute enough money to Prudence's family to ensure that her remains are transported to her home village.
- Prudence also has a loan from Faulu, a formal, Kenyan microfinance institution (MFI) that provides financial services to 250,000 poor people across Kenya. Prudence is using this loan to upgrade her house in order to rent out some rooms to secure regular income in her old age.
- Prudence has managed to save a few dollars that she keeps handy in a safe place in her house.
- Finally, Prudence has long-term savings locked up in the form of a cow that she owns and that her brother cares for back in her home village.

Prudence's story reveals a very rich survival strategy. She has managed to develop a fairly sophisticated portfolio of savings, loan, and insurance products from a diverse set of sources in order to secure lump sums for both her present and future needs. Helping poor people like Prudence to be able to do this more effectively is at the heart of microfinance.

What Exactly Is Microfinance?

Microfinance is an approach to poverty alleviation that seeks to establish financial systems for poor households and individuals. A "financial system" can be defined as any sustainable mechanism that enables people to create and access useful lump sums of money through savings, loans, insurance, or money-transfer services. A bank is an example of a financial system that is familiar to most readers. As discussed earlier, poor people often lack access to financial systems, making it difficult for them to acquire the lump sums they need in order to survive and to improve their lives. Microfinance tries to solve this problem by creating new financial systems or by adapting existing ones in hopes of improving the lives of poor people.

Most people equate the term "microfinance" with "microloans," but microfinance has become much broader than this, as researchers and practitioners have learned that poor households need a range of financial services, including savings, insurance, and money transfers.

Microfinance Is Not Just about Loans: The Importance of Savings Services

The common assumption is that poor people live hand to mouth, using every penny of income for immediate consumption. Indeed, for many decades microfinance efforts focused exclusively on making loans available to poor people, with many practitioners oblivious to the fact that poor people had the desire and capacity to save.

But years of research and practice have demonstrated that poor people actually do try to save for both daily needs and for larger lump sums of money. In the absence of banking services, poor people are forced to use considerable creativity to save. They sometimes hide a few dollars in their homes in bamboo poles, in jars buried underground, or in the hems of dresses. Others try to get the money out of their house by asking their neighbors to hold their savings for them or by lending their neighbors a few dollars, knowing that their neighbors will typically lend it back to them when they need it.[5] Others try to save in assets that they can eventually convert to cash, such as domestic animals, gold, or jewelry. And as we saw in the case of Prudence, some poor people are able to save in informal financial systems such as ROSCAs and ASCAs.

How badly do poor people want to save? As discussed earlier, there is evidence that poor people will pay as high as 80 percent APR for the privilege of saving, a clear indication that savings services are highly valuable to them.

Why is saving so important to poor people? As we saw in chapter 4, poor people are highly vulnerable. Even in the best of times their small incomes are irregular and unpredictable. Moreover, there are a host of events—sickness, famines, earthquakes, recessions, and violence—that can plunge them into a downward spiral. Faced with enormous uncertainty, poor people naturally try to reduce their risks, and saving is a less risky way of obtaining a lump sum than borrowing.

For example, a woman could either save or borrow to buy an oven to make baked goods to sell in the marketplace. If her child falls ill and she has chosen to save for the oven, she has the flexibility to delay her purchase and to use her savings to pay for her child's treatment. However, if she has borrowed to purchase the oven, then mandatory debt repayments might preclude her from getting medical care for her child.[6]

Indeed, research has found that the poorest households often perceive loans—particularly production loans with weekly repayment requirements—as too risky for them.[7] For example, one researcher has found that the hard-core poor in Bangladesh will not take microloans from Grameen Bank, the most famous MFI in the world, because they do not consider themselves capable of generating sufficient income to repay their loans.[8]

From the perspective of long-run development, there are at least four additional reasons that it is important to make savings services available to poor people.

First, using local savings as a source of capital is consistent with the **Asset-Based, Participatory-Development Principle**. Instead of poor people having to immediately look to outsiders for loan capital, they can turn to the savings services that communicate, "You have resources that can grow into something bigger."

Second, the process of savings fosters self-discipline and a forward-looking perspective that are both crucial to long-run progress. As discussed earlier, traditional religion teaches that the world is controlled by capricious spirits, implying that there is often little humans can do to effect change in their lives. This perspective sometimes undermines self-control and discipline, since life seems inherently uncontrol-

> ***Asset-Based, Participatory-Development Principle***
>
> Focus on local *assets* not just on *needs*; as much as possible, use *participatory* rather than *blueprint* approaches; do not use *relief* when the context calls for *development*.

lable. Furthermore, traditional religion's emphasis on appeasing ancestral spirits can result in a backward-looking perspective that can undermine planning for the future, making investments, pursuing education, and exploring new opportunities.[9] Of course, addressing traditional religion at its most fundamental level requires the transforming power of Jesus Christ. And as this happens, providing savings services can help to foster the behaviors that are consistent with this new life in Christ.

Third, the accumulation of physical capital (productive equipment) and human capital (education and knowledge) is essential to increases in income. But the only way to accumulate capital is to save or to borrow, and ultimately, even borrowing requires the ability to save. For example, consider a poor farmer whose income is $1 per day. Now imagine the farmer takes out a $25 loan to buy a new plow, which increases his income to $1.50 per day. The farmer cannot consume that entire $1.50, because he needs to repay the $25 loan. In other words, the farmer needs to consume less than he is earning—i.e., he needs to be able to save—in order to pay back the loan. If the farmer is not able to repay this loan, he will not be able to get additional loans to acquire more capital in the future. Thus, economic progress depends on the ability to save. When microfinance promotes savings services it fosters the patterns of behavior that are crucial for economic prosperity.

Finally, from a biblical perspective, we should certainly have hesitancy about rushing into debt. As Proverbs 22:7 states, "The rich rule over the poor, and the borrower is slave to the lender." Although this passage should not be construed to forbid all borrowing, it does provide a helpful warning about the dangers of indebtedness, particularly for poor people, who are already in a highly vulnerable state.[10]

Of course, saving is not easy for poor people. Like all human beings, poor people are tempted to spend their money on unnecessary or even harmful things. Moreover, when they do have the discipline to save, the absence of banks makes it difficult to store their money. Currency bills often rot when they are kept in a jar or buried underground. The lack of security in villages and slums makes it easy to steal money hidden inside a house or shack. Furthermore, friends and relatives who need financial assistance will often come calling whenever one has accumulated any funds. Even if one has saved by purchasing livestock, they

> ***Savings Principle***
>
> Poor people can and do save, but they need more effective systems for doing so.

might be forced to sell an entire animal in order to get a small amount of cash to assist a needy friend or relative. In addition, extremely high inflation rates in many countries devalue cash that is not earning any interest or income. In many instances, microfinance can help to overcome these problems by providing a financial system in which poor people can save, not just borrow.

In light of this discussion, we can now update the **Savings Principle** in the box above.

Microfinance Is Not Just About Loans: The Importance of Insurance Services

The extreme vulnerability of the poor also makes insurance a highly desirable intervention. In principle, poor households could greatly benefit from life, property, health, accident, disability, burial, and agricultural insurance.[11] Unfortunately, existing insurance products in most countries are not designed to meet the needs of poor households in terms of their prices and payment structures. Sometimes, poor people are able to creatively come up with their own partial solutions, as is the case with Prudence's funeral insurance group. And to some degree, savings and emergency loans can be a partial substitute for insurance, as both provide access to lump sums in a crisis.

However, formal insurance provides crucial benefits that neither savings nor emergency loans can: the ability for large groups of people to share the losses resulting from the occurrence of an uncommon event.[12] By including large groups of people in the insurance program, the amount of money that can be paid to the person experiencing the loss is far greater than the person could have saved or borrowed to cope with that loss on their own. Moreover, when the members of an insurance program are from diverse geographic regions, it enables the people in a region hit by a disaster to survive through the insurance premiums paid by people in regions not hit by that disaster.

Unfortunately, for a variety of technical reasons, it is very difficult and expensive to create formal insurance services for poor people. And even when microinsurance products are created, it is often difficult to get poor households to buy the products for at least three reasons:

- *Distrust*: How can poor people know that the insurance company is reliable?
- *Denial*: Human beings tend to not think about the bad things that can happen to them.
- *Misunderstanding*: It is difficult for many poor people to understand why they should pay money into an insurance program that they might never get back. To many it seems like just trying to save makes more sense. If the disaster happens, they can use their savings. And if the disaster does not happen, they can use their savings for something else.[13]

There are currently a number of creative efforts to overcome the obstacles of providing microinsurance to poor households. For example, MFIs that are trusted by their clients have the potential to distribute the products of formal insurance companies to poor people on a large scale. In India, this approach resulted in 900,000 poor people being provided with health microinsurance in 2006.[14] More creative efforts like this are sorely needed.

That having been said, a number of leading experts caution that the world is still a long way from being able to provide the insurance services that poor households need. In this light, they encourage the expansion of savings and emergency loan services, which can partially substitute for some of the benefits of insurance.[15]

Microfinance Is Not Just about Loans: The Importance of Money Transfer Services

If we talked with Prudence today, she might tell us that she now uses her mobile phone to receive "remittances," i.e., money earned by relatives who have migrated to Nairobi in hopes of increasing their earnings in the city. When these migrants are successful at finding work, they often send money back home to support relatives like Prudence.

Many Kenyans like Prudence receive their remittances via electronic money transfers in which they get an SMS text message telling them to visit an agent of M-Pesa to receive, say, a $30 remittance sent by the Nairobi relative. M-Pesa, a wildly successful mobile money company, serves over 15 million Kenyans and transfers over $50 million per day via its mobile phone network. The company has over 50,000 agents in almost every community who receive cash deposits from M-Pesa users. These users can then use their mobile phones to transfer money to other M-Pesa users' accounts. When users receive an M-Pesa SMS text message notifying them that a transfer has been made to their account, they can visit a local M-Pesa agent near them and withdraw the cash that has been transferred to them.

Many people also use the M-Pesa money transfer system to pay their electricity bills, school fees, and other bills.

While Kenya has by far the highest use of this money-transfer system, other African countries are also adopting this technology, and large foundations including the Gates Foundation are pushing it out around the world.

In addition to in-country money transfers, poor people can also benefit from easier and cheaper access to international remittances from relatives abroad. Over $400 billion in remittances was sent to low-income countries in 2012, primarily from relatives, and this is expected to increase to over $515 billion in 2015.[16] While some of this flow is underground, the above-ground remittances are usually very costly for both senders and receivers, averaging 9.1 percent of the value of the remittance.[17] Lower fees would be most helpful to poor households and to the economies of many countries in the Global South that have significant dependence on remittances.

The Continuum of Financial Systems

Microfinance establishes financial systems that provide financial services such as savings, loans, insurance, and money transfers to poor households. This section explores some of the financial systems that are the most relevant for poor households like Prudence's and introduces some key terms and concepts along the way. The discussion moves from simple to more complex financial systems.

Individual Financial Service Providers

As discussed earlier, individuals such as local moneylenders—i.e., "loan sharks"—and informal savings agents often provide poor households with access to lump sums. Similarly, pawnbrokers, traders, shop owners, friends, and family members can also serve as a source of loans or as a place to store money. Although none of these individuals seems like a bank, the fact is that they all represent informal "financial systems" in that all of them can be sustainable mechanisms that enable poor households to access useful lump sums of money. Of course, none of these individuals are ideal financial service providers. Many of them charge very high interest rates for their services; and mixing friends and family relationships with savings and loan services can be fraught with tensions.

ROSCAs

Prudence uses rotating savings and credit associations (ROSCAs) to obtain lump sums of money in order to restock her business and to pay her grandchildren's school fees. ROSCAs are indigenous financial systems that are governed and managed by the members themselves using their own savings—not outside resources—as the capital.

Each member of a ROSCA makes a contribution of a fixed amount to the group's pot at their regularly scheduled meetings. The members then take turns getting the pot, with one member getting the entire pot at each meeting. Recall that one of Prudence's ROSCAs meets weekly. Let us imagine that there are ten members in this ROSCA and that each member has agreed to contribute $2 at the weekly meeting. Then at each meeting one member will walk away with a lump sum of $20. Even after each member gets their turn at the "pot," they will continue to make the agreed-upon, $2 weekly pay-in until each person has rotated through and received their turn at the pot of money. If the ROSCA has worked well, the members will usually choose to repeat the cycle, although sometimes with membership changes or other modifications.

While it might not be obvious at first glance, a ROSCA is really a simple bank that provides savings and loan services to its members. To see this, let us assume that Prudence gets the pot the first week, that Josephine gets the pot the fifth week, and that Mary gets the pot the tenth week. There are seven other members of this ROSCA, but we will just focus on these three ladies. Tables 8.1–8.3 picture these three ladies' accounts with this ROSCA.

Prudence receives her lump sum of $20 in the first week, which consists of $2 of her own savings deposits into the ROSCA plus an $18 loan from the ROSCA, as indicated by her account balance of negative $18 at the end of the first week (Table 8.1). Where does this $18 loan come from? It comes from the savings pay-ins of the other nine members into the ROSCA. Just as a bank does, a ROSCA is collecting people's savings and lending these savings to borrowers. During weeks 2–10, Prudence's weekly, $2 pay-ins amount to her loan repayments, thereby enabling her to pay off her negative balance by the end of the ten-week cycle.

At the opposite end of the spectrum is Mary (Table 8.3), who gets the lump sum in week 10. Mary's lump sum is really just a withdrawal of her accumulated savings of $20. She never takes a loan. For Mary, the ROSCA functions purely as a savings mechanism.

In the middle is Josephine (Table 8.2), who gets her lump sum of $20 in week 5, consisting of $10 of her accumulated savings and a $10 loan. Her weekly pay-ins from weeks 6–10 amount to her repayment of her loan.

Table 8.4 summarizes the financial services—savings and loans—that this ROSCA provides Prudence, Josephine, and Mary.

While the dollar amounts in this example are purely illustrative, they are reflective of figures that are commonly observed in ROSCAs used by poor people in the Global South. To some readers it may seem unimpressive that the members of this ROSCA received lump sums of only $20. In reality, this small amount is indicative of the incredible power of this simple system. Poor people need access to savings and loan services that provide very small lump sums, *lump sums that virtually no bank in the world can afford to provide*. Invented, owned, and operated by poor people themselves, ROSCAs represent one of the only financial systems that can meet the banking needs of very poor people.

How can ROSCAs do this? Chapter 9 describes the key principles that make ROSCAs and all financial systems work. However, here we note that ROSCAs solve several of the most common problems of banking.

First, ROSCAs solve the need that banks have to select and monitor borrowers. A person will only be admitted into a ROSCA if the other members have some degree of trust in the person's integrity and ability to make the weekly pay-ins. And if a member fails to make a weekly

TABLE 8.1 Prudence's ROSCA Account

Week	1	2	3	4	5	6	7	8	9	10
Pay-ins to ROSCA	$2	$2	$2	$2	$2	$2	$2	$2	$2	$2
Lump Sum Received from ROSCA	**$20**	$0	$0	$0	$0	$0	$0	$0	$0	$0
Prudence's Account Balance	–$18	–$16	–$14	–$12	–$10	–$8	–$6	–$4	–$2	$0

TABLE 8.2 Josephine's ROSCA Account

Week	1	2	3	4	5	6	7	8	9	10
Pay-ins to ROSCA	$2	$2	$2	$2	$2	$2	$2	$2	$2	$2
Lump Sum Received from ROSCA	$0	$0	$0	$0	**$20**	$0	$0	$0	$0	$0
Josephine's Account Balance	$2	$4	$6	$8	–$10	–$8	–$6	–$4	–$2	$0

TABLE 8.3 Mary's ROSCA Account

Week	1	2	3	4	5	6	7	8	9	10
Pay-ins to ROSCA	$2	$2	$2	$2	$2	$2	$2	$2	$2	$2
Lump Sum Received from ROSCA	$0	$0	$0	$0	$0	$0	$0	$0	$0	**$20**
Mary's Account Balance	$2	$4	$6	$8	$10	$12	$14	$16	$18	$0

TABLE 8.4 Summary of Financial Services in ROSCA

	Savings	Loans
Prudence	$2	$18
Josephine	$10	$10
Mary	$20	$0

pay-in, the other ROSCA members will have a strong incentive to visit the delinquent member and to hold her accountable, since she has their money!

What prevents a person from getting an early payout and then running away? Of course, this sometimes happens, but ROSCAs are able to mitigate this problem. In collectively oriented communities, it is very shameful to break social bonds by not making ROSCA pay-ins. It is for this reason that it is more difficult for ROSCAs to work in highly individualistic cultures like the United States, except amongst some communal, immigrant populations.[18] In addition, failing to make payments typically causes a ROSCA member to be banned from future participation in the ROSCA, forcing this person to return to high-cost moneylenders or savings agents or to beg from friends and relatives whenever they need a lump sum of money.

Second, ROSCAs are also a creative way of solving another common banking problem: fraud. Because the entire pot is distributed each week, there is no money for a treasurer to steal!

Finally, ROSCAs address the need that all banks have to develop trust with their customers. ROSCAs build trust over time. Each week the members engage in an "action audit" in the sense that they observe the behavior of all the group members.[19] When the members see each other faithfully making their pay-ins week in and week out, trust is built, enabling the group to take on higher degrees of risk. For example, after several cycles, the members of Prudence's group might decide to increase their weekly pay-ins to $2.50, giving themselves access to larger sums of money as both their levels of income and trust rise.

ROSCAs can also serve functions that most banks do not. ROSCAs have weekly meetings that typically include singing and dancing in addition to the financial flows between savers and borrowers, and ROSCAs affiliated with a church, missionary, or ministry often include Bible study, prayer, songs of praise, and fellowship.

Of course, ROSCAs have their shortcomings as well. As shall be discussed further in chapter 9, when ROSCAs fail to follow the basic principles of finance, they can fall apart, bringing financial and relational harm to the members. Moreover, even when they work properly, the simplicity of ROSCAs has a downside: they are very rigid. In the previous example, what if Mary's child gets malaria during the fifth week, and Mary needs a lump sum of $8 to buy the medicine? Unless Mary is allowed to switch places with Josephine, Mary's child might die. Many ROSCAs members have designed innovative ways to determine the initial ordering of the members and to adjust the ordering if needed;[20] however, the fact remains that ROSCAs are sometimes too rigid to address poor people's needs for convenient, flexible, and reliable banking services. And that is where ASCAs come in . . .

ASCAs

Like ROSCAs, accumulating savings and credit associations (ASCAs) are informal financial systems that are owned and operated by their members and that rely solely on their members' savings for capital. Both provide savings and loan services to their members. However, ASCAs have four distinct advantages over ROSCAs.

First, at each ASCA meeting the group members decide how many loans to make, the sizes of each loan, and the terms of each loan. The group might decide to make multiple loans, one big loan, or no loans at all. This flexibility enables the ASCA to respond to the various needs and opportunities of its members in a more flexible fashion than the ROSCA, whose rigid structure gives the entire pot to a single person following the ROSCA's allocation rule.

Second, while the pot that gets distributed at each ROSCA meeting is fixed in size, an ASCA's pot of loanable funds grows over time. This growth enables the ASCA to provide bigger loans as their members' capacity to manage loans increases.

To see this, consider the following example. Assume that Prudence's ASCA has ten members who each contribute $2 of savings per week. At the first meeting, the group decides to make a loan to Prudence in the amount of $10 to enable her to purchase medicine. The group decides that Prudence will pay back her loan over the next four weeks in installments of $2.75 per week, for a total repayment of $11 on a $10 loan, which translates into an interest rate of 120 percent annually. This rate may seem high to readers, but in this context, it is not too high for services that are convenient, flexible, and reliable. For simplicity, assume that the group makes no additional loans over the course of the four weeks. Table 8.5 illustrates the status of the ASCA for the first five weeks of its life.

As illustrated by the last row in table 8.5, the total pot that the ASCA can use to make loans grows over time for three reasons. First, unlike the ROSCA, in an ASCA members repay the principal on their loans (row 2) in addition to paying in their regular savings contributions (row 1), enabling the pot to grow by more than just the amount saved. Second, in an ASCA, interest is often charged on loans, and that interest goes into the pot (row 2), thereby increasing the pot. Finally, the entire pot in an ASCA is not necessarily lent out each week (row 4), allowing leftover funds from the previous week to be available for lending the following week.[21]

Third, while members earn nothing on their savings in a ROSCA, in an ASCA the members can earn dividends on their savings that come from the interest that is charged on an ASCA's loans.[22] For example, the 130,000 women in PACT's Women's Empowerment Program in Nepal earned 18–24 percent interest on their ASCA savings.[23] And the 160,000 women in CARE's ASCA program in Niger averaged 76 percent APR on their savings.[24] These are outstanding returns on members' savings and represent a big improvement in a world in which poor people often have to pay 30–80 percent for the privilege of saving.

Finally, ASCAs provide more flexible savings services than ROSCAs. Subject to the rules of the group, an ASCA member can withdraw some

TABLE 8.5 Summary of Prudence's ASCA

	Week 1	Week 2	Week 3	Week 4	Week 5
+ Weekly Savings Paid In	$20.00	$20.00	$20.00	$20.00	$20.00
+ Loan Repayments Paid In					
(Principal plus Interest)	$ 0.00	$ 2.75	$ 2.75	$ 2.75	$ 2.75
– Loans Paid Out	$10.00	$ 0.00	$ 0.00	$ 0.00	$ 0.00
+ Leftover Balance in Pot from Previous Week	–	$10.00	$32.75	$55.50	$78.25
= Total Funds in Pot at End of Meeting	**$10.00**	**$32.75**	**$55.50**	**$78.25**	**$101.00**

of her savings when she needs them, thereby providing the key features that poor people say they desire in financial services: convenience, flexibility, and reliability.[25] Moreover, in the absence of formal insurance services, this flexible access to savings enables poor people to create simple forms of insurance. For example, a group member could choose to withdraw some of her savings only when there is a health emergency in her family.

ASCAs' ability to grow their pots of loanable funds, to pay dividends on savings, and to provide flexible lending and savings services make them much more powerful than ROSCAs. However, with this added power comes greater complexity. For example, in a ROSCA, the money all comes in and all goes out in the same meeting, so there is no need for the group to store any money. But in an ASCA, unlent funds must be safely stored and yet be accessible for members' needs in future weeks. In addition, ASCA leaders need greater bookkeeping skills to keep the more complex records. Finally, an ASCA's unlent funds create greater opportunities for fraud on the part of the treasurer or group leaders, requiring additional procedures to promote transparency and accountability.

Poor people have creatively designed many varieties of ASCAs to meet their wide range of needs for financial services, but there are two basic types of ASCAs: time-bound and non-time-bound.

At the outset, members forming a time-bound ASCA choose a date on which they will end the ASCA. The end date is usually around a religious holiday, like Christmas (as with Prudence) or Eid, or some other event that requires a lump sum of money, e.g., the date on which school fees are due. On their closing date, time-bound ASCAs return all savings and dividends to the members and all the books are cleared, which amounts to an "action audit" for the group. The ASCA then usually restarts again and closes on the new ending date. The repeated cycles can go on indefinitely.[26]

Non-time-bound ASCAs, which are also called "credit unions" in many countries, do not plan to end. As their funds continue to accumulate to larger and larger amounts, non-time-bound ASCAs are better able to meet the various financial needs of their members. However, with these growing funds, management and bookkeeping also become more complex, such that eventually all non-time-bound ASCAs require external technical support to help them manage their growth, bookkeeping systems, and other issues.[27] Some countries require non-time-bound ASCAs to register with the government as savings and credit cooperatives and then be regulated by government ministries.

While ROSCAs and ASCAs may sound like obscure concepts to some readers, for centuries poor people around the world have creatively used these simple financial systems to survive and to improve their lives, and the microfinance industry is building on this knowledge to help a growing number of people today. Consider the following:

- ROSCAs have existed in China since the middle of the Tang Dynasty, between AD 619 and 906.[28]
- People in Jamaica save 19 percent of their income in ROSCAs.[29]
- In Cameroon, approximately 54 percent of all savings in the country is placed into informal savings and credit associations.[30]
- It is estimated that there are well over 250,000 savings and credit associations in sub-Saharan Africa alone.[31]
- A number of Christian organizations are promoting various forms of *church-centered* savings and credit associations on a large scale. For example, at the time of writing, Five Talents International, HOPE International, Tearfund UK, and World Relief had reached a combined total of over 700,000 people in church-centered savings and credit associations.[32]
- The Village Savings and Loan Association model of VSL Associates is being used by a wide range of NGOs to help over 9.33 million people in at least sixty-one countries with time-bound ASCAs.[33]

As will be discussed in chapter 12, there is a tremendous opportunity for grassroots churches, missionaries, and ministries in the Global South to promote savings groups that incorporate evangelism, discipleship, prayer, singing, and fellowship as a means of holistic outreach. And there is a profound need for North Americans to support such efforts by helping to pay for training, praying for the groups, encouraging the leaders, and connecting them to additional resources when appropriate.

Microfinance Institutions (MFIs)

In addition to her membership in ROSCAs and ASCAs, Prudence also borrows money from an MFI called Faulu Kenya. MFIs are more complex financial systems than savings groups, and are usually legally recognized as semiformal institutions that are loosely regulated by their host governments. Some, like Faulu, become formal financial institutions and are regulated by their country's central bank.

MFIs come in a variety of types, from nongovernmental organizations (NGOs) that include microfinance as part of a multifaceted, poverty-alleviation strategy to specialized institutions that provide only financial services. When MFIs operate as parts of NGOs, they often do not have boards of directors, other than the board that oversees the NGO as a whole, but as they become regulated formal institutions, governments require MFIs to have their own, strong- functioning boards.

MFIs have some potential advantages over informal ROSCAs and ASCAs:

- Professional staff provides the financial services, so poor people do not have to run the financial system themselves as is the case with ROSCAs and ASCAs. Some MFI clients prefer simply buying the financial services from an MFI rather than going to a group meeting.[34]
- If the MFI is a formal financial institution regulated by the federal government, it will be able to offer a greater range of savings and loans products, and may even be able to offer insurance or money transfers.
- MFIs can offer bigger loans than either ROSCAs or ASCAs. For example, Prudence's MFI, Faulu Kenya, had an average loan size of $741 in 2012.[35]
- Most MFIs charge lower interest rates (typically 3 percent per month) than many ASCAs charge their members.

But MFIs have some disadvantages when compared to ROSCAs and ASCAs as well:

- Many MFIs only focus on "microcredit-for-microenterprises," thereby failing to meet the other financial-service needs of poor households.

- MFIs' financial services are usually rigid in their terms, whereas ROSCAs and ASCAs can be adapted to meet the particular needs of their members.
- MFIs that have not met the full regulatory conditions of the federal government usually are not permitted to provide savings services. And those MFIs that do provide savings services often do not pay interest on savings.[36]
- The loan sizes of MFIs are too large to reach the poorest people.
- MFIs typically cannot afford to reach into rural areas, where 70 percent of the world's poor live.
- MFIs can be tempted to focus on generating profits rather than on helping poor people.
- Because the MFIs provide the financial services, group members may not develop as many leadership skills as in ROSCAs and ASCAs.
- MFIs have to operate on a large scale in order to be viable, whereas ROSCAs and ASCAs can be conducted on a small or large scale.
- Christian MFIs often do not have time to incorporate evangelism and discipleship activities, as they are under pressure to lend as much money as possible in order to generate sufficient revenues to cover their costs.

Banks

The success of MFIs in sustainably serving poor people has challenged banks in some countries to make their financial services more accessible to poor people through such measures as reducing minimum balances on savings accounts and offering debit cards to poor people. And some MFIs are transitioning into becoming banks, as is the case with the Opportunity International network of MFIs.

In principle, as formal financial systems regulated by their federal governments, banks can offer a broad range of financial services to poor people. However, this remains a struggle for many banks because of the high costs of handling small deposits, of holding savings accounts with very low balances, and of making very small loans to poor people.

However, banks are increasingly moving toward serving poor people when they are able to develop efficient methodologies and technologies that enable them to significantly reduce costs. The Ghana Commercial Bank (n.d.) has a savings mobilization program of hiring and training respected and inexpensive community members to go door-to-door to collect savings from people. Private commercial banks in many countries have been using ATMs dispersed throughout cities, including some on wheels. The most recent technologies being developed and used in a few countries, e.g., Kenya and the Philippines, use money-transfer services via mobile phone networks. This technology holds great promise to enable banks to access significant numbers of poor people who have not been bankable before. Nevertheless, banks still lag behind MFIs, ROSCAs, and ASCAs in terms of the number of very poor people they serve, with a few exceptions such as Kenya's Equity Bank.

If they are able to become more accessible to poor people, banks offer some significant advantages. First, they are regulated by central banks, making them safer than informal systems, and additional security is provided by governmental deposit insurance funds. Second, banks usually offer many more types of savings and loan services than MFIs, ROSCAs, or ASCAs. Third, because banks have diverse sources of capital, they can offer much larger loans than ROSCAs, ASCAs, or MFIs. Finally, borrowers and savers just buy the financial services from banks. They don't have to manage them.

However, when we use the perspective of the theory of change for microfinance ministries described in chapter 7, banks have a number of distinct weaknesses. First, they almost never organize people into groups. Banks only know how to work with individuals. While this can be quite adequate for people that are not very poor, as we saw in Ministry Component #6, households that struggle with deep poverty can benefit from the social support that can come from being part of a group. Second, banks do not link people to the local church or provide evangelism and discipleship as part of their financial services (Ministry Components #1–#5 and #9).

Other Financial Systems

Individuals, ROSCAs, ASCAs, MFIs, and banks are only some of the many financial systems that exist. Figure 8.1 illustrates the rich diversity of

FIGURE 8.1 The Range of Financial Systems in the Global South

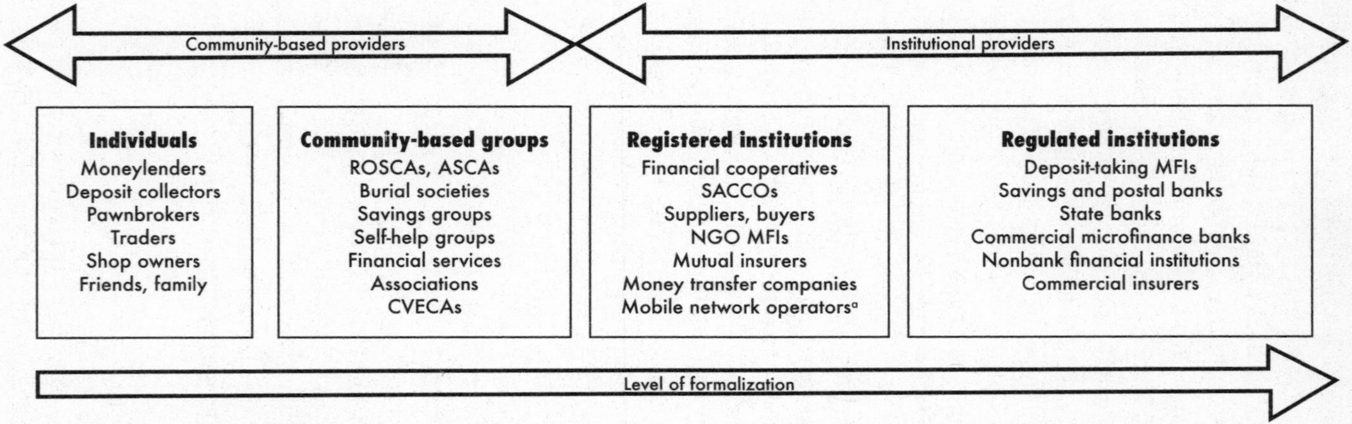

Note: ROSCAs = rotating savings and credit associations; ASCAs = accumulating savings and credit associations; CVECAs = caisses villageoises d' épargne et de crédit autogérés es; SACCOs = savings and credit cooperatives; NGO = nongovernmental organizations; MFIs = Microfinance institutions

a. Mobile network operators are regulated as communication companies; most are not licensed to provide financial services.

Joanna Ledgerwood with Julie Earne and Candace Nelson, eds., *The New Microfinance Handbook: A Financial Market System Perspective* (Washington, DC: The World Bank, 2013), 29, figure 1.3.

financial systems in the Global South, each of them having their own strengths and weaknesses for meeting the needs of poor households for lump sums of money.

What Is Microenterprise Development?

The term "microenterprise development" (MED) is often used interchangeably with the term "microfinance," even though they are not exactly the same thing. As we have seen, "microfinance" refers to the provision of a range of financial services to poor households. Microenterprise development focuses more narrowly on the businesses those poor households sometimes own, and consists of two types of interventions to help those businesses: financial and nonfinancial.

ROSCAs, ASCAs, MFIs, and banks can potentially address the financial services that microenterprises need. In this sense, as shown in figure 8.2, financial services to microenterprises are simply a subset of microfinance as a whole.

The nonfinancial component of microenterprise development, which is sometimes called "business development services," is very broad but often includes the following:

- *Market Access* services identify and/or establish new markets for business products or services.
- *Infrastructure* services include storage and transport, telecommunications, money transfer, internet, etc., that enable microentrepreneurs to increase their sales and income.
- *Policy/Advocacy* services carry out research and do subsector analysis to identify policy constraints and opportunities for microentrepreneurs. They also facilitate the organization of coalitions (business people, government officials, donors, academics, etc.) to carry out policy advocacy that promotes the interests of microentrepreneurs.
- *Input Supply* services help microentrepreneurs develop improved access to raw materials and production inputs.
- *Training and Technical Assistance* services develop the capacity of entrepreneurs to better plan and manage their operations

FIGURE 8.2 **The Economic Needs Addressed by Microeconomic Development and Microfinance**

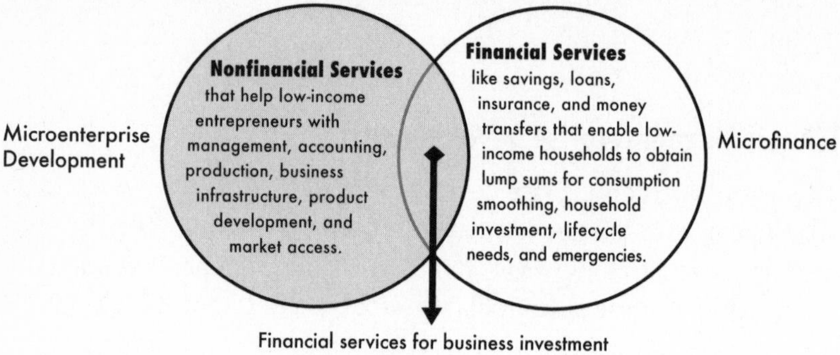

and to improve their technical expertise. This corresponds to Ministry Component #4 in chapter 7.

- *Technology and Product Development* services research and identify new products and technologies of microentrepreneurs.

It is important to realize that some nonfinancial services are likely already being provided in many communities. For example, seed and tool distributors often provide training to farmers or entrepreneurs in how to use the seeds and tools, and they sometimes help producers with market access. And infrastructure services are often being provided by bus and trucking companies, cellular telecommunications companies, and prepaid airtime card retailers.

However, where service gaps exist, there are opportunities to develop new ministries. For example, biblically based *Training and Technical Assistance* can be used to augment microfinance ministries, creating an opportunity to show the relevance of King Jesus to the affairs of everyday life (see Ministry Component #4 in chapter 7).

What Is Business as Mission?

Business as Mission (BAM) is a strategy that has become popular in the first decade of the twenty-first century with business people around the world, particularly North American business people who desire to use their wealth and business acumen as a tool for missions. "BAM" can be defined as "the use of for-profit businesses as instruments of global mission" and is a part of the missions movement that seeks to recognize Christ's preeminence over the marketplace.[37]

In contrast to microenterprise development, BAM does not typically focus on the businesses of poor people but rather on businesses established by missionaries to glorify God and to be intentional tools for the proclamation of the gospel. The companies established by BAM are sometimes called "Great Commission Companies" or "Kingdom Companies."[38] A famous example of BAM is a Korean businessperson who established a for-profit business in Central Asia that is ethically managed and profitable. The workers noticed that this business was run differently than many others and started attending Bible studies in which many became Christians. It is beyond the scope of this book to compare the pros and cons of BAM and microfinance. Indeed, there is a need for considerably more research before such a comparison could be made.

Summary

Microfinance is an approach to poverty alleviation that seeks to establish "financial systems," sustainable mechanisms that enable poor people to create and access useful lump sums of money through savings, loans, insurance, or money-transfer services. Consistent with the **Microfinance for Households Principle**, these lump sums assist poor households with consumption smoothing, business investments, household investments, lifecycle needs, and emergencies. The basic financial systems are ROSCAs, ASCAs, MFIs, and banks, each of which has different strengths and weaknesses. Other related interventions include business development services and Business as Mission.

Application Exercise

One mistake that can easily be made, especially if we focus on needs rather than assets, is to assume that few if any financial or nonfinancial services exist in the community we want to serve. As a result, we might fail to learn about what is already occurring in our ministry communities.

This can do real harm, for introducing new services can undermine existing assets and services. For example, introducing loans on very generous terms can reduce people's desire to save and can damage or ruin existing ROSCAs and ASCAs. It is vital to learn what assets and services God has already placed in the communities we want to serve.

Thus, it is absolutely crucial that microfinance and microenterprise development workers do a thorough "landscape assessment" of the services that might be operating in the community.[39]

Do a simple financial landscape assessment of your target community by having somebody—preferably a person indigenous to the culture of your target community—ask people about the financial services they are using. To assist you with this process, see the resource entitled *Financial Landscape Assessment* on the website associated with this book.

CHAPTER 9

THE THREE Cs: MAKING FINANCIAL SYSTEMS WORK

> Credit institutions must make sure that the loans get paid back in full, and in due time. If it does not happen that way, one should not be quick to blame the people for the failure; rather, one should blame the designer of the credit institution which fails to do the job.
>
> —*Dr. Muhammad Yunus, founder of the Grameen Bank of Bangladesh and Nobel Laureate*[1]

> Loans have been given to rural people without checking whether they had the capacity to repay.
>
> —*Senior rural development official in state government of Andhra Pradesh, India*[2]

The Great Recession that began in 2008 shook many wealthy countries, resulting in years of bankruptcies, high unemployment, and large government budget deficits. While a variety of factors led to the Great Recession, many of the problems stemmed from savers, borrowers, lenders, and insurers losing sight of some basic principles of finance. Trillions of euros and dollars were lost when individuals and financial institutions foolishly saved, lent, borrowed, and insured in highly risky ways.

While this was happening, poor people around the world continued to successfully save and borrow money through ROSCAs, ASCAs, and MFIs. How can this be? By following some basic financial principles, the microfinance movement has demonstrated that it is possible to provide financial services to hundreds of millions of poor people.

But none of this is automatic. As the Great Recession demonstrated, financial systems are fragile. If the basic principles of finance are not followed, financial systems can come crashing down, doing considerable harm to everybody involved. Indeed, churches, missionaries, and ministries often find that microfinance initiatives are far more difficult to operate than they had imagined. Good intentions are not enough. It is possible to hurt poor people in the process of trying to help them. This is true in general, and it is definitely true in the field of microfinance.

In an effort to equip readers with the knowledge they need to create sound microfinance systems, the first portion of this chapter discusses some of the basic principles of finance: the "Three Cs of Credit." Building upon the three Cs, the remainder of the chapter then examines six design features that are essential for making financial systems work for materially poor people.

Before we begin, we must make a brief comment about human behavior. The financial principles described in this chapter are rooted in economic theory, which assumes that human beings selfishly pursue their own self-interests. For example, economic theory predicts that if a person can default on a loan without suffering any consequences, then the person will default. In reality, human actions are influenced by many factors, including social ties, cultural norms, and moral convictions. Thus, a person might very well repay a loan simply because it is the right thing to do. While this broader range of human motives does operate, this chapter focuses on creating financial systems that work well even in the worst-case scenario in which people selfishly pursue their own financial self-interests.

Some Basic Principles of Finance

The Three Cs of Credit

Financial services are about saving and lending, which are "promises to pay" from one party to another *in the future*. Financial services are inherently complicated to provide, because it is difficult to know if the payer will actually keep their promise to pay. For example, when we receive a loan from a bank, we promise to pay the loan back to the bank in the future. But how does the bank know we will actually keep our promise to repay the loan? Similarly, when we deposit money into our savings account at the bank, the bank promises to pay us the money back at some point in the future. Note that our deposit is actually a loan to the bank. How do we know the bank will keep its promise to pay us back?

Clearly, the riskier the borrower, the higher will be the interest rate and fees on the loan, since the lender needs to be compensated for the additional risk they are incurring. In order to assess this risk, the lender needs to get information about what are often called the "Three Cs of Credit":

1. *Character*: What is the borrower's *character*? Does the borrower really intend to repay? How well has he or she repaid loans in the past?
2. *Capacity*: What is the borrower's *capacity* to repay? Does the borrower have the economic means—income and assets—to repay the loan?
3. *Collateral*: What *collateral*, assets of value, are available for the lender to seize in case the borrower does not repay?

Let us apply the three Cs to the case of going to the bank to get a loan for our small business.

To assess our *character*, the bank will try to learn if we have a history of faithfully repaying our loans to others. In some countries, the bank can run a credit check on us in a matter of seconds using internet-based credit scores. Our history of repaying our debts will be seen on the credit report. If we have a solid history, the lender will consider this to be strong evidence that we have good character and that we honestly intend to repay our loans.

In order to assess our *capacity* to repay the loan, the bank will look at our income, our assets, and how much debt we owe. Since this is a small business loan, the bank would also likely assess our business plan.

Finally, the bank will identify the value of our *collateral*, assets that it can legally seize in case we do not repay the loan. These assets can be the titles to real estate, automobiles, business equipment, or other property.

Once the bank evaluates our credit worthiness using these three Cs, it will then be able to decide what interest rate and fees it will charge us for the loan, taking into account the size of the loan and the term, i.e., the time period of the loan. As borrowers, we can then decide whether we want the business loan badly enough to accept the bank's offer.

Similarly, as savers we also need to apply the three Cs before we deposit our money into a bank, for our deposit represents a loan from us to the bank. We need to learn about the *character* of the bank, for modern history is replete with cases of corrupt organizations whose leaders had no intentions of returning savings and simply ran off with the money. We also need to learn about the *capacity* of the bank to repay us before we invest our savings. Some banks take very high risks with people's savings, lending them to borrowers with spotty repayment records. Finally, we should find out what *collateral* is available to us in case the bank cannot repay our deposits. Some country's central banks solve this problem by offering deposit insurance on bank savings, which amounts to a very strong form of *collateral*.

The more accurate and accessible the information is on each of these three Cs, the easier it is to determine the level of risk, to calculate the appropriate interest rates and fees, and to execute the financial transactions.[3]

Now, let us apply the three Cs to an example in microfinance.

A Case of Microfinance Gone Wrong: Long-Distance Microcredit

For several years, Riverbend Church, a wealthy congregation in the United States, had been sending short-term mission teams to Mount Zion Fellowship, a church located near a squatter community in Africa.[4] Desiring to make a longer-term impact, Riverbend Church offered to help Mount Zion start a microcredit program.

So on the next short-term trip, members from both churches developed a survey and jointly interviewed the residents in the squatter community to identify their business needs and openness to receiving a microloan to start or expand a microenterprise. The survey revealed that the local residents did not like the MFIs in the country because they required borrowers to form groups, and group members had to guarantee the loans of the other members of their group. If one member of a group could not repay their loan, the other group members were required to pay in that person's place. Until they did so, none of the members of that group could get any more loans. The residents did not like this system and wanted individual loans.

After examining the survey results, members of both churches identified twenty families from the squatter community who expressed an interest in having a microenterprise loan. Riverbend Church then sent $2,000 to Mount Zion Fellowship so that it could make $100 loans to each of the twenty families. Since the borrowers were very poor and since Riverbend was so wealthy, no pledge of collateral was required from the twenty families. As requested, the borrowers were not required to form groups, and the twenty loans were made to them as separate individuals. Each week a member of Mount Zion visited each borrower to pray with her and to collect the loan repayments.

The program seemed to get off to a good start, but after a few months problems began to emerge: about one-third of the borrowers were not making *any* loan repayments, and the remaining two-thirds were only paying back 50 percent of the scheduled amounts. Mount Zion learned that some defaulting borrowers had used their loans to buy household items rather than to invest in businesses. One husband had taken his wife's loan and had used it to have a drinking party with his friends. Some borrowers had invested in small businesses, but these businesses were slowly dying because of too much local competition. Other borrowers had used their loans to repay money they had borrowed earlier from local loan sharks. Some borrowers said they did not really believe that they had to repay the loans, since the money had come from a church in a wealthy country that was far away.

The leaders of both churches had numerous Skype calls about the problems. They soon realized that their survey tool had not really provided them with the information they needed to identify which borrowers were good credit risks and which were not. And now that some of the defaulting borrowers were coming to church, they were afraid to push for loan repayment lest they drive them away. Moreover, they realized that they really had no way of enforcing the loan repayment anyway, as no collateral had been identified at the outset. On the other hand, if they forgave the loans, they feared they might encourage attitudes of irresponsibility and dependency. It seemed like no matter what they did, some sort of unintended harm would occur.

What went wrong? The churches made mistakes in assessing the three Cs:

1. *Character*: How well did the lenders ascertain the *character* of the borrowers with respect to repaying their loans? It appears that they did not do this very well: One-third of the borrowers completely stopped repaying their loans; some of the borrowers did not take their loans seriously, treating them as easy money from rich foreigners; and some of the borrowers used the loans for purposes that they knew would not generate income to enable them to repay their loans.
2. *Capacity*: How well were the lenders able to ascertain the *capacity* of the borrowers to repay? It appears that their estimates of the businesses' success were not sound, as some borrowers invested their loans in businesses with stiff competition and high risks of unprofitability.
3. *Collateral*: How well did the lenders identify *collateral* that could be seized in case of nonrepayment? No collateral was identified at all, and borrowers were not organized into groups in which members would mutually guarantee each other's loans, which is part of the genius of microfinance.

The Genius of Group-Based Incentives in Microfinance

The churches used a survey tool to try and identify good borrowers, but their tool did not collect sufficient information about their borrowers' trustworthiness and ability to repay. This is not very surprising, for it is actually quite difficult and very time consuming to get accurate information on the three Cs for very poor people. Indeed, most banks in the Global South have found it to be much too difficult and costly to obtain such information, especially when these low-income borrowers are only going to borrow $100 anyway. As a result, most banks simply will not lend to people who are very poor.

The genius of microfinance is that it has discovered low-cost ways of learning about the three Cs for very poor people. Nobel Laureate Muhammad Yunus and the Grameen Bank of Bangladesh that he founded realized that people in poor communities have information about the three Cs for one another. Since they have often known each other since childhood, they are aware of each other's *character* and economic *capacity*. Furthermore, given their proximity to one another, they can fairly easily monitor each other's behavior. So Grameen created incentives for the community members to reveal their knowledge about each other's *character* and *capacity* and to create a new form of *collateral*.[5]

Here is how it works: Grameen requires people to form groups before they can borrow. If a group member does not repay her loan, the Grameen Bank will not make loans to any of the other group members until the defaulting loan is paid.[6] Some replications of Grameen's "joint-liability" model also require members to put "savings" on deposit with the MFI, money which serves as collateral that can be confiscated to cover any defaults.

Thus group members tend to form groups only with people whom they believe have the *character* and *capacity* to repay. Furthermore, when a loan is made to a group member, the other members have a very strong incentive to monitor the borrower's behavior to make sure that she invests the loan wisely. The group members might even monitor what happens with any profits generated by the loan to make sure they are used for loan repayment. Finally, group members might even repay loans on behalf of a delinquent borrower in order to make sure that the loans from Grameen keep on coming for the rest of them. All of these behaviors help to create *social collateral*, because very poor households usually lack *physical collateral*.

The genius of Grameen's approach is twofold: it recognizes that locals have vast information about one another, and it creates group-based incentives for this information to be used to address the three Cs. Without these group-based incentives, it would be nearly impossible for an outside organization to get this information quickly and cheaply, as both Riverbend and Mount Zion churches discovered the hard way. As the Grameen Bank's principles have become well-known, most microfinance programs, especially those serving very poor people, have adopted the group-based methodology as a primary tool to assess the *character* and *capacity* of borrowers and to create *social collateral*.[7]

As we can now see, the failure of Riverbend and Mount Zion churches to require their borrowers to form groups with appropriate incentive structures was a very bad move. It prevented these churches from accessing the inside information that people in the community had about each other's *character* and *capacity*, and it failed to create *social collateral* for enforcing the loan repayment. In addition, the ministry was even unwilling to enforce loan repayment out of fear of reducing church attendance. Indeed, there are both theological and practical reasons to believe that churches should not be lenders of money.[8]

The bad news for Riverbend and Mount Zion is that their microcredit program is highly likely to fail, which will do considerable harm to everybody involved. The good news is that by observing six essential design principles, microfinance ministries can successfully address the three Cs, resulting in programs that have a much greater chance of success. It is to those principles that we now turn.

Design Principles of Successful Microfinance Systems

Recall from chapter 8 that *"financial systems" are sustainable mechanisms that enable people to create and access useful lump sums of money through savings, loans, insurance, or money transfers*. In figure 8.1 we saw that there is a range of financial systems, from the simple ROSCA to the highly complex bank. Every financial system utilizes the following six design features to address the three Cs, but we shall be most focused on *micro*finance systems, namely ROSCAs, ASCAs, and MFIs. Space does not permit a complete discussion about how each of these principles contributes to addressing the three Cs, but if these principles are followed, there is a high likelihood that the three Cs will be satisfied and that the financial system will endure.

Design Principle #1: Trust, the Foundation of Microfinance

Trust is the foundation upon which every financial system is built. At the individual level, trust can be defined as the *confidence* that people will fulfill their *promises to pay*. At the financial-system level, trust can be defined as the *confidence* that the system will fulfill its promise to be a *sustainable mechanism* that provides financial services. Trust can be very difficult to build and maintain, but without it the financial system will typically collapse. Although trust needs to permeate the entire microfinance program, four interrelated dimensions in which trust needs to operate are highlighted here.

First, those who are lending need to have confidence that those who are borrowing will keep their promises to pay the money back in the future:

- ROSCAs, ASCAs, and MFIs must have confidence that borrowers will repay their loans before they lend them money.
- Savers must have confidence that the ROSCAs, ASCAs, or MFIs will return their money before they will make any deposits.

Second, borrowers need to have confidence that the financial system will endure in the future, or they will be less likely to repay their loans in the present. Remember, most of the loans in microfinance are not collateralized with physical assets. Hence, the primary economic incentive for borrowers to repay their loans today is their belief that by doing so they will be considered trustworthy and will be able to get additional loans in the future. But if for some reason the borrowers lose confidence that the lender will be around in the future, they will lose their hope of getting future loans from this lender. As a result, they may decide not to repay their loans today, an action that could cause the lender to go out of business. Note the self-fulfilling nature of this scenario: a loss of confidence that the lender will be around in the future results in a drop in loan repayments today, which actually increases the likelihood that the lender will go out of business.

Third, savers also need to have confidence that the financial system will endure into the future. If they begin to doubt this, they will be concerned that they will not be able to get their deposits back. This will cause them to withdraw their savings today, which can actually contribute to making the system insolvent. Again, the loss of confidence is self-fulfilling.

Finally, both savers and borrowers need to have confidence that the overall macroeconomic and political environment will enable the financial system to endure. Hyperinflation makes lending very difficult, as the real value of the money being repaid is undermined through rapidly rising prices. And political instability can wipe out financial systems through civil wars or by undermining the legal system needed to enforce contracts.

Broken Trust Can Do Real Harm

The importance of designing *financial systems* built on trust can be seen in the microcredit program created by a Christian NGO in Southeast Asia. After ten years of working in a community, this NGO announced to its staff and the community members that it would close down its operations in that community in eighteen months. The NGO also announced that its final project in the community would be a microloan program to help people start microenterprises to sustain themselves after the NGO departed. The NGO undoubtedly hoped that after ten years of providing educational scholarships, school uniforms, wells, and other assistance, the community members would have a sense of gratitude to the NGO and would feel an obligation to repay the microenterprise loans.

Is the NGO's financial system (its microloan program) built on trust—that is, *confidence* that the program will be a *sustainable mechanism*? Clearly not, for at the very outset of the loan program, the NGO announced that it was leaving! In other words, from the beginning the NGO announced that its loan program would *not* be a *sustainable mechanism*. And this announcement is likely to be devastating.

What do you think will happen in this scenario?

Imagine that we are one of the families that receives a loan from this NGO, and assume that we are pursuing our own financial self-interests. Knowing that the NGO will be gone in eighteen months, how strong is our economic incentive to *repay* the loan? With no trust—i.e., *with no confidence that this is a sustainable mechanism that will provide us additional loans in the future*—the economic incentive for us to repay the loan is gone, and we might take the loan and run! Furthermore, how strong is our incentive to invest the loan in a way that meets the NGO's desires? Again, this is also likely to be quite weak. Instead of investing in a business so that we can generate income to repay the loan, we might use the loan for whatever our most pressing need is at that moment. As a result, we may not generate the income to repay the loan.

Remember that the goal of poverty alleviation is reconciled relationships (see the **Poverty-Alleviation Principle**). In this light, how successful is the NGO's well-meaning program at alleviating poverty? Unfortunately, the program is likely to deepen poverty for everyone involved by damaging relationships:

- The NGO staff will likely have broken relationships with the borrowers who do not repay: "We've been helping these people for ten years, and this is how they thank us?"
- Some of the borrowers that repay their loans out of a sense of moral obligation may start to resent those that do not repay, putting strain on their relationships with one another.
- The borrowers who do not repay will have a damaged relationship with creation, as they have failed to be a proper steward of their resources.
- The financial supporters who donated to the program are likely to have a broken relationship with the NGO. Furthermore, it is likely that they will be somewhat disgusted with the borrowers who did not repay, thereby increasing their pride, i.e., a broken relationship with self.[9]

In addition, it is likely that the "credit culture" will be significantly damaged, making it difficult for other organizations to lend money in this region in the future. Once a sufficient number of borrowers in a region start to believe that loans do not really need to be repaid, it simply becomes too risky to create loan programs in that region. And this absence of financial services hurts everybody, including those who are honest.

Designing interventions in which materially poor people have strong temptations not to repay their loans is simply unwise. These are highly vulnerable people. Putting them in this situation is comparable to leaving a recovering alcoholic alone in a bar and telling him not to drink. Yes, it is still the alcoholic's sin if he gets drunk, but it was unloving to put him in that situation in the first place. The Christian NGO is making the mistake of believing that the good will that it has developed over the years with the members of this community will be strong enough to overcome the temptations it is creating for people to not repay their loans. It would be better if the program were designed to remove the temptation altogether.

Further Trust-Breaking Scenarios to Consider

To further understand why trust is so mandatory to making a financial system work, consider the following scenarios. In each case, ask yourself, "What might this situation do to trust, and what will be the impact on the financial system?" You might want to cover our "likely outcomes" for each scenario until you have formulated your own ideas.

- A ROSCA member begins to fail in her weekly contributions.

  Likely outcome: The other members will lose trust in her. Moreover, her lack of contributions undermines the ROSCA's ability to create lump sums over time for the other members, so they may lose trust in the ROSCA itself. This may cause them to stop making their own contributions, which will cause the ROSCA to collapse.
- A ROSCA admits a new member who takes her payout and never returns to the group.

  Likely outcome: Same as above.
- Despite repeated requests, the treasurer of an ASCA repeatedly fails to show the group the receipts verifying that she has deposited the group's funds in a local bank.

  Likely outcome: The group members will lose trust in the treasurer and have doubts about where their money is. They might stop making savings deposits into the ASCA. In addition, borrowers from the ASCA might stop repaying their loans, as their trust that the ASCA will be around to collect those loans is weakened. All of these actions can result in the eventual collapse of the ASCA.
- The ROSCA's or ASCA's record books are never available for members to examine.

  Likely outcome: Same as the previous scenario.
- The chairman of a financial cooperative uses the cooperative's funds to buy a plot of land.

  Likely outcome: Same as the previous scenario.

- The president of the country regularly asks a bank to make loans to his political cronies and family members. Fearing retaliation, the bank makes these loans as requested.

  Likely outcome: The president's actions undermine the three Cs and make it impossible for the bank to enforce loan repayment. When borrowers detect this, they lose confidence in the bank's sustainability and stop working hard to repay their loans. The bank starts to lose money, undermining the depositors' confidence that the bank is sustainable, so they start to withdraw their savings from the bank. The actions of both the borrowers and the savers will cause the bank to go out of business.

In each of these scenarios, trust has been broken, causing the system to collapse. This typically results in harm on multiple fronts: to savers, whose deposits are lost; to borrowers, who are taught that keeping their word is not important; to investors, whose money is squandered; to staff, who lose their jobs; and to interpersonal relationships, which become very strained. Moreover, the collapse weakens people's ability to trust in the future, thereby making it extremely difficult to start new financial systems that can provide the lump sums that people so desperately need.

Trust is the foundation of a microfinance system. Indeed, the other five principles are largely about building and maintaining trust.

Design Principle #2: Discipline

Discipline, faithfully obeying the rules, must be encouraged and enforced at multiple levels in order to build and maintain the trust that is essential for a financial system to work. At the individual level, discipline means that members of the microfinance group must keep their agreements if trust is to be maintained. When people say that they will save a certain amount, repay a certain amount, invest a loan a certain way, and attend meetings at a certain time, they actually must do so in order for trust to be built in their *character* and *capacity* and for social *collateral* to be formed. It is for this reason that most successful microfinance groups enforce fines for those who have unexcused reasons for failing to keep their agreements.

As we saw in the previous section, discipline is particularly important when it comes to individuals' savings contributions and loan repayments. In addition to damaging the reputation of the person, missing savings contributions or loan payments can undermine trust that the financial system will be able to continue providing financial services in the future. When group members see other members shirking, they start to lose trust in those people and in the system as a whole. It is important to remember that individuals are members of households, so discipline is really a family affair. For example, it is very tempting to take a "business loan" during the Christmas season to buy presents for the family rather than to invest in the business. But then it becomes very difficult to repay the loan in January and February.

Sometimes innovations in the financial system can help to create the discipline that builds trust. For example, many MFIs used to make $50 loans that were due in one payment, say fifty weeks later. For the entire term of fifty weeks, both the MFI and the other poor members of the borrower's group were likely wondering, "Will this person repay? What will we do if she cannot repay?" The Grameen Bank then discovered an innovation that could increase discipline and build trust by requiring borrowers to make small, frequent, and regular loan payments, e.g., requiring weekly payments of $1 plus interest for fifty weeks. By watching the borrower faithfully demonstrate the discipline of making these weekly repayments, both the Grameen Bank and the other members of the borrowing group increased their trust in her and in the system. Moreover, this innovation reduced the risk to Grameen by enabling it to identify possible repayment problems much earlier than waiting until the end of the fifty-week term to discover a problem.

In addition to discipline at the individual and household levels, the financial system itself must have discipline in several important ways.

First, the lender must be disciplined enough to not lend more money than the borrower has the *capacity* to repay. In 2008, American and British credit markets were roiling under the weight of undisciplined lending due to banks lending more money for home mortgages than borrowers could ever hope to repay. Similarly, MFIs are also tempted to overlend to poor people, since the loans generate the interest income that enable MFIs to increase their revenues. As discussed in chapter 4,

MFIs in the Andhra Pradesh state of India faced a severe crisis, partly because they overburdened poor households with too much debt.

Second, the microfinance system must be sufficiently disciplined not to take more savings or to lend more money than its management and accounting systems can handle. For example, if the microfinance system requires weekly pay-ins, the system must be able to grow its bookkeeping capacity as it grows the number of weekly transactions. If it fails to do so, the lack of sound recordkeeping will eventually lead to a breakdown of members' trust, which will undermine the entire system. This issue often presents a challenge for ASCAs, which often have many illiterate members, and for smaller MFIs, which often lack sound accounting systems.

Third, the financial system should be disciplined in lending only in ways that it fully understands. For example, adding a new type of individual loan product when the MFI only has a history of making group loans can be tempting and dangerous if the MFI does not have good information-gathering systems, collateral systems, and strong ways to enforce contracts.

Finally, the financial system must have the discipline to enforce all of its policies with respect to savings, loans, and meeting attendance. For example, fines are often used to encourage members to be disciplined, and it is imperative that the financial system faithfully enforces these fines. If members perceive that the financial system is not serious about enforcing its policies, it will encourage them to be less disciplined in their own behaviors, which will undermine confidence in each other and in the system, causing it to collapse. Having the discipline to enforce policies—including fines—can be particularly difficult for church-centered microfinance ministries, which should have a bent toward showing love. But God does not see discipline—appropriately applied and tempered with grace—as inconsistent with love; rather, God sees them as complementary to one another (Hebrews 12:5–11).

Design Principle #3: Financial Sustainability

Financial sustainability is absolutely essential to building the trust that is at the heart of a financial system, i.e., the confidence that the system will be able to provide ongoing services. At the household level, financial sustainability simply means that the amount of money flowing into the household must be greater than the amount of money flowing out of the household across time. A constant danger in microfinance is that the household might take a loan that is bigger than it can actually handle. In particular, if the household takes out a business loan and if the business then struggles or even fails, the household may fail to be financially sustainable. And if this happens for many borrowers, it will undermine the sustainability of the financial system itself, which relies on the loan repayments from its borrowers in order to be financially viable.

Similarly, financial sustainability for the financial system means that the system is generating sufficient revenue to cover the costs of providing the financial services.[10] The Chalmers Center has found that a simple way of explaining this to materially poor people in microfinance groups is through the idea of a cooking pot.[11] In order to be able to continuously serve stew, the inflow of ingredients into the cooking pot must be greater than or equal to the amount of stew being ladled out. Similarly, if a financial system is to endure, the amount of money paid into the system must be greater than or equal to the amount of money being paid out.

In every financial system, including ROSCAs, ASCAs, or MFIs, there are *pay-ins* and *payouts*. The pay-ins are cash inflows: member savings contributions, repayment of principle and interest on loans, interest earned from any bank accounts that the group holds, etc. Payouts are all of the cash outflows from the system: loans, savings withdrawals, dividends earned on savings, costs of notebooks for record keeping, pencils, etc. Inflation, an overall increase in the price level, reduces the value of the group's funds over time. Hence, while it is not actually "paid out" to members, inflation is like a crack in the pot through which value leaks out. A financial system "pot" must stay full in order for it to continue providing services to its members.

Figure 9.1 displays a quick summary of the main pay-ins and payouts of ROSCAs and MFIs. Clearly there are many more pay-ins and payouts needed for a complex MFI than for a simple ROSCA. Thus, the management, administrative, and bookkeeping skills of the MFI staff must be well developed, especially when the MFI gets very large and needs to record tens of thousands of transactions every week.

FIGURE 9.1 Comparison of ROSCA and MFI Pay-Ins and Payouts

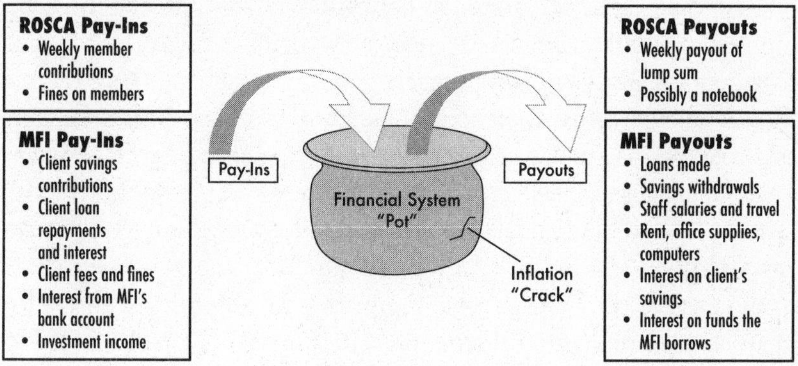

Note that one of the primary sources of pay-ins for MFIs (and for ASCAs, not pictured) is the interest on loans, which is a problematic subject for Christians, since the Bible warns against charging interest from people who are poor (Exodus 22:25; Leviticus 25:35–37). Space does not permit a complete discussion of all the theological issues involved, but it is important to distinguish between a loan for business or other investment purposes and a loan for a destitute person who needs to buy food. The Bible prohibits charging interest on loans to the destitute for food; it does not forbid interest on loans for investment purposes. Therefore, it is advisable for microfinance ministries to have funds available to make no-interest loans or gifts to people in destitute circumstances.[12]

But why are microfinance systems charging interest at all? Is not the whole idea to help poor people? Does not the fact that MFIs charge interest (typically 36 percent per year[13]) show that they are just in it for the money and that they do not care about poor people? It is certainly the case that some MFIs are exploiting poor people. But if the MFI does not charge for its services, it will cease to be able to serve poor people across time! Lenders charge interest to cover their costs of doing business, i.e., to keep the pot full, so that they can continue to provide loans to more people in the future. Just as a furniture maker prices his products to cover the costs of production so that he can stay in business, a lender of money sets the price of the loan to meet the cost of providing that service so that it stays in business and serves more people. Financial systems that cannot cover their expenses via interest are usually not able to even survive, much less grow to serve new people that they want to reach.

It is virtually impossible to overstate the next point: it is absolutely essential that all parties believe that the microfinance program is financially sustainable. Indeed, if enough borrowers start to doubt that the system is financially sustainable, that doubt alone will likely cause the financial system to crumble. Remember what we saw earlier in the case of the NGO in Asia: the primary economic incentive for borrowers to repay their loans today is their belief that by doing so they will be able to get additional loans in the future. If borrowers lose confidence in the financial sustainability of the lender, they will not have an incentive to repay their loans today, because they do not believe that the lender will be around in the future to provide additional loans. But if enough borrowers stop repaying their loans, the pot will become empty and the system will collapse. *Widespread belief in the financial sustainability of the system in the future is crucial for the system to be able to survive today.*

To better understand the principles of *discipline* and *financial sustainability*, consider the following scenarios. In each case, ask yourself, "What might happen next?"

- At a ROSCA meeting, it is Jonathan's turn to get the payout. He puts the money in his pocket and pledges, along with the rest of the members, to return next week. But as Jonathan leaves the meeting he overhears some members whispering that they are really struggling financially and are unlikely to be able to make their contributions to the ROSCA in the future.

  Likely outcome: Since other people will be stopping their pay-ins (lack of *discipline*), Jonathan knows that the pot will soon become empty (lack of *sustainability*). Given that he is unlikely to get any more payouts, he might simply take his money and run. When the group meets the next week and Jonathan is absent (lack of *discipline*), trust will start to weaken and the ROSCA might soon collapse as people stop contributing.

- An ASCA puts a sign on the door of its meeting room, telling its members that no new loans can be made until members make more savings pay-ins and more loan repayments are received.

  Likely outcome: Borrowers from the ASCA will probably stop repaying their loans, since they believe the ASCA will not be around to give them additional loans in the future (lack of *sustainability*). Members will likely stop making savings pay-ins (*lack of discipline*), since they have no confidence that their money is secure, given that loans are not being repaid. The ASCA pot will eventually become empty, and the ASCA will crumble.
- An MFI reduces sizes of new loans and delays loan releases to its existing clients for one to two months because cash is a little tight.

  Likely outcome: Sensing that the pot is running dry and that the MFI might have to close (lack of *sustainability*), existing loan holders will stop repaying their loans (lack of *discipline*), as they believe the MFI will not be around to grant them loans in the future. These actions will actually cause the pot to become empty, causing the MFI to go out of business.

Design Principle #4: Leadership, Management, and Governance

The leadership, management, and governance of a financial system are crucial to its trustworthiness. Leadership relates to modeling behavior, servanthood, and visioning; management deals with human resources, logistics, and organization; and governance relates to accountability of the people who are in leadership positions. At a minimum, leadership, management, and governance have the following key tasks:

- Protect the money and interests of the members or clients, especially from loss or fraud.
- Hold participants accountable for their savings and repayment of loans.
- Build leadership skills and capacity of others.
- Move the system beyond relying on a visionary or champion.
- Help assess the risk of loan requests and the plans of the members or clients.

- Uphold the vision.
- Approve strategic direction.
- Ensure that accurate records are kept.

It is vital that those in a position of governance know enough about the basic principles of financial systems to be able to hold the leaders and managers accountable. In particular, churches, missions, and ministries might have some learning to do about the principles of finance before they can allow their staff or members to establish microfinance systems. In addition, they must be able to determine if a microfinance ministry—which requires a very high degree of discipline and accountability—fits with their organization's vision, mission, capacity, and organizational culture.

Furthermore, it is absolutely imperative that the leadership, management, and governance provide sufficient organizational stability to communicate permanence to the savers and borrowers. As we saw in the case of the NGO in Asia, as soon as the leadership of the NGO communicated that it was leaving in eighteen months, it undermined people's incentives to repay their loans. In other words, in addition to financial sustainability, the governance, leadership, and management need to communicate and demonstrate overall organizational sustainability into the foreseeable future.

We can see the effects of weaknesses in leadership, management, and governance by estimating what might happen when there are breakdowns. For each of the following scenarios ask yourself, "What might happen next?"

- A ROSCA organizer fails to visit members who are struggling to make their pay-ins.

  Likely outcome: The struggling members may miss more weeks of payment, which will result in the ROSCA pot not being full enough to make its scheduled payouts. Members who pay in on time will likely become discouraged, and they might stop paying. All of this can cause the financial system, the ROSCA, to break down.
- The president of an ASCA loses the only copy of the group's records.

Likely outcome: The group will not be certain how much each person has saved and how much is still owed on each loan. Some disagreements will probably erupt between members and leaders, damaging relationships. Some people will likely stop making their savings and loan pay-ins, and the pot will start to empty. Trust in the ASCA's sustainability will plummet, and it will likely fall apart.

- The pastor of a church that launched an ASCA catches the treasurer committing fraud by unauthorized "borrowing" of the group's funds.

  Likely outcome: In this very difficult situation, if the treasurer is unrepentant or is not held accountable, the ASCA members will probably stop making pay-ins of their savings and their loan repayments. The group's pot will run dry; trust will be broken; and the ASCA will likely close.
- The CEO of an MFI facilitates a noncollateralized loan to his cousin that is much bigger than the loans given to other clients.

  Likely outcome: The MFI's clients in the cousin's borrowing group will note his big loan and will wonder what will happen. If the cousin misses a couple of payments, the members will carefully watch what the CEO does. If the CEO does not hold the cousin accountable, the group members will lose trust in the CEO's ability to enforce discipline and will likely stop repaying their own loans. If this news spreads to other groups, they may stop repaying their loans as well. Faced with declining revenues, i.e., a pot that is drying up, the MFI could go bankrupt.

Design Principle #5: Transparency

All decisions and transactions about handling money in financial systems should be transparent—that is, they should be done in the open in front of multiple sets of eyes. In the case of ROSCAs, ASCAs, and MFIs, this should occur at four levels.

First, all cash transactions for pay-ins to and payouts from the financial pot should be done in the open in front of multiple people rather than outside of meetings where only two parties are involved. It is much more difficult to accuse another person of fraudulent activity when money changes hands publicly than when it is changed behind closed doors.

Second, transparency in decision making is particularly important in group-based microfinance. If decisions about allocating loans are made in private, without the full knowledge of the group, then the group members may not fully trust the process that was used. For example, rumors could begin circulating that loans are being made on the basis of kinship, tribe, or other forms of favoritism, which could cause the group members to lose confidence in the system; and as we have seen, when trust is lost, the group members will often stop their pay-ins of savings and loan repayments, which will cause the pot to go dry and the system to collapse.

Third, all financial systems should be able to produce accurate and meaningful records and reports on a timely basis for their members or for other involved parties. This means that members in a ROSCA, ASCA, or MFI should be able to see—on demand—accurate records regarding their attendance, pay-ins, and payouts.

Finally, the financial system needs to communicate the terms of its services in ways that are understandable to the participants. Savers need to understand exactly how much they will earn on their deposits and the conditions that must be met for withdrawal. Borrowers need fees and interest expressed in ways that make the full cost of taking a loan easy to determine.[14]

Weaknesses in transparency can stimulate very quick declines in trust. If members have not seen transactions with their own eyes, it can be much harder for them to believe that the financial system is well managed and governed, which can weaken their commitments to keep their own agreements and to pay on time. The system can then quickly crumble, doing harm to everyone involved.

Design Principle #6: Fit the Target Population

There is incredible diversity amongst the 2.6 billion people in the world who live on less than $2 per day. Hence, there is no "one-size-fits-all" set of services that can meet their needs. For example, a thirty-year-old father with a high-school education who is operating a profitable microenterprise is very different from a seventy-year-old, illiterate widow who daily picks food out of the trash. If a microfinance ministry fails to take these differences into account, the financial services that it offers will not match the needs of its target population. At best, this will result in very few participants in the program. At worst, this will bury the participants in debts that they cannot afford to repay, doing significant harm to the borrowers, their families, and the program as a whole. For example, see the quotes at the very start of this chapter about this type of harm in India.

As we saw in figure 4.1, working-age people living on less than $2 per day have very different primary occupations: 610 million are smallholder farmers; 370 million are casual laborers; 300 million are salaried; 180 million are microentrepreneurs; 100 million are unemployed; 80 million are fishermen and pastoralists. Each of these types of economic activities requires different types of financial services. For example, the long gaps between planting and harvesting in agricultural work require loans with much longer repayment terms than a lady selling perishable items in a busy market (see Pumza in chapter 4).

In addition, variations in income and wealth for people within these different income-earning categories significantly impact the types of financial services they desire. For example, as a person's income and wealth increase, they are more likely to have both the desire and the capacity to take out larger loans. Figure 9.2 summarizes how the microfinance-related services desired by poor households typically vary across income levels.[15] The "poverty line" in this table differs from one country to the next, depending on local prices for such things as essential food.

The services in figure 9.2 fall into two categories:

- *Financial services*: savings; insurance; and loans for business investment, household investment, and contingencies (emergencies, consumption smoothing, lifecycle needs). See the **Microfinance for Households Principle**. Not shown are money-transfer services, for it is too early to determine how well these services will meet the needs of people in various levels of

FIGURE 9.2 Microfinance-Related Services Desired by Households of Different Poverty Levels

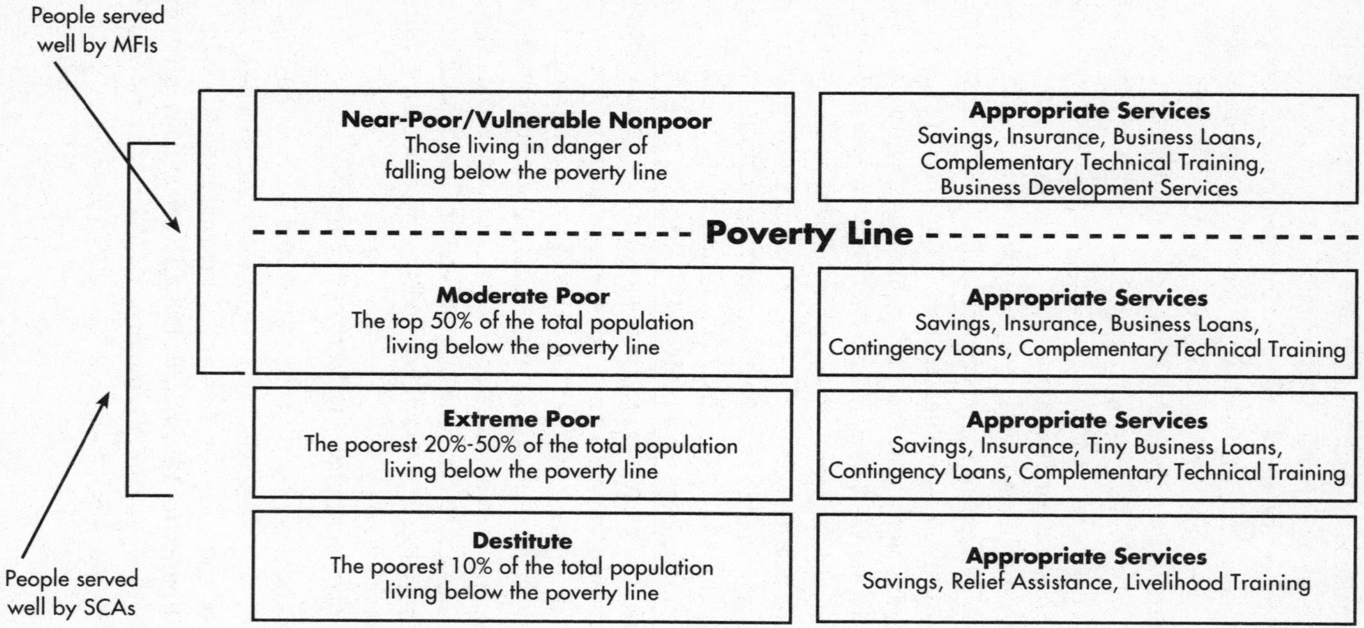

Adapted from Monique Cohen, *The Impact of Microfinance*, CGAP Donor Brief (Washington, DC: CGAP, July 2003), 1.

poverty, but it is likely that they will be desired by most people above those who are destitute.[16]

- *Nonfinancial services*: complementary technical training in agriculture, business, home, health, etc. (see Ministry Component #4 in chapter 7); and other business development services such as market access, infrastructure, and advocacy (see figure 8.2 and the related discussion in chapter 8).

As we move into deeper levels of poverty, the demand for business loans decreases, while the demand for contingency loans (emergencies, consumption smoothing, and lifecycle needs) and for very tiny business loans (e.g., $10) rises. People who are in "extreme" poverty or who are "destitute" are highly vulnerable. As a result, the business loans of $50 or more that are typically offered by MFIs are simply too risky for them. SCAs such as ROSCAs and ASCAs are able to provide the savings and types of loans desired by the "extreme" poor.

Microfinance services are usually not appropriate for "destitute" households, with the exception of providing savings services in coordination with relevant training and broader relief ministries such as food aid. However, since the mid–1990s, several large MFIs in Bangladesh (Grameen Bank and BRAC) have found ways to combine livelihood training, savings, and sometimes loans with relief-type, safety-net programs in ways that graduate "destitute" people to becoming "extreme" poor. The Consultative Group to Assist the Poor (CGAP) and the Ford Foundation have expanded this "graduation model" to eight additional countries and have produced a technical manual to help others to implement this strategy.[17]

In addition to occupation and income levels, appropriate microfinance services can also be influenced by marital status, religion, and cultural characteristics. For more information, see the resource entitled *Target Community* on the website associated with this book.

Financial Systems Design Principle

In order to be successful, a financial system must maintain all of the following features:

1. Trust
2. Discipline
3. Financial Sustainability
4. Leadership, Management, and Governance
5. Transparency
6. Fit the Target Population

FIGURE 9.3 House of Principles

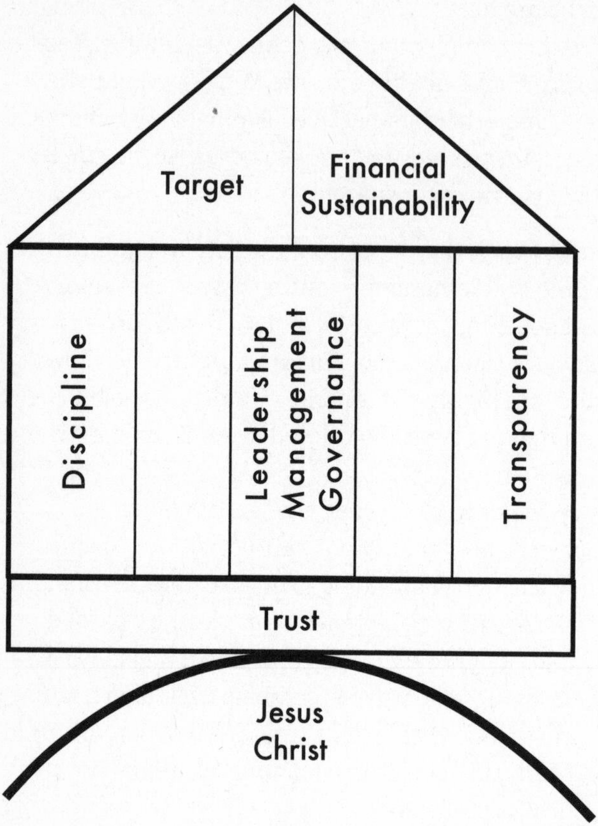

In summary, we can now introduce the **Financial Systems Design Principle**.

The House of Principles

Explaining these principles in simple terms to very poor people is not easy, but it is absolutely essential that they understand them in order for microfinance ministries to be successful. The Chalmers Center has found that the House of Principles pictured in figure 9.3 is a useful training tool for equipping very poor churches for ministry.[18] If any portion of the house is removed—the foundation, pillars, or roof—the house will eventually collapse, hurting the people inside and perhaps beyond. Similarly, if any of the six design features are not in place, the financial system will collapse, hurting the members and others associated with the system.

The house is built on the rock of Jesus Christ, for it is through his power alone that the group will be able to maintain the six design principles and to function successfully.

Summary

Financial services are inherently difficult to offer because they involve "promises to pay" in the future. As a result, there is some risk involved in finance. The three Cs of a borrower—character, capacity, and collateral—must be clearly known in order to ascertain the risk involved in lending money and to calculate the appropriate interest rates and fees. Unfortunately, it is very difficult and costly to determine the three Cs for materially poor people, which is the primary reason that banks will generally not lend to them. The microfinance movement has developed relatively low-cost ways of addressing the three Cs, often using group-based incentives based on joint liability for loan repayment. Although all financial systems are fragile, by following six key design principles, the three Cs can be successfully addressed and the system can function successfully: trust; discipline; financial sustainability; leadership, management, and governance; transparency; and fit the target population. If these principles are not followed, it is likely that the system will fail, doing considerable harm to everybody involved. Ultimately, the success of the system depends upon the power of Jesus Christ to make it work.

Application Exercise

While this chapter has tried to simplify the concepts and principles, it might be good to practice a bit. Hence, try to assess a microfinance system operating in your context to see how consistent it is with the principles in this chapter. Select a ROSCA, ASCA, MFI, or similar system to study. If you are not in a Global South context, you can gather information on ROSCAs and possibly ASCAs from immigrants to your country who have come from the Global South. We have found that immigrants are often quite happy to answer all sorts of questions about the informal financial systems they used in their home countries and that they still might be using in yours. To help you with this assessment, a tool entitled *Microfinance System Assessment* can be found on the website associated with this book.

PART 4

THE THREE MICROFINANCE MODELS

CHAPTER 10

THE PROVIDER MODEL OF MICROFINANCE

People treat their own money differently than they treat other people's money. And when something comes to you at no cost, you value it differently than you do if it cost you something.

—Head of a Christian foundation in the United States who has studied failed Provider Models in the Global South[1]

I can pay [my loans]. My business is coming on. But I won't cover [the loan defaults] for those ones again.

—Borrower from an MFI in Ghana who spent about $1,000 to repay loans for defaulting members of her borrowing group[2]

We have covered a lot of ground, and now it is time to get very practical. If your church or organization is interested in pursuing a microfinance ministry, it has three strategies from which to choose: *provide, partner, or promote*. The primary purpose of the next three chapters is to help you to make this choice wisely.

In addition, your ministry might want to consider offering the nonfinancial services that were discussed earlier:

1. Complementary technical training in such things as managing business, household, or health. See Ministry Component #4 in chapter 7.
2. Additional business development services. See figure 8.2 and the related discussion in chapter 8.

These complementary services will also be discussed at appropriate points in the next three chapters.

This chapter focuses on the Provider Model of microfinance. Throughout the discussion, it will be helpful to keep the **Financial Systems Design Principle** in mind.

Financial Systems Design Principle

In order to be successful, a financial system must maintain all of the following features:

1. Trust
2. Discipline
3. Financial Sustainability
4. Leadership, Management, and Governance
5. Transparency
6. Fit the Target Population

An Introduction to the Provider Model

Long-Distance Microcredit Revisited

In chapter 9 we discussed the troubled microcredit program started by Riverbend Church and Mount Zion Fellowship in a squatter community in Africa. Let's continue their story. As Riverbend and Mount Zion were trying to determine the best way forward, somebody introduced them to the group-based lending methodology of the Grameen Bank. The church leaders soon became quite enamored with Grameen's story: founded in 1976, Grameen has 8.6 million poor members, having lent $15.5 billion since its inception, with an average repayment rate of 97 percent![3] That sounded pretty good to the church leaders, so they decided to try the group-based lending methodology as well.

Because they feared that their reputation had been a bit damaged in the squatter community, the leaders of Riverbend and Mount Zion decided to get a fresh start in a different community. Representatives from Riverbend and Mount Zion churches met with community leaders and members over the course of several months, explaining to them how the loans would work: if a group member does not repay her loan, no new loans will be given to any of the other group members. They then encouraged community members to form groups in order to receive loans. Riverbend gave another $2,000 in loan capital to Mount Zion to get things started, and Mount Zion provided two volunteers from its congregation, Mary and Bethany, to train the groups and to administer $100 loans. The program got off to a slow start, as community members initially seemed a bit skeptical. But as the community members saw loans being granted and repaid and new loans being issued, their excitement increased. Soon, many groups were forming, and membership in the program was increasing rapidly.

From the start, it was clear that these participants were acting in more disciplined ways than those in the squatter community, as nearly everybody was repaying their loans on schedule. In addition, a subset of the participants was very entrepreneurial. This subset had very good business ideas and was very focused on improving and growing their businesses. In fact, it was not long before the entire $2,000 had been lent out, and there was no end in sight. New groups were forming rapidly, each of which needed loans. In addition, some of the more entrepreneurial members had businesses that were really starting to take off, and they wanted bigger loans. The business people at Riverbend grew very excited by all of this, and they soon donated an additional $15,000 to increase the amount of money that Mount Zion could lend.

Although they were a bit tired, Mary and Bethany were very excited as well. They loved seeing renewed hope in the borrowers' faces, and they were particularly pleased about the businesses that were expanding. In addition, Mary and Bethany were seeing evidence of spiritual impact, as some borrowers were starting to attend worship services at Mount Zion. The leaders of Mount Zion and Riverbend were understandably elated. Unfortunately, their joy might be short-lived, for this microfinance ministry is at great risk. Do you know why? Stop and think about the **Financial Systems Design Principle**. Do you see violations of any of the six components of this principle?

Not as Easy as It Looks

Riverbend and Mount Zion are pursuing the Provider Model of microfinance, and they are not alone. Enamored by the success of the Grameen Bank and other large-scale MFIs, many organizations—including churches, missionaries, small parachurch ministries, and small NGOs—are also trying to implement the Provider Model, an approach in which the organization sells financial services (savings, loans, insurance, and money transfers) to poor people for a fee.[4] Most of the churches, missionaries, small parachurch ministries, and small NGOs that are using the Provider Model focus on offering loans, usually for business purposes, rather than on providing savings, insurance, or money-transfer services; therefore, most of the discussion that follows will focus on being a provider of business loans. For the remainder of this chapter, unless we use more specific language, we shall use the term "ministries" to refer to both small parachurch ministries and small NGOs, even though the latter are typically a bit larger and more sophisticated than the former.

It is very important to note that in the Provider Model, the organization lending the money, e.g., Mount Zion Fellowship, owns the loan capital, which it normally gets from a donor such as Riverbend Church.[5] The organization then lends this capital to materially poor people and tries to collect it back with interest. The donor might also give some money to help with the initial start-up of the program. See figure 10.1.

Grameen has made the Provider Model look easy, but it is not. As mentioned earlier, financial systems are inherently very fragile. If all six components of the **Financial Systems Design Principle** are not executed properly, the system will likely collapse, doing considerable harm to everybody involved. Indeed, the landscape is littered with the carcasses of failed Provider Models started by churches, missionaries, and ministries.

The primary purpose of this chapter is to explain why it is so difficult to implement the Provider Model successfully. *In fact, we highly recommend that churches, missionaries, and ministries not utilize the Provider Model.* You now already have the main conclusion of this chapter, but we know from years of experience that many readers are not yet convinced, so

FIGURE 10.1 The Provider Model of Microfinance

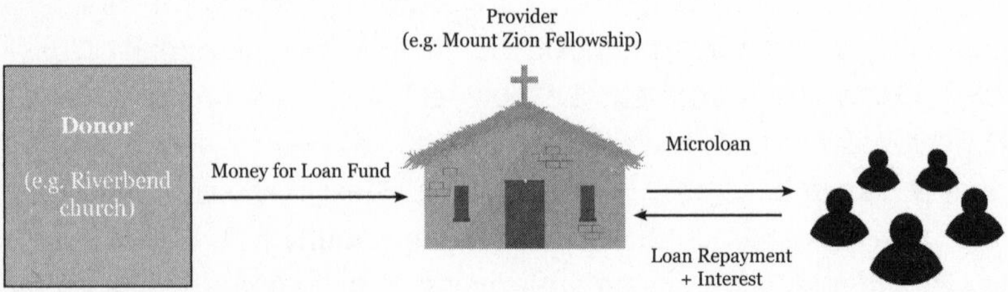

read on! And if you are already convinced, you should read the rest of this chapter anyway, as it will be important to help you understand the Partnership and Promotion Models discussed in chapters 11–12.

To begin to understand the difficulties of implementing the Provider Model, let us begin by examining table 10.1, which shows the range of microfinance providers.

The smallest type of microfinance provider is the Relational Loan Ministry (column 1), in which a church or missionary makes just a few loans to some people whom they typically know pretty well. This model has virtually no overhead costs and can be used in virtually any setting. The borrower usually has no economic incentive to repay the loan, as the loan is often not collateralized in any meaningful sense, and there is also not much chance of receiving additional loans in perpetuity; hence, loan repayment depends upon the borrower's integrity and the value that they put on their personal relationship with the lender.

The Relational Loan Ministry seems like a very easy model to implement, but many churches and missionaries have found out the hard way that it is not so easy to get their loans repaid! Lending on the basis of personal relationships can be very tricky, as the borrower might see the loan as really just a "gift," and the lender might find it very difficult to demand repayment from a friend.

Small-Scale Microcredit Programs (column 2) try to serve anywhere from dozens to hundreds of borrowers. Mount Zion Fellowship's loan program falls into this category, as do the loan programs of many churches, missionaries, and ministries. Because Small-Scale Microcredit Programs are larger than Relational Loan Ministries, it is very difficult for them to obtain loan repayments on the basis of personal relationships; thus, it becomes even more important for them to provide proper economic incentives for borrowers to repay. Unfortunately, as we shall see below, it is nearly impossible for Small-Scale Microcredit Programs to provide such incentives, which makes this model so risky to pursue.

Medium-Scale MFIs (column 3) reach tens of thousands of people. Most of the microfinance programs that are operated by the major international Christian relief and development organizations fit into this medium-scale category, as do some Christian organizations that

TABLE 10.1 The Continuum of Microfinance Providers

	Relational Loan Ministries	Small-Scale Microcredit Programs	Medium-Scale MFIs	Large-Scale MFIs
Examples	• Benevolence fund in a church • Missionary making a few loans	• Mount Zion's microfinance ministry • Small parachurch ministries • Small, often indigenous NGOs	• Major, multisectorial Christian relief and development organizations • Most Christian MFIs	• Grameen Bank • Some Christian MFIs
Context Where It's Found	Anywhere	Wide range of contexts	Mostly stable macroeconomic contexts	Stable macroeconomic contexts
Number of Clients Reached	Just a few	Dozens to hundreds	3,000–100,000	> 100,000
Interest Rates	Usually very low, sometimes 0%	Low interest rates, sometimes below inflation rate	"Market rate" that other MFIs charge in the region	"Market rate" that other MFIs charge in the region
Funding Sources	Rely on their available cash	Usually ongoing reliance on outside grants	Start-up grants replaced with loans and equity investments as they grow	Few grants. Access capital markets for loans and equity investment
Services Provided	Typically microcredit	Microcredit that is often integrated with multiple services	Often minimalistic, focusing only on microfinance, particularly loans for business investment	With increased profitability, they can offer new financial services and sometimes nonfinancial services
Loan Repayment Rates	Sometimes okay, but often very low	Sometimes okay, but often very low	Very high or they will go out of business quickly	Very high
Staffing	Volunteers	Few paid staff, often working in multiple programs	Hundreds of staff, mostly nationals, doing only microfinance	Thousands of specialized national employees
Sustainability	Subsidized by volunteers and supporters	Not sustainable. Funding of multiple ministries is often combined, and none of them are sustainable on their own	Sustainability reached after 3–7 years or the program will likely collapse	More than sustainable and use profits to fund expansion into new geographical areas, additional financial services, and sometimes nonfinancial services

focus on microfinance (e.g., HOPE International).[6] Because Medium-Scale MFIs are far too large to depend on personal relationships for loan repayment, they must rely on economic incentives. Amongst other things, this implies that they are under enormous pressure to rapidly become very large so that they can earn sufficient interest revenues to be financially sustainable. Achieving such scale requires MFIs to become quite complex institutions, for they have to execute, record, and monitor a very large number of financial transactions. As a result, these programs tend to be "minimalist"—that is, they usually focus solely on providing financial services rather than on offering additional interventions such as agricultural assistance, business training, healthcare, or education. In addition, in their drive to grow to scale, Christian MFIs often struggle to find the time and money to engage in evangelism and discipleship.

Medium-Scale MFIs have tended to focus on loans for businesses, i.e., the "microcredit-for-microenterprises" approach. As we saw in figure 9.2, this makes Medium-Scale MFIs best able to serve the "moderate poor" or "non-poor" rather than the "extreme poor." However, a number of Medium-Scale MFIs have recently started to offer savings and even insurance services, enabling them to serve deeper levels of poverty through the "microfinance-for-households" approach.

Large-Scale MFIs (column 4) such as the Grameen Bank are financially sustainable and can develop a diverse set of financial products—loans, savings, and insurance—that tightly fit the assets and needs of their target group and that can evolve as the target group matures. The MFIs in this category are able to use their profits to innovate, creating new financial products, and they can sometimes move beyond minimalist microfinance into addressing a wider range of household needs.

It may seem strange to readers to include both a missionary making a few personal loans and the Grameen Bank all in the same table. The reason for putting them together is that all of the individuals and organizations in this table share two features: (1) They are all providing financial services for a fee, usually business loans that charge interest; and (2) They must all follow the six components of the **Financial Systems Design Principle**. If they do not follow all six components, they will experience low repayment rates on their loans, and the system will likely collapse. Indeed, as we shall see in the next section, many of the microfinance ministries started by churches, missionaries, and ministries are often at high risk of failure.

Beware of Implementing the Provider Model

Applying the Six Components of Healthy Financial Systems

In order to increase our understanding of the difficulties of being a microfinance provider, let us examine the ways in which MFIs address the six components of the **Financial Systems Design Principle**. For simplicity, we will talk about both the "medium" and "large-scale" MFIs in columns 3 and 4 of Table 10.1 as one group called "MFIs." As we examine each of the six components, we will also explore some of the particular challenges that churches, missionaries, and ministries have in mimicking the techniques of the MFIs, using the case of Mount Zion Fellowship's microfinance ministry to illustrate.

Design Principle #1: Trust is the Foundation of Microfinance

MFIs' loan programs intentionally use three mechanisms that build trust, each of which is difficult for churches, missionaries, and ministries to emulate:

1. *Selecting borrowers who are likely to repay:* By requiring borrowers to self-select into groups with joint liability for loan repayment, MFIs are able to increase trust that the borrowers are likely to repay their loans. When churches, missionaries, and ministries engage in a Relational Loan Ministry (column 1), they might know enough about the *character* and *capacity* of their potential borrowers to be able to select them well. However, as they move into Small-Scale Credit Programs, the growing number of clients makes it less likely that churches, missionaries, and ministries will have such information on potential borrowers. Unfortunately, like Riverbend and Mount Zion in the squatter community, many such programs make the mistake of providing individual loans rather than group-based loans with joint liability.[7] This approach fails to weed out those borrowers who are unlikely to repay, as the lender does not have sufficient information on the three Cs to select good borrowers.

Furthermore, even when churches, missionaries, and ministries do use groups, they often fail to create proper incentives for the group-formation process to weed out the borrowers who are unlikely to repay. For example, churches might simply decide to lend to all the people in a preexisting group such as a Bible study, a woman's association, or a nutrition program. But lending into groups is not sufficient to address the three Cs. The groups must self-select for the purposes of cross-guaranteeing each other's loans so that borrowers with "bad Cs" do not receive loans. The fact that a group of people are willing to be in a Bible study together does not automatically mean they should cross-guarantee loans for one another.

2. *Creating institutional permanency:* With well-trained staff, visible buildings, formal boards, and professional operations, MFIs communicate that they are permanent institutions from which well-behaved clients can get loans indefinitely. As discussed in chapter 9, it is this hope of ongoing loans that provides the economic incentive for borrowers to repay their current loans.

In contrast, churches, missionaries, and ministries are less professional and often have programs that come and go as funding sources dry up, volunteers get tired, and family considerations lead missionaries to return home. Indeed, Mary and Bethany were already getting tired. What would happen if they needed to quit? Would other volunteers step up to take their place?

3. *Providing access to larger loans:* MFIs build trust in their ability to provide ongoing services by offering progressively larger loans to borrowers who faithfully repay. Creating such confidence in future services is an extremely important motivator for borrowers to repay in the present. The small programs run by churches, missionaries, and ministries may not have sufficient funds to continue to grow their loan sizes as the borrowers' capacity grows. Indeed, Mount Zion was starting to face this problem, as the successful entrepreneurs were seeking bigger loans. Will Riverbend continue to fund a growing loan pool, and if it does, will Mount Zion have the ability to administer these growing funds well? If not, the entrepreneurs might start to see

this loan program as irrelevant, which would reduce their incentive to repay their current loans, putting the entire program at risk.

Design Principle #2: Discipline

A microfinance provider must enforce discipline. Many MFIs have experienced initial clients who intentionally test the program's commitment to repayment discipline to see if they can get away with not repaying. This requires the MFIs to quickly and decisively enforce client discipline. Some East African MFIs require their client groups to seize and sell assets from defaulting group members in order to repay their loans. A Christian MFI in Southeast Asia requires its field staff to visit the homes of defaulting members in order to shame the client into repaying by waiting, sometimes for hours, without eating or drinking until the client finds the money to repay.

One leader of a Christian MFI explains the tensions this way:

> One of the greatest hurdles I have faced in administering an MFI is finding the proper balance between compassion and firmness. A borrower, especially in countries with a history of continual aid, is watching when a program is beginning to see if this is really a bank or if it is just another charity. He will never be any more interested than you are in repayment. And yet we want to show the love of Christ in every part of a program. This balance calls for much prayer.[8]

The challenges for churches, missionaries, and ministries in enforcing discipline in loan repayment are manifold. Their organizational cultures are generally quite different from those of a high-accountability financial institution, and their staff members are often more accustomed to delivering free food to poor people than to seizing their assets!

Indeed, Mount Zion has already shown its inability to enforce loan repayment in the squatter community. The fact that Mount Zion is now using groups in the second community can help with this problem, as groups have incentives to hold their members accountable. But using groups does not remove the problem altogether. Eventually, Mount Zion will need to hold a group accountable to repay a member's loan, and the evidence from the squatter community suggests that Mount Zion will—quite understandably—struggle to do this. And remember, Mount Zion did not come up with these loan funds in the first place. When collecting loans gets difficult, it would be entirely within the realm of human nature for the leaders of Mount Zion to say to themselves, "Riverbend Church has so much money, and these borrowers are so poor. It won't hurt Riverbend if we just forgive some of these loans. They were not expecting to get their money back anyway." Humans tend to handle other people's money differently than they handle their own money, and both the borrowers and Mount Zion are handling other people's money.

The difficulty of getting staff to enforce discipline is worsened by the fact that potential borrowers come with preexisting expectations about churches, missionaries, and ministries. Indeed, these organizations are widely known for giving things away for free. This general problem is exacerbated when an organization uses the same staff members to run both the "handout" ministries and the loan program. In the highly relational cultures that characterize much of the Global South, it is a bit much to expect borrowers to understand and believe that the same person who gives them free food in the morning will seriously try to enforce loan repayment in the afternoon.

Design Principle #3: Financial Sustainability

It is imperative for MFIs' revenues to exceed their costs so that the program can continue to provide financial services, which is the primary economic incentive for loan repayment (see figure 9.1). In addition, pressures from competitive markets and donors have forced MFIs to increasingly adopt businesslike operations in which they seek to maximize revenues and to decrease costs through a variety of methods:[9]

- *Charging interest rates sufficient to cover costs*: MFIs charge interest rates that cover the costs of capital, operating costs, and losses to inflation. Typically this involves a "flat rate" of 36 percent per year, which translates into an annual percentage rate of 65.7 percent.[10] These high interest rates are needed to cover the very high costs of making small loans to materially poor people.
- *Increasing loan sizes*: It is cheaper to lend $100 to one person than $10 to ten people, as the former requires fewer transactions; hence, MFIs have strong incentives to encourage clients

to borrow the maximum amount of money they can handle. It is for this reason that MFIs' loan products are typically too large to serve the "extreme poor" in figure 9.2.

- *Growing to scale*: MFIs usually strive to become very large. By pumping out more loan capital, they can increase their interest revenues, enabling them to cover their overhead costs.
- *Offering only minimalist services*: By cutting out additional services that do not generate revenues and focusing solely on lending money and collecting it back, MFIs can reduce costs.
- *Focusing on regions with high population density*: Lending in heavily populated areas reduces transportation costs.
- *Using group-lending methodologies*: Peer groups reduce the transaction costs of providing services since field staff can work with twenty to forty borrowers in one meeting rather than having individual meetings with each borrower. In addition, the self-selection process reduces the costs of discovering and weeding out bad borrowers.
- *Standardizing products*: Cost reductions are large when staff can be trained and systems developed for only a few financial products and delivery methodologies.
- *Increasing use of technology*: MFIs are increasingly training their clients to use cell phones or point-of-sale cellular devices as means of repaying loans and making other payments, both of which can lower the costs of delivering financial services.

The microfinance programs of churches, missionaries, and ministries usually cannot achieve financial sustainability, which is one of the biggest threats to their success. Because these programs are too small to generate the revenues needed to cover their costs, they require ongoing subsidies to stay afloat. If the subsidies dry up or are even irregular, the programs will likely collapse. Mount Zion's program is at great risk in this regard. Mary and Bethany are subsidizing the program by volunteering their time, but they are already getting tired. If they quit, the program will not have any money to hire their replacements, and loan repayments will likely plummet.

There is one caveat. As mentioned earlier, although financial sustainability is generally necessary for loan repayment, *sometimes* Relational

Loan Ministries are able to get loans repaid despite the fact that they are not financially sustainable. In such cases, the personal integrity of the borrowers or their desire to maintain a healthy relationship with the lender can substitute for their lack of economic incentives to repay the loan. However, this caveat does not negate the fact that the Relational Loan Ministry often fails to maintain the other five components necessary to create a successful microfinance ministry, which often results in their suffering from very low repayment rates.

Design Principle #4: Leadership, Management, and Governance

As discussed in the previous chapter, it is imperative that leadership, management, and governance provide the organizational stability, accountability, and discipline necessary for a well-functioning financial system. This is not always easy to find. Indeed, a survey of over 300 microfinance practitioners from 74 countries identified management quality and corporate governance as the top two risks in microfinance.[11]

Most churches, missionaries, and ministries will find this to be an extremely difficult problem to solve. Authority in such settings is often largely in the hands of a single individual—the pastor, the missionary, the visionary ministry leader—and even when the authority is more widely dispersed, it is unlikely that it has the necessary expertise to oversee a microfinance system.

For example, the regional leadership of a denomination in a country in the Global South decided to start a Small-Scale Microcredit Program to serve their region. One of the authors visited the loan officer of this ministry, which operated out of the denomination's regional offices. The ministry was making individual loans throughout the region, using funds donated by a partner church in the United States. Borrowers were asked to specify some physical asset as collateral. When asked if she would actually seize the collateral if a borrower failed to repay, the program officer replied:

> The committee overseeing this program consists of the head of the region for the denomination, his assistant, and a pastor from the region. They have decided that because we are a church and these are very poor people, we will not actually seize any collateral. But this is a secret policy that nobody knows about.[12]

Well, it was a secret policy that nobody knew about *yet*. It would be just a matter of time before a delinquent borrower learned that their collateral was not real collateral, and as this news spread to other borrowers, the entire program would be at risk. The committee governing this ministry was ineffective, because power was not shared sufficiently broadly, and it lacked the expertise necessary to oversee a microfinance program. Indeed, we can see similar dynamics at work in the loan program of Riverbend and Mount Zion. There is no clear structure for leadership, management, and governance, so these responsibilities are defaulting to the church leaders, who have no experience in finance, and who have—understandably—demonstrated great hesitancy in enforcing loan repayment.

Similarly, when a foreign missionary raises all of the support needed to pay his or her own living expenses and starts a Small-Scale Microcredit Program, it is often the case that there is no real governance in place. The missionary's financial supporters are usually widely dispersed and do not know enough about microfinance principles to ask the missionary any hard questions. Moreover, many mission agencies also have very loose supervisory structures, and most of the time these structures have few if any people with any financial background. As a result, some microfinance missionaries run by missionaries operate completely on their own with no governance at all. This is a very dangerous situation.

Even many small parachurch ministries and small NGOs that establish microcredit programs struggle in this regard. Often their boards of directors, either national or international, have little or no expertise in microfinance or even in finance in general. Sometimes the management in such organizations believes that the microfinance program will generate enough profits to help subsidize the non-microfinance operations of the ministry or NGO, despite the fact that the microfinance program is too small and too inefficient to even approach financial sustainability, much less generate profits. There have even been cases in which managers of small NGOs have withdrawn loan capital out of their microfinance programs in order to cover staff salaries in other programs of the NGO, a move which puts the microfinance program and the organization as a whole at considerable risk.

It is extremely difficult for churches, missionaries, and ministries to develop the leadership, management, and governance to successfully implement the Provider Model of microfinance. The good news is that there are other microfinance models that churches, missionaries, and ministries can use very effectively, as we shall see in chapters 11 and 12.

Design Principle #5: Transparency

Transparency in all financial transactions and in decision making must be done in public to build trust. MFIs typically do this in the context of the meetings of the borrowing groups: everybody knows the rules, and everybody can see them being consistently applied and enforced.

Although this type of transparency is possible for churches, missionaries, and ministries, it may require a shift in culture settings in which the pastor or other leader is accustomed to making decisions behind closed doors and just announcing those decisions to the congregation or staff. In particular, trust will be broken if it is even perceived that the pastor or leader is steering loans to relatives or close friends or giving them particular leniency in repaying their loans.

Design Principle #6: Fit the Target Population

MFIs develop very specific products and then use techniques to screen out candidates who do not match those products well. On the one hand, MFIs want to weed out borrowers who do not have the character, capacity, or collateral to repay the loans being offered. On the other hand, MFIs also want to screen out borrowers whose income or wealth give them too much capacity to repay the particular loan size being offered. Such people are likely to have access to other sources of credit, thereby increasing the likelihood that they will not repay the small loans being offered by the MFI, as they can just get bigger loans elsewhere. In addition, such people may become impatient with very poor group members who are struggling to make payments, thereby undermining the social cohesion that is so crucial to building trust in the group.

MFIs use a number of tools to create fairly homogenous groups that are well suited for the particular financial service being offered. Group lending with joint liability tends to weed out those with bad three Cs.

In addition, the use of weekly meetings, small initial loan sizes, and cost-recovering interest rates, which tend to be rather high, tend to deter non-poor people from joining, as they have access to other, larger sources of capital that require less time and have lower interest rates.[13]

Because they lack expertise, it is difficult for churches, missionaries, and ministries to target their customers well. Note that Mount Zion offered the same loan size of $100 in both communities, even though the communities appear to have very different populations. In addition, the borrowing groups in the second community were clearly not homogenous, as some of the members were far more entrepreneurial than others and were already seeking larger loan sizes than Mount Zion's standard loan of $100. It takes expertise to create a good fit between the financial service being offered and the customers who are buying it.

In summary, churches, missionaries, and ministries face enormous challenges in addressing the six components of the **Financial Systems Design Principle**. In addition, these organizations find it increasingly difficult to obtain funding to be providers, a topic to which we now turn.

Donor Expectations for Providers

The expectations of donors for microfinance are changing, which has tremendous implications for Christian microfinance providers of all sizes.

First, donors are increasingly demanding high degrees of technical competency and efficiency. We are rapidly approaching the end of an era in which Small-Scale Microcredit Programs have been able to access funds from relatively uninformed foreign donors, who were often more committed to the Christian vision of these microfinance programs than to their financial performance. The economic growth in Western nations over the last thirty years has created a large cohort of wealthy Christian businesspeople, who are eager to use their time, skills, and wealth to promote business development and microfinance in the Global South.[14] These people's business expertise not only impacts their personal giving, but also that of the missions committees and foundations on which they serve. This is resulting in greater concerns that the microfinance providers they support are technically competent and financially sound. Thus, small microfinance providers are likely to find that the capital of these businesspeople—and the capital of the organizations that they are influencing—are not easy to access.

In addition, the growth of web-based funding portals like Kiva is increasingly driving microfinance providers to higher technical standards. Kiva has created a web-based structure in which even a small individual donor can select a materially poor borrower to whom they would like to make a microloan. MFIs that are able to meet Kiva's criteria are allowed to post some of their borrowers' profiles on the Kiva website. A donor sends money online to Kiva, earmarked for the MFI and borrower of their choice, and Kiva bundles this donor's money together with the money from other donors and transfers the funds to the MFI. Once the MFI's borrower repays her loan to the MFI, the donor can get their money back with no interest, but most allow their money to be recycled to other borrowers.

Kiva has helped to open up new ways for donors to invest God's resources into ministry, as many of the organizations on Kiva are Christian MFIs. But smaller providers will find it difficult to access such funds, as they are unlikely to be able to meet Kiva's technical standards. Unfortunately, Kiva's technical standards—as well as those coming from the major government donors—are making it increasingly difficult for Christian MFIs to include evangelism and discipleship in their programs.[15] MFIs are being required to grow very rapidly so that they can achieve financial sustainability in as little as two to three years. In contexts in which there are few Christians, such rapid growth often forces Christian MFIs to hire unbelievers as staff. Furthermore, to reduce costs, each staff member is being asked to handle a very large number of borrowers, especially if those borrowers are very poor. It is not unusual for there to be a ratio of 400 borrowers per staff member, which provides little time for staff members to engage in evangelism, discipleship, or virtually anything else other than making loans.

The end result is that even many Christian MFIs end up being "minimalist," simply lending money and collecting it back. Providing such loan services is an important thing to do, but it falls far short of what is necessary to alleviate poverty, as described in the theory of change outlined in chapter 7.

Do No Harm

The message of this chapter may be very discouraging to some people: *churches, missionaries, and ministries should usually not try to pursue the Provider Model in which they lend money to poor people*. Indeed, some readers may already be involved in this approach and now feel very threatened or even angry. It is not our intent to discourage or to offend readers; rather, we truly want to help both the church and the poor to move from dependence to dignity, and that requires us to help readers to avoid what can be a very harmful approach to microfinance.

And make no mistake about it. A failed microfinance program can do considerable harm to everyone involved: to the poor; to the church, missionary, or ministry; to the donors; to other organizations trying to provide financial services in the same region; and ultimately to the very name of Jesus Christ. And as one donor to a failed Provider Model stated, "All of this gives Satan a foothold."[16]

As depicted in Chambers's Web of Deprivation (figure 5.1), poverty is multifaceted, implying that a portfolio of interventions is needed to improve people's lives. Churches, missionaries, ministries, and MFIs all have profoundly important roles to play, but none of them can get the job done on their own. Churches, missionaries, and ministries are not good lenders of money, while Christian MFIs often struggle to do much beyond lend money. By working together, it is possible for them to do more than they can on their own, which is the subject of the next chapter.

Summary

Enamored by the success of the Grameen Bank and other large-scale MFIs, many churches, missionaries, and ministries are also trying to implement the Provider Model, an approach in which the organization sells financial services—savings, loans, insurance, and money transfers—to poor people for a fee. In most cases, small providers have focused on providing loans, primarily for business purposes. Relational Loan Ministries with just a few borrowers can sometimes leverage personal relationships and the borrowers' integrity to obtain loan repayment; however, this approach can get intertwined with complex interpersonal dynamics that can weaken loan repayment and strain relationships. Small-Scale Microcredit Programs, with anywhere from dozens to hundreds of borrowers, are less able to rely on personal relationships and usually must depend upon economic incentives to encourage loan repayment. This presents a tremendous challenge, because most churches, missionaries, and ministries are unable to properly address the six components of the **Financial Systems Design Principle**, resulting in unsound financial systems that are at great risk of failure. Successful Medium-Scale and Large-Scale MFIs are able to execute all six components well, but churches, missionaries, and ministries do not have the capacity to grow and operate programs of this size. Hence, rather than pursuing the Provider Model, they should consider the Partnership and Promotion Models, which are described in the next two chapters.

Application Exercise

1. If you are thinking of using the Provider Model, please carefully review the problems described in this chapter that most organizations face in successfully maintaining the six components of the **Financial Systems Design Principle**. How will you be able to successfully address each of these six principles?

2. If you are thinking of using the Provider Model of microfinance, please consider the following additional questions:

- Have you developed a financial model that carefully details all of the costs that you will incur and how your revenues will cover those costs? Can you realistically hope to implement this financial model? A financial model for estimating sustainability can be downloaded at www.microfin.com.
- Is your organization willing to charge the interest rates that MFIs are charging in the region in which you want to provide?
- Are you prepared to enforce discipline on borrowers to get them to repay their loans, including seizing any collateral that is available?
- If you are working with very poor people, are you prepared to use group-based methodologies with joint liability for loan repayment?

- Have you received training to be a provider of microfinance services?
- Are you part of a network where you can get assistance when you need it for methodology, systems development, and repayment crises?
- Do you have staff with the temperament and skills to enforce discipline?
- Are your microfinance staff different from the staff of your other programs?
- Has your organization avoided giving lots of handouts in the past?
- Do you have a governance structure in place that understands microfinance well?
- Do you have the knowledge of your target community's financial service needs?
- If your answer is "no" to *any* of these questions, you are probably not ready to be a microfinance provider. If your answer is "yes" to *all* of these questions, please get further counsel from microfinance experts before proceeding.

3. If you are a church, missionary, or small ministry that is already using the Provider Model, try to learn more about any MFIs that might be operating in the same location as your microfinance program. If any of these MFIs are sound and share your values, prayerfully consider linking your borrowers to them so that they can do the difficult job of making and collecting loans. Note that you do not have to abandon the people to whom you are ministering; rather, you can walk with them through the linking process and can continue to minister to them afterwards. Both the next chapter and the Chalmers Center's *Handbook for Partnering with Microfinance Institutions*, which is available on the website associated with this book, can help you through this process.

4. If you are a church, missionary, or small ministry that is already using the Provider Model and are unable to link your borrowers to a sound MFI, do not panic. God can help you. Prayerfully review the problems described in this chapter for each of the six components of the **Financial Systems Design Principle**. What are specific actions you can take to strengthen your program in order to reduce the chances of harm? Is there any expert you could ask for advice about the best way forward?

CHAPTER 11

THE PARTNERSHIP MODEL OF MICROFINANCE

> Every week during our church's testimony time I hear praises and expressions of gratitude to God for this [microfinance program].
>
> —*Pastor in Liberia, commenting on his church's partnership with an MFI*[1]

> Yes, we go to church more now. Our loan officer is always encouraging us to go to the church.
>
> —*Member of a borrowing group in Uganda that is part of a church-MFI partnership*[2]

The pastor of a church in a low-income community in East Africa once asked a foreign microfinance expert for a grant to enable the church to enlarge its microcredit loan fund.* The deacons of the church were using this fund to make interest-free loans to members of their church as a means of ministry. The pastor lamented that the fund was just too small to meet all of the loans desired by these church members. This is not very surprising, for at zero interest, these loans were substantially cheaper than the other sources of credit in the community.

The microfinance expert was immediately concerned, for he was well aware that churches are rarely able to implement the Provider Model very well, as we saw in chapter 10. In fact, there was already evidence that this program was likely to fail, for zero-interest loans would prevent the program from ever being financially sustainable, a

* *The authors thank Luke Kinoti of Fusion Capital in Nairobi, Kenya, for his helpful comments on this chapter.*

key component of a successful financial system (see #3 in the **Financial Systems Design Principle**).

Looking for a better approach, the specialist asked, "Are there any MFIs operating in the area from which the church members could borrow?"

"Yes," the pastor replied, "there are several MFIs, but they are inflexible and charge very high interest rates." With a dismissive wave of his hand, he continued, "They are just businesses, and all they care about is money."

The pastor's response is very common. Rather than seeing MFIs as assets in the fight against poverty, churches often view MFIs—even Christian MFIs—as exploiters of the poor. Similarly, as discussed in chapter 6, MFIs often view churches as hindrances or even threats to their work. Each side has some legitimate frustrations with the other. MFIs can become so focused on loan repayment that they sometimes lose sight of the ultimate goal of helping the poor. And churches often have such a profound misunderstanding of financial principles—particularly when it comes to the necessity of charging interest—that they and their members often become the MFIs' worst borrowers.

But the mutual disdain also flows from a deeper problem: both churches and MFIs often suffer from different understandings of the nature of poverty and its alleviation. In other words, churches and MFIs are often operating from very different "theories of change," each of which is somewhat flawed. One implication of this is that neither party truly appreciates their need for one another. And that is one of the reasons that chapters 5–7 are in this book.

But it doesn't have to be this way. It is possible for churches and MFIs to collaborate in the Partnership Model of Microfinance, a microfinance ministry in which churches and MFIs work together in such a way that the **Integral Mission Principle** is achieved.

> ***Integral Mission Principle***
>
> The *global* body must function in such a way that the *local* church is able to use its gifts to engage in integral mission: proclaiming and demonstrating among people who are poor the good news of the kingdom of God in a contextually appropriate way.

Unfortunately, such collaborations are far too rare, but by combining their respective gifts, churches and MFIs can pursue ministry together that is far more powerful than anything they could accomplish on their own. Toward that end, this chapter explains the basic ideas of the Partnership Model, including its structure, benefits, requirements, obstacles, and key steps. Although the discussion will focus on churches partnering with MFIs, most of what follows would apply to missionaries and small ministries partnering with MFIs as well.

What Is the Partnership Model?

What Do We Mean by Partnership?

The term *partnership* gets used in many different ways. At its most basic level, a partnership between an MFI and a church occurs when the MFI provides financial services while the church provides nonfinancial services to the same group of poor people. But within that definition, there is a continuum of degrees of partnership between the church and the MFI.

At one end of the continuum are partnerships that require a very low level of collaboration. For example, the partnership could simply be the church encouraging its members to become MFI clients. In this approach, the MFI and church each go about their ministries almost as if the other did not exist. At the other end of the continuum are high-collaboration partnerships, which missions expert Daniel Rickett describes as a "complementary relationship driven by a common purpose and sustained by a willingness to learn and grow together in obedience to God."[3] This type of partnership requires common goals, a close trusting relationship, and very high levels of cooperation and interdependence. Although the Partnership Model of microfinance could fall anywhere on this continuum, this chapter is primarily focused on models that involve relatively high levels of shared vision and collaboration, which would be consistent with the **Church and Parachurch Principle**.

Church and Parachurch Principle

Parachurch ministries must be "rooted in and lead back to" the local congregation(s) that minister in the same location.

An Example from Liberia

The West African country of Liberia was absolutely devastated by two civil wars between 1989 and 2003. Hundreds of thousands of people were killed, and millions were forced to leave their homes. The conflict featured horrific atrocities, including the widespread use of rape, mutilation, and child soldiers. In the midst of this carnage, a Christian MFI partnered with local churches to pursue integral mission.[4] The MFI intentionally held its loan group meetings in or near churches to make it easier for the churches to minister to the group members. And the churches embraced the idea that this partnership was an integral part of their churches' ministries. Pastors and church staff led Bible studies during the group meetings and visited and counseled individual members outside of the meetings. And rather than express disdain for the MFI, the pastors encouraged borrowers to repay their loans as a matter of integrity.

The overall impacts of this partnership were quite remarkable. Group members were able to generate enough income from their businesses to avoid starvation. As one borrower explained, "Before [the microfinance ministry], I prayed to God to take my life because I didn't want to suffer anymore. My children were malnourished and complained of headaches. When they were hungry, they frowned and couldn't smile. [Now] we always have something to eat."[5] In addition, surveys also found evidence of improvements in participants' access to education and health care, sense of dignity and responsibility, relationships with people from other tribes, and spiritual maturity.

The pastors were very pleased with the impact that this partnership had on their churches. MFI borrowers who were church members used their increased skills, confidence, and spiritual maturity to advance the full range of their churches' ministries. In addition, the churches experienced increases in giving ranging from 30–100 percent. One pastor stated, "All our ministries are benefiting from this increased giving—our schools, our outreach activities, our building programs."[6]

Many people believe that MFIs and churches simply cannot work together. As the executive director of the Liberian MFI stated, "We've seen that myth overturned."[7]

The Basic Structure of the Partnership Model

The Partnership Model allows MFIs and churches to focus on their primary areas of giftedness. MFIs concentrate on providing financial services such as loans, savings, insurance, and payment services. Recall from chapter 10 that MFIs commonly use this "minimalist" strategy, focusing solely on offering financial services that generate revenues in order to achieve financial sustainability. In particular, MFIs have tended to focus on providing loans for business investment—the "microcredit-for-microenterprises" approach described in chapter 4—although some of the larger ones are now offering additional financial services as well.

Churches in the Partnership Model focus on providing nonfinancial services to the borrowing groups, including such things as evangelism, discipleship, Bible study, counseling, prayer, complementary technical training,[8] nonfinancial business development services,[9] and other services that reduce vulnerability, such as medical care. In addition, as will be discussed in chapter 12, there may be opportunities for the church to "promote" rather than "provide" additional financial services that the MFI is unable to offer.

Figure 11.1 pictures the Partnership Model, focusing on the most common case in which the MFI is providing loans. The MFI obtains loan capital from a donor and lends this money to materially poor people, collecting it back with interest. Larger MFIs can also obtain the loan funds from equity investment or by borrowing from capital markets. Churches then complement the MFIs' loans with valuable nonfinancial services.

There are two variations on this basic model. First, churches will sometimes minister to the staff of the MFI rather than to the borrowing groups themselves. For example, a Christian MFI in the Philippines asked a local pastor to lead evangelism and discipleship Bible studies for its staff.[10] Second, churches will sometimes minister to *both* the staff and clients of the MFI.

The Theory of Change and the Partnership Model

The best motivation for churches and MFIs to form a high-collaboration partnership is that their theories of change make them realize that

FIGURE 11.1 The Partnership Model of Microfinance

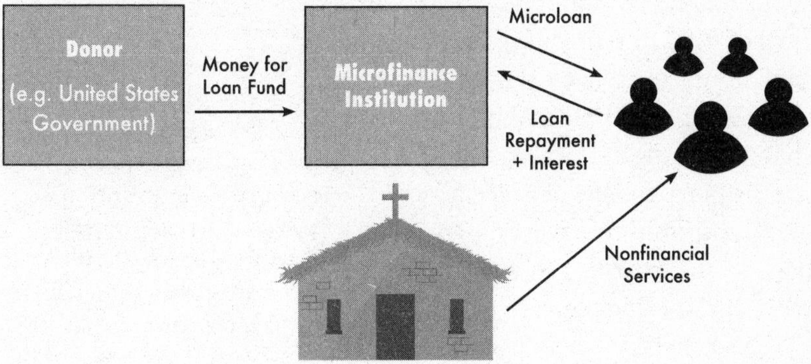

they need each other. Recall that a theory of change describes how the particular intervention(s) will improve the lives of poor people. Implicit in a theory of change is a diagnosis of the causes of poverty and of what the ultimate goal of poverty alleviation is.

At a most basic level, in order for a church to want to partner with an MFI, the church's theory of change must include the idea that poor people's lives will be better if they have access to the MFI's financial services. And in order for the MFI to want to partner with a church, the MFI must believe that poor people's lives will be better if they have access to the church's spiritual services.

Of course, the more that the church and the MFI share the same theory of change and the more that this shared theory of change creates a deep appreciation for their respective contributions, the deeper the collaboration is likely to be. Toward that end, chapters 5–7 outlined a holistic theory of change for microfinance ministries that is rooted in a biblical understanding of human beings, of the cosmos, and of God's relationship to both of them. This theory of change recognizes that poverty is due to broken individuals, broken systems, and demonic forces, implying that poverty alleviation must address all three. The good news of the gospel is that King Jesus has power over all three, and he is using that power to bring about a new heaven and a new earth in which his people will be fully restored as image bearers.

In contrast to secular approaches to poverty alleviation, this theory of change takes the supernatural actions of the Triune God seriously, believing that these actions are relevant for the here and now of the "real world." In particular, we saw that being united to the person of Jesus Christ is God's theory of change, making the local church and the ordinary means of grace absolutely essential to poverty alleviation, as summarized in the **Union with Christ Principle**.

> ***Union with Christ Principle***
>
> Being united to King Jesus — and his body, the church — is God's theory of change for addressing the broken individuals, broken systems, and demonic forces that cause poverty. This union is received and nurtured through faith as the Holy Spirit applies the church's "ordinary means of grace" to people's lives.

This holistic theory of change for microfinance ministries should give both churches and MFIs a deep appreciation for one other. Indeed, as Table 11.1 summarizes, by working together in the Partnership Model, it is possible for a church and an MFI to address the ten Ministry Components of a microfinance ministry described in detail in chapter 7, thereby participating in the work of King Jesus in addressing broken individuals, broken systems, and demonic forces.

It should be acknowledged that these ten Ministry Components represent the "ideal" microfinance ministry (although the authors readily admit that even this description of the ideal is far from perfect). In practice, a microfinance ministry will often fall short of this ideal model, but that does not mean that the ministry is doing no good or that it is not worth pursuing. God achieves his purposes despite all of our imperfections.

For example, some Christian MFIs operate in countries in which there are so few Christians that they have difficulties in hiring Christian field staff. This provides a tremendous opportunity for churches and missionaries to minister both to the group members and to the staff themselves.

In addition, even if the MFI is not explicitly Christian, it still might be possible to implement a beneficial microfinance ministry. A church could invite such an MFI to provide valuable financial services to the people to whom the church is ministering. As long as the MFI is not saying or doing things that are harmful to the church's ministry or to the group, this low level of collaboration could be used as part of the

TABLE 11.1 The Partnership Model and the Holistic Theory of Change

	Role of Local Church	Role of MFI
MINISTRY COMPONENT #1: **Connect People to the Local Church and the "Ordinary Means of Grace"**	▪ Church staff or volunteers minister to microfinance group, encouraging participants to attend church. ▪ Church members can become participants in the microfinance group, enabling them to develop relationships that can connect people to the local church. ▪ Church provides its facilities for meetings of the microfinance group. ▪ Church faithfully administers the "ordinary means of grace."	▪ MFI invites church staff to minister to the microfinance group. ▪ MFI encourages church members to join a microfinance group. ▪ MFI encourages members of microfinance groups to join local church. ▪ If possible, MFI staff are members of the churches with which they are partnering. ▪ MFI staff see themselves as supporting the integral mission of the local churches.
MINISTRY COMPONENT #2: **Foster Whole-Person Discipleship in King Jesus Using Adult Education Principles**	▪ Church staff or volunteers conduct Bible studies and/or other training that emphasize the relevance of King Jesus to all aspects of life. MFI allows time in group meetings for Bible studies and/or other training and sees this as an integral part of the group meetings. ▪ Church staff or volunteers use principles of adult education in all training.	▪ MFI staff could be trained to use adult education principles in the processes of forming groups and in administering ongoing financial services.
MINISTRY COMPONENT #3: **Use Technical Training on Microfinance that Is Integrated with a King Jesus Worldview**	▪ Church staff or volunteers provide biblical instruction about finances and the importance of keeping promises to repay.	▪ MFI trains participants to understand its financial services and their responsibilities.
MINISTRY COMPONENT #4: **Use Complementary Technical Training that Is Integrated with a King Jesus Worldview**	▪ Church staff or volunteers provide complementary technical training on such topics as business, home, health, etc., using curricula integrated with a biblical worldview about the relevance of King Jesus to all of life, including his power over demonic forces. ▪ In some cases, churches might be able to provide additional business development services (see figure 8.2 and related discussion in chapter 8).	▪ MFI allows time in group meetings for complementary technical training and sees this as an integral part of the group meetings. ▪ Depending on their time, MFI staff could be trained to deliver some of this complementary technical training to group members.

TABLE 11.1 The Partnership Model and the Holistic Theory of Change *(continued)*

	Role of Local Church	Role of MFI
MINISTRY COMPONENT #5: Connect People to the Ecosystem of the Church Family	■ Same roles as in Ministry Component #1 above. ■ Church staff and members look for additional ways to minister to group members. ■ Church creates a welcoming and nurturing environment.	■ Same roles as in Ministry Component #1 above.
MINISTRY COMPONENT #6: Use Supportive Group Structures for Delivery of Microfinance Services	■ Church staff, volunteers, and group members foster an environment of support, encouragement, and accountability in the microfinance groups. ■ Church reinforces the importance of repaying loans as a matter of integrity.	■ MFI takes lead in the group-formation process, balancing the necessary messages of accountability and discipline with support and encouragement.
MINISTRY COMPONENT #7: Encourage Group Members to Address Broken Systems	■ Church encourages group members to see themselves as image bearers, asking them to consider what they could do to change the systems around them. ■ Church can consider joining with group members to address these additional broken systems.	■ MFI encourages group members to see themselves as image bearers, asking them to consider what they could do to change the systems around them. ■ MFI's leadership can consider using their influence to address additional broken systems.
MINISTRY COMPONENT #8: Use Microfinance to Create Financial Services	■ Church staff, volunteers, and group members support the MFIs' need to uphold all components of the **Financial Systems Design Principle**. ■ Microfinance group members who are from local churches need to be exemplary participants in microfinance groups.	■ The MFI provides sound, honest, and appropriate financial services, using the **Financial Systems Design Principle**. ■ Church can explore possibility of promoting additional microfinance services, as described in chapter 12.

church's pursuit of integral mission. The church should narrate that the financial services—like all good things—are gifts from King Jesus so that the problem of the "excluded middle" is avoided (see figure 7.3 and the related discussion in chapter 7). And the church can complement these financial services by performing the other roles described

TABLE 11.1 The Partnership Model and the Holistic Theory of Change *(continued)*

	Role of Local Church	Role of MFI
MINISTRY COMPONENT #9: **Teach People to Forsake the Practices of Traditional Religion and to Put on the Whole Armor of God**	▪ Church staff and volunteers instruct microfinance group members to forsake the beliefs and practices of traditional religion and to put on the whole armor of God. The complementary technical materials in Ministry Component #4 in chapter 7 can aid in this process. ▪ Church members who are in microfinance groups provide examples of godly living.	▪ MFI staff reinforce the church's instruction.
MINISTRY COMPONENT #10: **Immerse the Entire Ministry in Ongoing Prayer**	▪ Church staff, volunteers, and church members engage in regular prayer.	▪ MFI board, staff, and financial supporters engage in regular prayer.

in table 11.1. This situation is certainly less desirable than one in which the church and the MFI are linking arms in ministry, but it may be better than not engaging in any microfinance ministry at all.

Requirements for the Partnership Model to Work

There are seven basic requirements for the Partnership Model to work:

1. Clearly there must be a viable MFI and a church working in the same area. If there is a church but no MFI, the church could possibly invite an MFI in a nearby region to open up operations in the church's community.
2. For there to be a high-level collaboration, the church and MFI must have some degree of commitment to the holistic theory of change for microfinance ministries. They do not have to agree on every last detail of the model presented in this book, but a high level of collaboration necessitates that they have sufficient agreement to see one another as essential to the process of poverty alleviation.

3. Both the MFI and the church must be credible to people in the community, and neither can be perceived as dishonest or corrupt.
4. The church must accept that the MFI will likely have a different organizational culture than the church. In particular, the church members need to accept that the MFI must operate by strict business principles in order to survive. This businesslike behavior is essential in order for the MFI to uphold the **Financial Systems Design Principle** and to be viable in what may be a highly competitive environment. Amongst other things, this implies that the MFI cannot easily change its target group, cannot adjust its interest rate or other policies, and cannot relax its loan-repayment requirements, no matter whether the borrower is a church member or not. Rather than being angry at the MFI for its rigidity, the church needs to be grateful that the MFI is doing the hard work of providing the financial services, work that the church is uniquely *not* qualified to do!
5. The church and the MFI must build and maintain trust about each other's intentions, competencies, and perspectives.[11] If the partnership is only a simple transaction in which each party provides a service for the other—e.g., the church just providing a meeting place for the MFI—then little trust is required. However, if the partnership involves a high degree of collaboration in which both rely on the other, then higher levels of trust are required, since both partners stand to lose if something goes bad. For example, when the MFI really depends on a church to provide evangelism and discipleship to the group, it must be able to trust this church will not destroy the client group's cohesion by "sheep stealing," i.e., the church should not encourage group members who are from other churches to join its church. The church must also trust the MFI to provide its microfinance services with complete integrity and fairness. Open and honest communication between the church and the MFI are essential to building trust.

6. Each organization will likely need a "champion" who promotes and fosters the partnership, diligently working to make it succeed. Amongst the many helpful things that champions do, one of their central tasks is to maintain regular and effective communication between the two organizations.[12]
7. The church and the MFI must have the same target group within the community. Figure 9.2, which is reproduced in figure 11.3, summarizes the microfinance-related services desired by households of different poverty levels. Note that if the church desires to serve the "extreme poor," it is unlikely that a partnership with an MFI will work, as the MFI's loan sizes are likely to be too large for these very poor people. And as discussed in chapter 4, even in the categories of "moderate poor" or "near poor," only a small percentage of people fit the profile that are well-served by MFIs, because most poor people are not microentrepreneurs needing business loans.

There are two caveats to this. First, in some cases MFIs are able to provide savings, insurance, and possibly even money-transfer services in addition to business loans. These services can address both a wider range of household needs and more levels of poverty than business loans can, sometimes reaching even to the "extreme" poor. Second, as discussed in chapter 9, some MFIs are now experimenting with a "graduation" model in which they combine livelihood training, savings, and sometimes loans with relief-type, safety-net programs targeting the "destitute."

Thus, it is important to keep in mind that figure 11.3 is only a general guide. Because many MFIs are creatively experimenting with new financial products, a church should keep abreast of the latest services being offered by the MFI(s) in its area, lest it miss an opportunity to introduce a valuable service to the people it is trying to help. And the church and the MFI will need to work together to determine the best complementary services that the church can offer, given the target community's exact needs and the capacities of both the MFI and the church.

FIGURE 11.3 Microfinance-Related Services Desired by Households of Different Poverty Levels

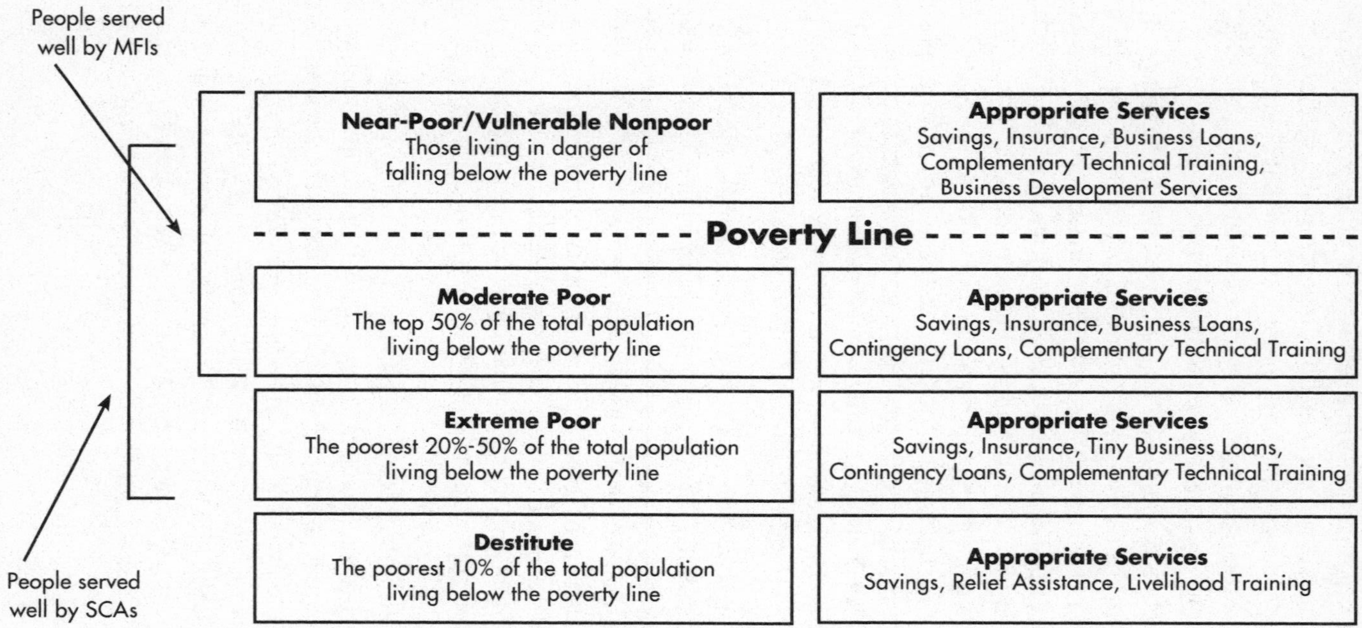

Adapted from Monique Cohen, *The Impact of Microfinance*, CGAP Donor Brief (Washington, DC: CGAP, July 2003), 1.

Primary Obstacles to the Partnership Model

As we saw in chapter 10, it is extremely difficult for churches, missionaries, and ministries to implement the Provider Model of microfinance. Given this fact, it seems like the Partnership Model would be a very attractive alternative, as it allows each party to focus on their respective gifts. Unfortunately, there are a number of obstacles that have often prevented the Partnership Model from being pursued in the field.

Obstacles to Partnership on the Part of Churches

There are five primary obstacles that have frequently made it difficult for churches to partner with MFIs:

1. Churches often believe that they should care only for people's spiritual needs. But as discussed in chapter 2, Jesus did not ignore the physical needs of the poor and the sick; rather, he used both words and deeds to bring restoration to the whole person as a foretaste of the comprehensive restoration that his kingdom will bring when it is fully consummated. As his body, bride, and fullness, the local church is to be concerned with restoring the whole person as well. See the **Integral Mission Principle**.
2. Similarly, churches sometimes have a sacred-secular view of the world in which they view the church as good and other parts of society as somehow "dirty." As a result, they tend to view MFIs as "just businesses" that are involved in worldly activities like charging interest rates and enforcing loan repayment. Indeed, this was the case in the opening story of this chapter. But as we saw in chapter 6, Colossians 1 teaches that King Jesus is the creator, sustainer, and reconciler of all things. As a result, being a loan officer can and should be done for his glory, just as being a pastor can and should be done for his glory. Of course the Fall happened, so no part of culture is free from sin; thus, MFIs—as well as churches—need to be constantly seeking to be restored more and more to what Christ is calling them to be and to do. But this caveat does not change the fact that both churches and MFIs fall under the

Lordship of Jesus Christ and can operate in ways that bring glory to him.

3. Churches have often become very accustomed to handouts, making it very difficult for them to adjust to a high-accountability ministry like microfinance. As discussed in chapter 7, if churches or church members have received *relief* for long periods of time, when they actually needed *development*, it is likely that they will not be accustomed to being asked to do something in order to receive a service (see the **Asset-Based, Participatory-Development Principle**). In particular, they will likely expect low interest rates and will not really believe they need to repay their loans. These two expectations conflict with *discipline* and *financial sustainability* in the **Financial Systems Design Principle**.

> ***Financial Systems Design Principle***
>
> In order to be successful, a financial system must maintain all of the following features:
>
> 1. Trust
> 2. Discipline
> 3. Financial Sustainability
> 4. Leadership, Management, and Governance
> 5. Transparency
> 6. Fit the Target Population

As pictured in the House of Principles in figure 9.3, if even one component of the **Financial Systems Design Principle** is violated, the system is likely to collapse, doing harm to everybody involved. It is absolutely crucial that church leaders communicate respect for the MFI and its policies to their members. In particular, they need to instruct their members that keeping their agreements to repay their loans is part of living with integrity as a Christian.

4. Some churches believe that charging interest is always a sin. As discussed in chapter 9, although the Bible forbids charging interest from destitute people who need money for food, it does not forbid the charging of interest on loans for other purposes, such as business investment. If a church continues to believe that the charging of interest is wrong, it would be better for this church not to participate in microfinance at all. It is extremely harmful when church leaders create a culture in

which their members do not feel obligated to repay their loans because they have been taught that such loans are immoral due to their interest charges.

5. A powerful pastor or church leader with a history of accessing outside resources and of controlling how those resources are used can create partnership challenges. If a pastor or his parishioners see him as a patron, then it is possible that this pastor will desire to take on roles that normally belong to an MFI.[13] Conflict will inevitably result if this pastor seeks to choose loan recipients, to determine the size of loans, or to decide how strongly to enforce loan repayment. The problem is enhanced by the fact that most MFI field staff are younger people in their twenties, who might not feel they have the authority to challenge pastors, who are their social superiors.

Obstacles to Partnership on the Part of MFIs

There are five primary obstacles that have often made it difficult for MFIs to partner with churches:

1. The need to become financially sustainable puts considerable pressure on MFIs to rapidly grow to scale and to cut costs wherever possible (see component #3 of the **Financial Systems Design Principle**). As a result, it is difficult for MFIs to find the time and money to help churches to overcome their obstacles to working with MFIs. Similarly, MFIs struggle to find the resources to pursue an intentional, highly collaborative partnership with churches.
2. Some MFIs fear working with churches because they have already had bad experiences with them. For example, if a pastor pressures even one MFI staff member to forgive a loan to one of the church members, it will likely sour the staff member's attitude toward the church. If the MFI's management fails to counteract this bad attitude, it will likely spread to the other MFI staff, undermining their desire to partner with local churches.
3. Many MFIs fall seriously short of having a holistic theory of change for microfinance ministries, like the one outlined in

chapters 5–7. Instead, many MFIs simply assume that poverty is primarily caused by a lack of access to loan capital. MFI staff may need training in these issues if they are to recognize how desperately they need to partner with churches in order to address both the multifaceted nature of poverty and its underlying causes.

4. Under pressure to become financially sustainable, MFIs do not always maintain timely communication with churches when the MFIs' operational needs require them to make decisions that can strain a partnership. For example, if the MFI decides to change the date of an MFI client group meeting without talking with the church, the church will be frustrated if its pastor or volunteers were scheduled to attend the group meeting to provide complementary services.
5. Like many Christian organizations, MFIs often struggle to find mature Christian leadership. And in the increasingly competitive world of commercialized microfinance, the necessity of mature Christian MFI leaders is more crucial than ever before.[14] If MFI leaders do not have an appreciation for the God-ordained role of the local church, then partnering with the MFI will be quite difficult. Even more broadly, if MFI leaders do not personally exemplify a holistic vision for physical, social, economic, and spiritual transformation of clients in their day-to-day management, then partnership can be difficult. What do MFI leaders pray for, and what do they celebrate and publicize? Is the local church on those lists? When the CEO visits clients with her field staff, does she ask any questions about the spiritual situation of the clients that they visit or about any local churches that they might attend? How often does the board of the MFI ask how many clients have become believers or how many churches are now partnering with the MFI?

The struggles we have briefly outlined suggest that it might take some time for a church and an MFI to develop a sufficient relationship to form a solid partnership. This is particularly true if there is distrust between the two parties resulting from previous experiences. For example, the church may be uncomfortable with some of the ways it has seen MFIs enforce loan repayments in the past, giving it some pause about working with the MFI. Or there may be a history of other churches criticizing the MFI, which could make the MFI leery of getting too close to the church. Ongoing communication between the church and the MFI is extremely important. They should meet regularly in order to understand what each other is doing and to build and sustain their trust in each other.

The Process of Forming a Church-MFI Partnership

The Nine Basic Steps

There are nine basic steps for a church and an MFI to follow in order to form a partnership:

1. The church leaders must develop in the congregation a holistic vision of poverty and an appreciation of the role of microfinance in poverty alleviation; in other words, the church needs a holistic theory of change for microfinance ministry.
2. The church leaders must develop in the congregation and the target group an understanding of the reason that MFIs must function in a businesslike manner (see the **Financial Systems Design Principle** and the House of Principles in figure 9.3). In particular, the church leaders and members need to understand the reason for charging interest and that loan repayment is absolutely essential.
3. The church should assess the MFI(s) in its area to learn about their target group, financial services, vision, reputation, and credibility. Is the MFI following the principles outlined in chapter 9? Does the MFI have a holistic vision of poverty and an appreciation of the essential role of the local church? Do the MFI's services match the needs of the church's target population?
4. The church should assess itself to decide what ways—if any—it might like to partner with the MFI.
5. The church should identify who its "champion" will be. Eventually, the MFI should choose a champion as well.

6. The church leaders and champion should spend time developing a relationship with the MFI, seeking to come to a better understanding of one another and to build trust.
7. The church and the MFI should come to an agreement about their partnership and respective roles and then write it down to make it formal.
8. The church and the MFI should each do their best to execute their agreed-upon roles.
9. The church and the MFI should intentionally communicate with each other and monitor and assess the partnership on a fairly regular basis.

Institutional Considerations

In addition to these nine steps, churches and MFIs will need to work through their organizational structures to make a partnership work. If the church is part of a denominational structure that requires local pastors to get approval from denominational leaders, then the partnership might require spending time to build trust with those leaders as well. Similarly, the manager of an MFI's branch office also reports to superiors, who might need to approve any official partnership. While these organizational structures can complicate and slow down the formation of partnerships, they can also solidify the partnership by building overall organizational "buy-in."

If the branch manager of the MFI faces significant organizational barriers to partnering, it might be easier and more appropriate to test a partnership as a pilot project rather than as a top-to-bottom change in the MFI.[15] Once a pilot project is shown to be successful, the branch manager can then solicit the MFI's management to make a more formal agreement with the church or its denomination.

Summary

As we saw in the previous chapter, churches, missionaries, and ministries are not good providers of financial services. In contrast, successful MFIs are very good at providing financial services, but they often struggle to do much more than that. Hence, by working together, it is possible to accomplish more than either party could on their own. The MFIs can provide the financial services, and the church, missionary, or ministry can provide evangelism, discipleship, and complementary nonfinancial services. Such a partnership can address all ten Ministry Components of a microfinance ministry.

In practice, a number of obstacles often prevents such partnerships from forming. In particular, high-collaboration partnerships require the church, missionary, or ministry and the MFI to have theories of change that are sufficiently holistic that they value what the other contributes in the fight against poverty. In addition, it is often the case that the church, missionary, or ministry has a target population that is not well served by the MFI's financial services, a problem that the Promotion Model in the next chapter can sometimes address.

Application Exercise

If you are a church, missionary, or ministry and you are interested in pursuing the Partnership Model, you should do some more research about any MFIs in the area of your target community using the tool entitled *Partnership Model Assessment*. If you decide to move forward with a partnership, the Chalmers Center's *Handbook for Partnering with Microfinance Institutions* can walk you through this process. In addition, you can complement the MFI's financial services with the Chalmers Center's curricula on business, home, and health, as described in Ministry Component #4 in chapter 7. All of these resources are available on the website associated with this book.

CHAPTER 12

THE PROMOTION MODEL OF MICROFINANCE

Our parishioners who are in savings groups are being transformed. They now have purpose in their lives. They see God as the one from whom these blessings flow. They have become benefactors and leaders in our church.

—*Joseph, pastor of a Rwandan church that has four savings and credit associations as part of The PEACE Plan of Saddleback Church*[1]

Having been part of savings groups for thirteen years ... I came wondering what you could teach me. But now I see what the other groups had been missing—the House of Principles and focus on Christ.

—*Indian national being trained by HOPE International to facilitate church-centered savings and credit associations*[2]

Maria walked to the front of God's Compassion Church of Manila and testified, "My child would have died had it not been for the help of the members of the [ASCA]. I was able to get a loan for the medicine, and they also prayed for me, and visited my sick child."* Maria sat down, and then Camilla stood and explained how the ASCA members had encouraged her to borrow some money so that she could start a small cookie-selling business. She went on to share that the profits from this business were enabling her to meet the daily needs of her children.

The three hundred people in the church listened intently as Maria, Camilla, and the other twenty-four members of the church's ASCA

---

* *The authors thank Smita Donthamsetty of the Chalmers Center for helping to write an earlier version of this chapter.*

shared how God had used the ASCA to bless their lives. The economic benefits were obvious to all in attendance. Lacking access to formal banking services, these mothers had always struggled to save and were usually unable to borrow at all, unless they opted to use expensive and risky loan sharks. In contrast, the ASCA had enabled the mothers to save and to lend these savings to one another. The results had been nothing short of phenomenal. A total of forty-one relatively low-interest loans had been made with a 100 percent repayment rate. The interest paid on these loans had enabled the ASCA members to earn dividends on their savings that averaged 50 percent in annual terms.

But the blessings were more than economic. The ASCA members also testified that they had developed a strong community as the mothers prayed for each other and their families. And God had regularly answered their prayers, providing jobs for their husbands, healing their children, and mending their broken relationships.

The ASCA had enabled its members to be salt and light in the community as well. Neighbors of the ASCA members had commented about the love and concern that the members showed to one another, so the ASCA members had invited these neighbors to attend their weekly meetings and Bible study. These nonmembers were allowed to borrow money from the ASCA at an interest rate much lower than that available from local loan sharks. And when the ASCA started its second cycle, these nonmembers were allowed to become members.[3]

God's Compassion Church and its ASCA represent the Promotion Model of microfinance, which we first encountered in the Masai church in chapter 1. In the past decade the Promotion Model has become increasingly popular in the microfinance movement. In particular, many churches and missionaries are finding it to be a better option for them than the Provider Model, given the difficulties they have in lending money successfully.[4] Whether or not the Promotion Model or the Partnership Model is preferable depends on a number of contextual factors, as will be described further below.

This chapter describes the basic structure, variations, strengths, and weaknesses of the Promotion Model and describes how to choose between it and the Partnership Model. Consistent with the primary purpose of this book, the discussion in this chapter focuses on churches and missionaries, but large portions of what follows would apply to small parachurch ministries as well.

What Is the Promotion Model?

The Basic Structure of the Promotion Model

As pictured in figure 12.1, the Promotion Model consists of an organization—in this case a church or a missionary—facilitating the formation of a savings and credit association (SCA). The SCA is owned and operated by the SCA members themselves, with the church or missionary providing sufficient technical training to enable the group to function properly on its own. Note that in the Promotion Model, the loan capital is coming from the savings of the group members themselves. In contrast, in the Provider and Partnership Models, the loan capital is coming from an outside donor or investor (compare figure 12.1 with figures 10.1 and 11.1).

In addition to facilitating the formation of the SCA, the church or missionary might provide the same nonfinancial services as they do in the Partnership Model: evangelism, discipleship, Bible study, counseling, prayer, complementary technical training,[5] nonfinancial business development services,[6] and other services that reduce vulnerability, such as medical care.

Like the Partnership Model, one of the advantages of the Promotion Model is that the church or the missionary never has to touch any money, shielding them from the difficulties that can arise when they are put in the position of holding savings or making loans. Indeed, as

FIGURE 12.1 The Promotion Model of Microfinance

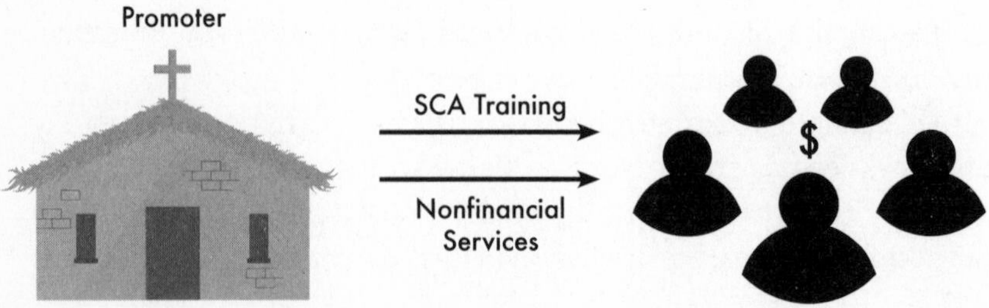

discussed in chapter 10, churches and missionaries are generally not good at providing financial services, and in the Promotion Model they do not need to do so. Rather, they can focus on helping poor people to provide those financial services for themselves.

Why is it that poor people are often better able to provide these financial services than churches or missionaries? It comes down to this: people generally treat their *own* money differently than they treat *other* people's money. Because the SCA members are lending their *own* money to one another, they treat it differently than they would if the loan capital was coming from an outsider, such as a church or a missionary. Indeed, the members of the SCA have very strong incentives to ensure that the requirements of the **Financial Systems Design Principle** are met so that the SCA is sound and their money is safe. Readers interested in learning more about how SCAs meet all six components of the **Financial Systems Design Principle** can read the resource entitled *What Makes SCAs Work?* on the website associated with this book.

A Good Idea Rediscovered

At the heart of the Promotion Model is a "savings-led" approach to microfinance. In contrast to the credit-led approach, savings-led microfinance emphasizes the following:

- Poor people would often rather save than borrow; they just need a good way to do so. See the **Savings Principle** and the discussion in chapter 8.
- The savings of the poor can be used as the source of loan capital instead of outside money from donors or investors.
- The poor need lump sums of money for a range of household needs, not just for investment in microenterprises. See the **Microfinance for Households Principle**.

The credit-led approach of the "microcredit-for-microenterprises" strategy has largely dominated microfinance for much of the past forty years. However, research demonstrating the importance of savings services, concerns about the negative effects of overindebtedness, and the success of several NGOs in promoting SCAs on a massive scale are combining to increase the popularity of the Promotion Model.[7]

For example, one of the most popular approaches to promoting SCAs is the Village Savings and Loan Association (VSLA) model produced by VSL Associates.[8] Originally developed by CARE International in Niger in 1991, this model is now being used by a wide range of NGOs to reach over 9.33 million people in at least sixty-one countries across the Global South.[9] This very rapid expansion suggests that many poor people were not being well served by the "microcredit-for-microenterprises" approach. This should be expected, for as described in chapter 4, only a relatively small portion of the world's poor needs the type of business loans typically offered by MFIs, while nearly all poor people need access to convenient, flexible, and reliable savings services for a wide range of household needs. See the **Microfinance for Households Principle**.

In terms of the contemporary microfinance movement, savings-led approaches are relatively new, but churches and missionaries have been using savings-led approaches to microfinance for quite some time. Two hundred years ago, William Carey, who is considered to be the father of modern missions, started savings banks for Indian farmers. And researchers are discovering that missionaries and churches in the Global South were using various savings-led approaches throughout the past two centuries.[10]

Moreover, poor people themselves have been creatively designing various types of SCAs as a means of survival for even longer. ROSCAs go at least as far back as the middle of the Tang Dynasty in China between AD 619 and 906,[11] and researchers have documented the incredible ingenuity that many poor people around the world are currently using to create SCAs that address their need for convenient, reliable, and flexible financial services.[12] In fact, there are local names for SCAs in many countries of the Global South, as SCAs have often been present for centuries, long before any missionaries or NGOs arrived on the scene.[13] Many poor people have participated in SCAs or know people who have. They will know of good and bad experiences with SCAs, but they are not always sure what factors contributed to their success or failure. In addition, while poor people are often familiar with one type of SCA (e.g., a particular type of ROSCA), they may not be aware of different versions of the ROSCA or of alternative forms of SCAs such as ASCAs.

In this light, there is a sense in which the Promotion Model builds upon what many poor people already know to some degree, affirming them by recognizing that their knowledge is a valuable asset that can be developed further. Starting with what they already know, the Promotion Model can then ask the group members to reflect on the key determinants of their past successes and failures in SCAs, make them aware of new possibilities, and help them to improve upon their past. This approach to development may sound less exciting than pumping in capital and all sorts of new technology, but it is consistent with how the human brain is actually wired to experience positive change, as depicted in the Learning Cycle in figure 7.4. And since people are at the heart of poverty, this is an approach that is essential to successful and sustainable poverty alleviation.

The Theory of Change and the Promotion Model

The holistic theory of change for microfinance ministries articulated in chapters 5–7 seeks to take the supernatural actions of the Triune God seriously, believing that these actions are relevant for the here and now of the "real world." In particular, we saw that being united to the person of Jesus Christ is God's theory of change, making the local church and the ordinary means of grace absolutely essential to poverty alleviation, as summarized in the **Union with Christ Principle**.

In this light, the general statement of theologian Lesslie Newbigin about the church and parachurch rings true in the field of microfinance as well: *parachurch ministries "have power to accomplish their purpose only as they are rooted in and lead back to a believing community."*[14] We captured this idea in the **Church and Parachurch Principle**.

These considerations make the Promotion Model quite appealing, for it can be structured in such a way that, from the very outset, the

Union with Christ Principle

Being united to King Jesus — and his body, the church — is God's theory of change for addressing the broken individuals, broken systems, and demonic forces that cause poverty.

Church and Parachurch Principle

Parachurch ministries must be "rooted in and lead back to" the local congregation(s) that minister in the same location.

parachurch—i.e., an SCA—is "rooted in and flows back to" the local church in a deeper way than is typically possible in the Partnership Model. Indeed, as the stories of God's Compassion Church in Manila and the Masai Church in Kenya (chapter 1) illustrate, although SCAs are parachurch ministries in the sense that they are not owned and operated by the local church, they are connected to the local church in such an intimate way that people often see the SCAs as an expression of the local church, and more importantly, of the Triune God that this church worships. Indeed, the ultimate goal of any ministry is for people to give glory to God, not to the NGO, the SCA, or even the local church or missionary.[15]

An Example: The Chalmers Center's Promotion Model

The Chalmers Center is a research and training organization that equips churches and missionaries for integral mission. Toward that end, the Center first designs strategies that churches and their missionaries can use, then implements those strategies in field tests, and finally trains churches, missionaries, and church-equipping organizations to use those strategies on their own. Sometimes these field tests can be fairly large. For example, the Center is currently developing and refining a distribution model in West Africa that has equipped churches to promote SCAs to nearly 13,000 people thus far. More will be said about that project in the next chapter. However, the Center's primary replication strategy is to use the lessons from these field tests to train others. Indeed, this book and the resources on the associated website are one of the ways that the Chalmers Center provides such training.

The Chalmers Center began field testing the Promotion Model with churches and missionaries in Africa, Asia, and Latin America in 2000. The authors have been heavily involved with the Chalmers Center's work since its inception, so we are admittedly very partial to it. However, although the Chalmers Center has learned a great deal, we are painfully aware that there is still so much more that we do not know. In fact, the Center is constantly revising its training and curricula in light of what it is learning both from its own experiences and from the experiences of other organizations that are trying to do similar things. Hence, what follows should not be taken as the "final word" on

Why Use the Promotion Model?

A number of international organizations are equipping churches to use the Promotion Model. We asked leaders from some of these organizations how doing this enabled them to further their mission.

To answer that question, I'll begin with another question, one that is strategic for HOPE: Is this HOPE's SCA project or is it the church's SCA ministry? We believe the latter is the better view, and that ultimately, church-centered SCAs should become *vibrant, holistic, and sustained ministries of the church.* That belief impacts all that we do, from program design to curriculum to training and, most importantly, to capacity building. Our partnership with the Chalmers Center has been a vital part of this journey. Consider this: do churches speak about their women's ministry as "the women's project sponsored by Women, Inc." or their children's ministry as "the children's project sponsored by Children's, Inc."? Obviously, the answer is "no." These ministries are an integral part of the church's ministry and calling, part of their DNA. We believe the SCA ministry should be no different. So since our entry into the arena of church-centered savings in 2007, and supported by an integral partnership with the Chalmers Center, we have continued to seek God's direction as we hone our focus on seeing the church embrace SCAs as a *vibrant, holistic, and sustained ministry* to the church and community. In doing so, HOPE is joyfully fulfilling its mission to the fullest.

Phil Smith, director of savings and credit associations for HOPE International

The mission of World Relief is to empower the local church to serve the most vulnerable. Toward that end, World Relief implements a Church Empowerment Zone (CEZ) model in which the programs are designed and implemented in cooperation with local church leadership. Our Savings for Life program (SFL), which promotes savings groups, is a great addition to CEZ because it allows churches to submit volunteers, who then bring savings services — a felt need in many of the communities we work in — to their neighbors. An initial mindset transformation for pastors and church leaders has the goal of helping the participants to understand: (1) we have problems in our community, but (2) we also have resources available to us to help solve some of these issues. After this, SFL is a perfect program to help mobilize resources among the church and community members themselves to allow them to achieve their own financial dreams, support others in the community, and give back more tangibly to the church.

Courtney O'Connell, Savings for Life senior technical advisor for World Relief

the Promotion Model or even as the best model in existence. There are simply too many unknowns in this field at the moment for anybody to be able to make such statements. Rather, the following model is included as an example of a church-centered microfinance ministry that is very intentionally designed to be consistent with the holistic theory of change in chapters 5–7. Readers are encouraged to explore other models from other organizations in order to discern the best approach for their context.

Because the Chalmers Center's mission is to equip churches and their missionaries for integral mission, the Center's process involves steps and components that would not be present if the goal were simply to provide financial services to the poor. In particular, it is necessary to help church leaders and members—most of whom are typically very poor themselves—to understand integral mission, to embrace the promotion of SCAs as a part of that mission, and to be able to successfully facilitate the formation of a holistic SCA.

Toward that end, the Chalmers Center's process involves training a member of a local church—i.e., a "church-based facilitator" (CF)—to be the point person for walking the church and the SCA through a series of steps. In the case of a missionary working where there is no church, the missionary could take on most of the roles of the CF or could train others to take on that role. The process is as follows:

1. ***Orientation:*** Sessions are held with church and lay leaders to help them to consider how the SCA might be a tool that their church can use for integral mission and to identify CFs that can be trained.
2. ***CF Training:*** The CF is trained in the SCA methodology in order to take it back to the local church, find group members, and implement the SCA as a church ministry.
3. ***Group Formation:*** The CF walks the SCA through a process of determining its rules in the areas of membership criteria, financial rules, and management, including the election of group leaders.
4. ***Group Leadership Training:*** The CF trains the leaders of the SCA to run and manage the group: conducting group meetings, bookkeeping, monitoring, biblical leadership, and conflict resolution.

5. *Ongoing Training for the Group:* The CF uses the SCA's meetings to provide appropriate technical training:
   - The key ideas of the **Financial Systems Design Principle** are reinforced using the House of Principles (see figure 9.3) throughout the first savings-and-loan cycle.
   - After the first savings-and-loan cycle is completed, additional complementary training in business, home, and health topics can be used. See the description of these curricula in Ministry Component #4 in chapter 7.
6. *Group Reforms:* After finishing the first cycle, the group can decide to end or to make any changes necessary to improve their policies and procedures for the next cycle.

   As described in greater detail in Ministry Components #2–#4 in chapter 7, there are some distinct features of the Chalmers Center's training and curricula for the Promotion Model:
   - Adult education principles are used throughout to engage people's minds, hearts, and actions.
   - A biblical worldview about King Jesus is applied to the practical issues of people's everyday lives.
   - Emphasis is placed on understanding people's four key relationships with God, self, others, and the rest of creation and on prayerfully asking King Jesus to heal these relationships.
   - An asset-based, participatory philosophy permeates both the design and content of the entire process.

By God's grace alone, thousands of churches and missionaries are using this process and curricula to minister to hundreds of thousands of SCA members across the Global South. By far the largest distributor to date is HOPE International, which is dramatically scaling up its equipping of churches to use the Promotion Model. The Chalmers Center is deeply grateful for its partnership with HOPE International, and it continues to learn from HOPE's experiences as well as from those of the other churches, missionaries, and church-equipping organizations with which the Center works.

A Church-to-Churches Approach

By Joel Assaraf, leader of the poverty initiative of The PEACE Plan of Saddleback Church

In 2006, Pastor Rick Warren spoke from the pulpit about a vision he had for our church and global missions—The PEACE Plan. Our creed: "Ordinary people, empowered by God's Spirit, to do extraordinary things, through the local church."

In late 2011, I became the lay leader for the PEACE Plan's Poverty Initiative. One of our pastors suggested that I start with SCAs. I did some research and found the Chalmers Center and its *Savings Group Handbook: A Church-Centered Approach to Savings Groups.* The Chalmers Center's SCA curriculum is outstanding and overlaps 100 percent with the values of The PEACE Plan—"Christ-centered, church-centered." The local church, the body of Christ, gets the glory.

In early 2012 I received training from Chalmers, consisting of online training and assigned readings. Also, I started and facilitated some SCAs through a local church in bordering Mexico. It took about six months for me to feel adequately trained to be able to equip local churches in a foreign country to start SCAs.

We launched SCAs in Rwanda in the summer of 2012. We were blessed to hire an experienced SCA trainer, a Rwandan named Emmanuel, who had previously implemented an SCA program with the Anglican Church. We have worked with him to train many church-based facilitators across Rwanda. As a result, churches have started over 500 SCAs with roughly 15,000 members who have saved over $500,000 to date. Lord willing, we hope to double this number over the next year and to keep on growing from there. We have also started to introduce additional training into these groups using the Chalmers Center's business, home, and health curricula.

The Ten Ministry Components

As described in table 12.1 (see page 262), the Promotion Model can be implemented in a way that is consistent with the ten Ministry Components from the holistic theory of change described in chapters 5–7. The table uses the Chalmers Center's model described above as an example, but the church-centered models of other organizations would include many of these components as well. In the case of a missionary working in an unreached region, the missionary could take on many of the roles of the church-based facilitator (CF) or could train a number of people to act as CFs.

When we ask members in our SCAs to share the greatest impact that the SCA has had on their lives, they talk about far more than money; they talk about their lives being transformed:

> After the genocide I was a lonely person. I belonged nowhere. I started going to church and heard about the savings groups. The group helped me to build my farm from a small plot into a bigger farm and profitable business. I can now buy health insurance for my family. This group has become my family and has resurrected me.
>
> —*Beatrice, a genocide survivor*

> My life has been transformed. I used to be poor and was ashamed to go out in public. But now, through my church and my savings group, God has blessed my family. I have gone from subsistence farming to owning a restaurant. We have food, school fees, and health insurance. We have enough to give offerings to the church. The church is our second family. I am no longer ashamed to go out.
>
> —*Clementine, a wife and mother of seven*

Circumcised hearts. Transformed lives. Mine included. I think Emmanuel sums it up best: "Joel, the glory is not yours. It's not mine. It's not The PEACE Plan's. It's not Chalmers'. The glory is God's. The glory is with his church. He opened our eyes. He got us trained. He gave us the will and energy to serve. We're just ordinary people equipping his local church. All we did was obey."

Variations in the Promotion Model

A number of international NGOs are implementing the Promotion Model on a large scale, including a number of Christian organizations: Five Talents International, Food for the Hungry, HOPE International, Salvation Army, Tearfund UK, World Concern, World Relief, World Renew, and World Vision.[16] There are many variations in the ways that these organizations, including Christian NGOs, implement the Promotion Model, but there are three differences that are particularly noteworthy for the purposes of this book:

1. *Community-Based vs. Church-Centered*: In a community-based approach, an NGO promotes the formation of SCAs in a poor community either directly or through existing community-based associations. In a church-centered approach, the NGO equips local churches and missionaries to promote SCAs as part of their ministries.
2. *Evangelism and Discipleship*: Some NGOs very intentionally incorporate evangelism and discipleship into the life of the SCA using biblically integrated training and curricula, while others use training and curricula that are primarily technical in nature. In addition, even amongst those organizations that use biblical integration, there are wide variations in the approaches being used. For example, some focus on addressing deep worldview issues, while others focus more on behavioral changes. And some are very intentional about pointing people to Jesus Christ, while others are less explicit.
3. *Degree of Participation*: Some NGOs use participatory approaches in which most of the decisions about policies and procedures are made by the SCA members themselves, and others use an approach in which the NGOs make most of those decisions for the SCA members in advance.

TABLE 12.1 The Promotion Model and the Holistic Theory of Change

MINISTRY COMPONENT #1: **Connect People to the Local Church and the "Ordinary Means of Grace"**	▪ CF or other trainer orients the church leadership and members to see SCAs as part of integral mission. See step #1, "Orientation," in Chalmers's Promotion Model. ▪ CF forms and trains the SCA, intentionally expressing the SCA as a ministry of the local church and seeking to point people to the church. ▪ Church members join the SCA, enabling them to develop relationships that can connect people to the local church. ▪ Pastor or other church staff can minister to the SCA members. ▪ Church might provide its facilities for the meeting. ▪ Church faithfully administers the "ordinary means of grace."
MINISTRY COMPONENT #2: **Foster Whole-Person Discipleship in King Jesus Using Adult Education Principles**	▪ CF uses principles of adult education in all training. ▪ Curricula focus on showing the relevance of King Jesus to all aspects of life.

MINISTRY COMPONENT #3: **Use Technical Training on Microfinance that Is Integrated with a King Jesus Worldview**	■ CF walks the SCA leaders and members through the entire process of forming, leading, maintaining, and reforming the group using curricula integrated with a biblical worldview about the relevance of King Jesus to all aspects of life. See steps #2 – #5 in Chalmers's Promotion Model.
MINISTRY COMPONENT #4: **Use Complementary Technical Training that Is Integrated with a King Jesus Worldview**	■ CF provides complementary technical training integrated with a biblical worldview about the relevance of King Jesus to all of life, including his power over demonic forces. See Chalmers's business, home, and health curricula. ■ In some cases, the church, missionary, or CF might be able to provide additional business development services (see figure 8.2 and related discussion in chapter 8).
MINISTRY COMPONENT #5: **Connect People to the Ecosystem of the Church Family**	■ Same roles as in Ministry Component #1 above. ■ Church staff and members look for additional ways to minister to group members. ■ Church creates a welcoming and nurturing environment.
MINISTRY COMPONENT #6: **Use Supportive Group Structures for Delivery of Microfinance Services**	■ The CF and church members foster an environment of support, encouragement, and accountability in the SCA. ■ Church reinforces the importance of repaying loans as a matter of integrity.
MINISTRY COMPONENT #7: **Encourage Group Members to Address Broken Systems**	■ CF encourages SCA members to see themselves as image bearers, asking them to consider what they could do to change the systems around them. ■ Church can consider joining with the SCA members to address these additional broken systems.
MINISTRY COMPONENT #8: **Use Microfinance to Create Financial Services**	■ CF trains the SCA members to provide these financial services for themselves by following the concepts in the **Financial Systems Design Principle**. ■ Group members from the church need to be exemplary SCA members. ■ Over time, CF can help the group to consider linking to MFIs, banks, or other institutions that can provide additional financial services.
MINISTRY COMPONENT #9: **Teach People to Forsake the Practices of Traditional Religion and to Put on the Whole Armor of God**	■ Church and CF instruct SCA members to forsake the beliefs and practices of traditional religion and to put on the whole armor of God. The Chalmers Center's business, home, and health curricula in Ministry Component #4 can aid in this process. ■ Church members who are in microfinance groups provide examples of godly living.
MINISTRY COMPONENT #10: **Surround the Entire Ministry with Ongoing Prayer**	■ All of the staff, volunteers, church members, and financial supporters engage in regular prayer.

> ***Asset-Based, Participatory-Development Principle***
>
> Focus on local *assets* not just on *needs*; as much as possible, use *participatory* rather than *blueprint* approaches; do not use *relief* when the context calls for *development*.

Let us explore the issue of participation a bit more deeply. Even though many practitioners embrace the **Asset-Based, Participatory-Development Principle**, there are differences of opinion about how to apply this in the context of the Promotion Model. Unfortunately, there is a lack of research to sort out these differences.

For example, one of the most popular approaches to promoting SCAs is the Village Savings and Loan Association (VSLA) model produced by VSL Associates.[17] Originally developed by CARE International in Niger in 1991, the model is being used by a wide range of both secular and Christian NGOs to reach over 6 million people in at least 61 countries across the Global South.[18] NGOs doing VSLA always call their SCAs "savings groups," and their "savings groups" are always time-bound ASCAs.

The process used by VSLA is fairly standardized, leaving relatively few policy decisions to be made by the members of the SCA. For example, during the first cycle, group members are told that they will meet weekly, that they will form an ASCA, that loan sizes can be a maximum of three times the value of the borrower's savings, that loans will be repaid monthly, etc. In subsequent loan cycles, the group is allowed to make some adjustments, but only to very few of these policy decisions and usually without any advice from VSLA NGOs. The standardization of the process makes it possible to form the groups relatively quickly. Moreover, because the group-formation lessons are highly scripted, even a person with very low levels of education can start a group.

In contrast, the Chalmers Center's process is more participatory, allowing group members to make many more policy decisions about their group's purpose, policies, and procedures. Because the Chalmers Center's model is less prescriptive than VSLA, it usually takes more time to form the group and to support it through the end of the first cycle and the re-formation process, requiring more effort on the part of the facilitator. Indeed, although the jury is still out, it is likely that a more participatory process costs more per SCA member than a standardized process, at least in the short run. So why bother? There are several reasons.

First, a participatory approach allows the group greater flexibility to tailor its policies and procedures to meet the specific needs of the members. For example, VSLA prescribes that the group will form an ASCA and will remain an ASCA forever. In contrast, the Chalmers Center's training process helps group members to assess their ASCA at the end of the first cycle and then to modify their policies based on that assessment. At that point the group can choose to remain an ASCA, can become a straight-savings group in which no loans are made, can form a ROSCA, or can evolve into some combination of the three. The group uses its knowledge of the members' three Cs, time constraints, occupations, and local circumstances to make this decision. For example, a group of mothers with school-age children might add a straight-savings group to accumulate enough money for school fees. A group of fruit vendors might decide to become a ROSCA that meets every market day to buy produce from wholesalers. A group of farmers might want to add a ROSCA to their ASCA.

Second, allowing the group to make more of its own decisions is rooted in the conviction that the goal of poverty alleviation is to help restore people as image bearers by reconciling the four key relationships (see the **Poverty-Alleviation Principle**). While creating access to financial services is an extremely important part of such restoration, the way that those services are created matters as well. For example, many poor people have never been given the opportunity to have their knowledge respected, to voice their opinions, and to make choices, all of which are inherent to image bearing. Similarly, many poor people have had very limited opportunities to engage in the ongoing process of formulating ideas and of testing these ideas out in order to discover how God's world works, which is an essential part of having a proper relationship to creation (see the Learning Cycle in figure 7.4). Yes, the group will make some policies that do not work so well, and they will need to fix those mistakes over time. But engaging in such a process is an essential part of image bearing.

Third, greater participation increases the group members' sense of ownership, which both increases the likelihood of the ministry's sustainability and unleashes latent assets. The members are not just clients of somebody else's microfinance program. This is *their* group and *their* ministry. It is a place where they can use *their* gifts and *their* abilities to minister to others and to effect change in the world around them.

On the other hand, it is possible to have too much participation. Too many options can sometimes be overwhelming for participants, so reducing the number of choices could be very useful in some contexts. And there may be situations in which people simply do not have the capacity to make some of the decisions very well at all or where high levels of distrust make it easier to get SCAs started using more standardized group policies. Finally, a more scripted process requires less capacity on the part of the church-based facilitator, making it easier to use and to replicate. Some trial and error is required to determine the optimal level of participation in each setting. For example, although the Chalmers Center's curriculum is more participatory than VSLA, the Center had to adjust its curriculum to be a bit more prescriptive in certain aspects of the initial group-formation process in its current field project in West Africa.

One final note: If a church or missionary decides to use VSLA, there is the additional problem that VSLA is not written from a Christian perspective and is not intentionally designed for use as part of a church's ministry. However, a number of Christian organizations have supplemented VSLA with additional biblical worldview training and are using these augmented materials for church-centered ministry. Although this approach does not allow for a complete integration of biblical concepts with the technical SCA training, it may be the best option for some organizations and contexts. In fact, the Chalmers Center is currently testing this approach with a major Christian NGO at the time of the writing of this book.

Provide, Partner, or Promote?

Should a church or missionary pursue the Provider, Partnership, or Promotion Model of microfinance? As argued in chapter 10, churches and missionaries are not good lenders of money, so they should usually avoid the Provider Model. But both the Partnership and Promotion

How Are Church-Centered SCAs Different?

A number of international organizations are very intentionally equipping churches to use the Promotion Model. We asked leaders from some of these organizations: Are your SCAs different from those promoted by secular NGOs? If so, how?

Indeed, they are different. First, the training is based on a biblical worldview, because we are seeking holistic transformation. Second, we really want the SCAs to be able to manage themselves over time. Hence, we place a great emphasis on the facilitation of a group constitution as opposed to prescribing a format. Provisions are made in the constitution for changes so that the group can agree to change an interest rate, fine, membership criteria, etc., at any time. Finally, we place a heavy emphasis on planning to be a blessing to others through an emergency fund. Close to 100 percent of our groups have this type of fund. This is a practical way to live the gospel message to love and care for our neighbors. As one SCA member stated, "Our group is based on love; if we were here just for money we would be finished."

Suzanne Schultz-Middleton, program director for Five Talents International

Tearfund's SCAs[19] are places where members experience love, joy, spiritual and material well-being. They are driven by relationships rather than money. When money is raised, it is used well due to the trust and relations created.

Donald Mavunduse, head of east and southern Africa team for Tearfund

Yes, they are, and this stems from our distinctly evangelical Christian mission and mandate. Our goal is to have holistically different savings members. This includes not only financial lives but also social, emotional, spiritual lives. We seek whole-person development, not just economic development through savings. The more our Savings for Life (SFL) curriculum can highlight this and the more the programming in the community can be integrated in a way that doesn't include just savings, then all the better. In order to contribute toward holistically changed savings members, the Savings for Life methodology teaches the group how to function with principles derived from the Village Savings and Loan Association's model along with faith messages that supplement the financial practice being taught that day, e.g., taking a loan, repaying a loan, etc. Additionally, we have penned a Bible study that each group can use at the beginning of their meeting to get the group together looking at the Word of God.

Courtney O'Connell, Savings for Life senior technical advisor for World Relief

Models are viable options, so which is the better choice? If there is not a financially sound MFI in the region, as will often be the case in rural areas, then the Partnership Model is not even an option. But what if there is a good MFI available; should the church or missionary choose to partner or to promote?

The answer to this question largely hinges on the financial service needs of the target community. The church or missionary needs to learn about the financial services that the local MFI is providing and the types of clients the MFI is targeting. Does it appear that the MFI has services that meet any of the financial-service needs of the target population of the church or missionary? Figure 9.2, which is reproduced in figure 12.2, summarizes the microfinance-related services desired by households of different poverty levels.

For example, recall that many MFIs focus on providing loans for business purposes, typically for people with incomes in the category of "moderate poor" or above. If the target population could be well served by such business loans, then the Partnership Model could be pursued, either on its own or in combination with the Promotion Model. As described in the **Microfinance for Households Principle**, poor people need more than business loans; they desire a range of savings, insurance, loans, and money-transfer services to enable them to access lump sums for a wide range of household needs. Therefore, the church or missionary might work with the target population to design an SCA to meet some of its nonbusiness financial needs—e.g., savings and small loans for emergencies—and then partner with an MFI to obtain business loans. This is where the flexibility of SCAs is so useful. They can be adjusted to meet a wide range of household needs, and they can be adapted to reach all levels of poverty other than the destitute.

Microfinance for Households Principle

Poor households need convenient, flexible, and reliable financial services for:

1. Consumption Smoothing
2. Business Investments
3. Household Investments
4. Lifecycle Needs
5. Emergencies

If the target population is in the category of "extreme poor," then partnering with an MFI may not be possible, as the MFI's services

FIGURE 12.2 Microfinance-Related Services Desired by Households of Different Poverty Levels

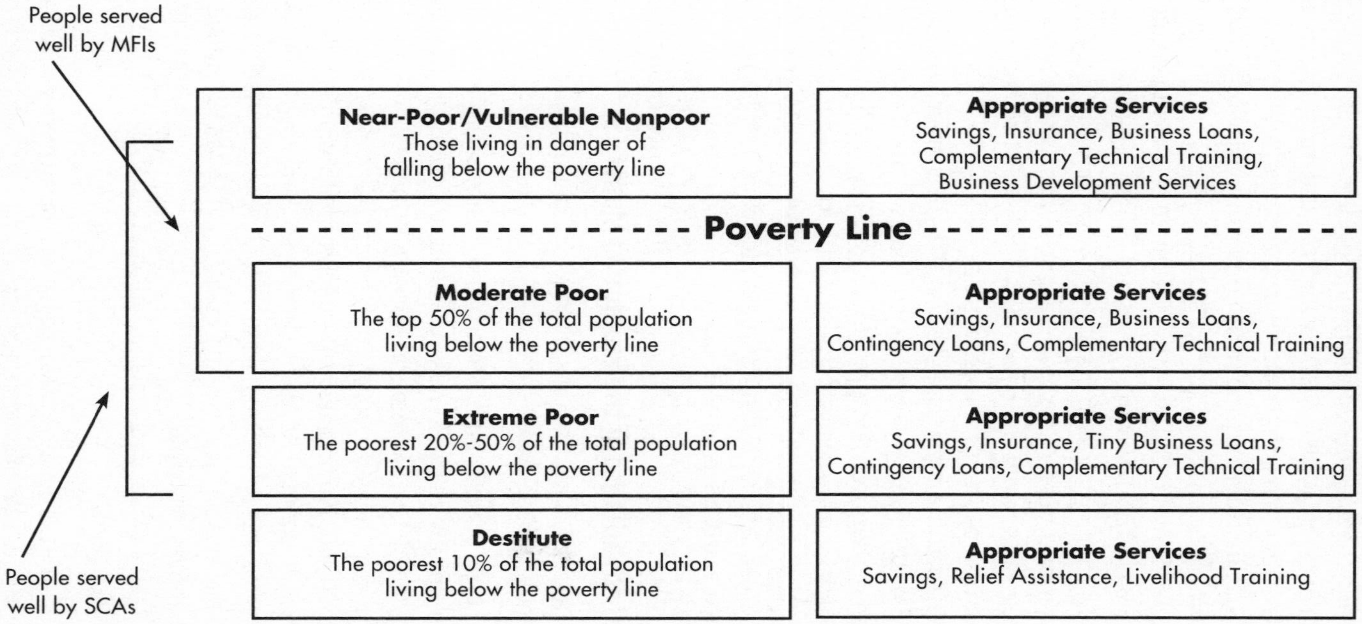

Adapted from Monique Cohen, *The Impact of Microfinance*, CGAP Donor Brief (Washington, DC: CGAP, July 2003), 1.

typically cannot serve this population. Indeed, most of the people in the SCAs being promoted by NGOs, churches, and missionaries across the Global South are much poorer than the typical MFI clients.

Table 12.2 illustrates this point by comparing data from field tests of the Chalmers Center's Promotion Model in Kenya, the Philippines, and the Dominican Republic with data from MFIs working in the same regions. Note that the average savings and loan sizes of the ASCAs are only small fractions of those in the MFIs.[20] While these smaller amounts might seem unimpressive to some readers, in reality they represent a huge success: SCAs are able to provide sustainable financial services that serve much poorer people than these MFIs can.

However, there are exceptions. As discussed in chapter 10, some MFIs are very innovative and are now offering savings, insurance, and even money-transfer services, some of which can reach the "extreme poor," even when their business loans are targeting those in the category of "moderate poor" and above. Hence, churches and missionaries need to carefully research the MFIs in the region to see if they have financial services that could be helpful to the target community.

Additional Advantages of the Promotion Model

The discussion thus far has described a number of positive features of the Promotion Model:

- It is a viable option for churches and missionaries to use to communicate the good news of the kingdom of God in word and in deed. See the **Integral Mission Principle**.
- It builds on indigenous knowledge, which is consistent with the **Asset-Based, Participatory-Development Principle**.
- It is highly compatible with the holistic theory of change.
- It is very flexible, so it can be adapted to meet a wide range of financial service needs as articulated in the **Microfinance for Households Principle**.
- It can minister to a range of poverty levels, including the "extreme poor."

In addition, there are several additional positive features of the Promotion Model that should be noted:

TABLE 12.2 Comparing Savings and Loan Sizes in Chalmers Center's ASCAs with MFIs

Chalmers Center's Field Testing Country	Average Saving Account Balance in Chalmers's ASCA	Average Savings Account Balance in MFIs in the Region	Average Loan Size in Chalmers's ASCA	Average Loan Size of MFIs in the Region
Kenya	$7.90	$68.00	$8.67	$348.00
Philippines	$14.41	$100.00	$16.07	$224.00
Dominican Republic	$58.04	$548.00	$57.37	$1,238.00

Data for MFIs is from Microfinance Information Exchange (2006).

- *Low Cost*: When done on a large scale, the Promotion Model typically has lower costs per person served than the Provider Model. For example, CARE, a secular NGO, found that it cost them between $15 to $60 to serve a person by promoting SCAs, while it cost them an average of $250 per client to establish a sustainable MFI in Africa.[21]
- *Variety of Scales*: Unlike the Provider Model, the Promotion Model can be implemented on either a small or large scale. It is entirely possible for a missionary or a volunteer in a church to promote the formation of a single SCA, providing an excellent opportunity to minister holistically to the group members. On the other hand, it is also possible to use the Promotion Model on a large scale. For example, HOPE International has worked with the Anglican Church of Rwanda to reach over 198,000 people in church-centered SCAs, with total savings of over $5 million.[22]
- *Adaptable*: The Promotion Model is extremely adaptable to a wide range of contexts, including those that are typically not conducive to credit-led microfinance: rural settings; countries with high inflation; regions with political instability; and target populations comprised of the elderly, orphans, handicapped, or HIV victims. In addition, the Promotion Model is being used both by established churches as well as by missionaries as a "pre-evangelism" strategy amongst unreached people groups.

- *Savings Rather than Over-Indebtedness*: As discussed in chapter 8, emphasizing saving rather than borrowing has additional advantages: it encourages discipline and a forward-looking perspective; it is consistent with the **Asset-Based, Development Principle**; and the Bible warns about the dangers of debt (Proverbs 22:7). Moreover, the payouts that members receive from saving in an SCA can be used to help them to escape or avoid overindebtedness to other lenders.
- *Simple*: It is much easier to promote the formation of an SCA than to set up an MFI. Indeed, poorly educated people can operate SCAs without having to get extensive technical training.
- *Avoid Dependency*: Because SCAs require no outside loan capital to get started, even a poor church or indigenous missionary can start one without having to rely on funds from outsiders.
- *Self-Replicating*: Once a group is trained to start an SCA, it is very common for the members to spawn additional groups. For example, in the 1990s CARE promoted SCAs to approximately 100,000 people in Niger. Researchers later discovered that on average each group had promoted an additional SCA on their own, bringing the total number of people reached to roughly 200,000.[23] The Chalmers Center has seen self-replication in church-centered SCAs as well.
- *Dividends on Savings*: Poor people often have to pay 30 percent to 80 percent for the privilege of saving with informal savings agents; in contrast, in ASCAs the group members earn interest on their savings. While the amount earned varies by SCA, the organizations using VSLA report an average return of 35.4 percent.[24]

Key Weaknesses and Primary Obstacles in the Promotion Model

Key Weaknesses

Of course, like all interventions, the Promotion Model has some weaknesses, two of which are described here.

First, the capital buildup in SCAs, especially if the members are very poor, is likely to be slow. This can create frustrations, especially for any group members who are a bit better off financially or who are more entrepreneurial.

To offset this problem, some churches, missionaries, and NGOs have tried to inject outside money into the SCAs in order to give them more loan capital. The evidence suggests that this is a bad idea. Research on several dozen SCA programs around the world has found that SCAs with no outside funds or loans have the best track record in becoming solid financial systems.[25] Outside funds can attract group members who think they are going to get something for nothing, and their subsequent behaviors weaken trust and group cohesion. In addition, people handle other people's money differently than they handle their own money, which reduces the incentives of the group members to work hard to make sure that all the components of the **Financial Systems Design Principle** are being met. Unfortunately, there are no shortcuts. It simply takes time for the group to develop the necessary trust and to accumulate sufficient assets to be able to make larger loans.

Second, although SCAs are more flexible than some of the standardized financial services of MFIs, some inflexibility is inevitable. For example, if a member in a time-bound ASCA wants to borrow to produce pineapples, which take twenty months to grow, but the ASCA only lasts twelve months, there is an obvious mismatch. The savings limits, loan sizes, and repayment terms may not fit the financial needs of everyone in a particular community or target group.

Primary Obstacles

There are also a number of common obstacles to churches and missionaries moving forward with the Promotion Model.

First, if people have come to expect lots of handouts from the church or missionary, it can be hard to shift to an approach in which poor people are being asked to save and lend their own resources to one another. In particular, if "relief" has been used for long periods of time with people who are not in a crisis, it can be very difficult for the church or missionary to move into the more "developmental" approach that is inherent in the Promotion Model (see the **Asset-Based, Participatory-Development Principle**).

Second, the commitment of church leaders is crucial. Pastors that are accustomed to being channels of outside resources to their communities are often not very excited by a microfinance ministry model that has no outside resources flowing in. Similarly, church leaders might be hesitant to try a high-accountability ministry such as microfinance if they are accustomed to relief-type benevolence ministries in which the "beneficiaries" are given goods or services with little or nothing expected in return.

Third, at a theological level, some church leaders do not embrace the idea of integral mission, believing that the church should confine itself to a preaching ministry and not get involved in deed ministry. There are certainly limits to what the local church—as an institution—should undertake directly, which is the reason there is a profound role for parachurch ministries such as the SCAs in the Promotion Model. But often the objection is not rooted in ecclesiology but rather in a lack of understanding of the comprehensive nature of Christ's kingdom, reducing his reign to the spiritual dimension, as in "evangelical gnosticism" (see figure 5.4). It has been the Chalmers Center's experience that emphasizing a theology of the kingdom of God is often the key ingredient in getting churches to move forward.[26]

Fourth, men often do not appreciate the value of savings-led microfinance approaches and would rather have large injections of outside capital in order to more quickly access large loans for businesses. This entrepreneurial spirit should be encouraged, not crushed. The problem is that providing such loans is not easy, as discussed in chapter 10. In order to get moving, the Chalmers Center has learned through experience that orienting the women in the church is often essential for generating interest in the Promotion Model. Because formal church leaders are often men, it may take a special effort to connect with the informal female leaders in order to bring them into the process.

For all of these reasons, working with local churches and their leaders can be a longer and slower process than the secular NGO programs that directly promote SCAs on a massive scale. On the other hand, once church leaders catch the vision, things can really take off, as it is possible to leverage denominational infrastructure, social capital, and the individual congregations' facilities, people, and spiritual resources to promote SCAs on a large scale, even in hard-to-reach places.

For example, it took a microfinance consultant from 2003–2005 to get the Promotion Model started with the Free Pentecostal Fellowship of Kenya (FPFK), a denomination that had about five hundred mostly rural churches at the time. As the consultant explains, one of the major obstacles in the process was getting church leaders to "understand how the promotion of tiny savings and credit groups would contribute to FPFK's mission of building God's kingdom."[27] But once the leadership was convinced, the program grew to an estimated 12,000 participants in 2011 and is a prime example of how a network of rural churches can be leveraged to create financial services for very poor people in even remote regions.[28] The "Masai Missions" story in chapter 1 is about one of the FPFK churches involved in this microfinance ministry.

Summary

Because even very poor churches and missionaries can promote SCAs on their own, the Promotion Model is a particularly attractive option for integral mission. Indeed, the model is highly consistent with the holistic theory of change articulated in chapters 5–7. In addition, it is relatively easy to use, does not depend on outside resources for loan capital, is highly adaptable, is consistent with asset-based participatory development, and can reach very poor people in even remote areas. Finally, it can address the wide range of household needs for financial services, not just the need for loans for business purposes. The major weakness with the Promotion Model is its slow capital buildup, which can be an obstacle to its adoption by those churches, missionaries, and target populations that have grown accustomed to rapidly receiving lots of material resources from outsiders. In fact, as we shall see in the next chapter, histories of handouts can be the main obstacle to effective and sustainable distribution of the Promotion Model.

Application Exercise

If you are considering pursuing the Promotion Model, you should explore this possibility in greater detail with your target population using the tool entitled *Promotion Model Assessment*. If you believe that God is calling you to move forward with the Promotion Model, the Chalmers Center's *Restore: Savings* handbook can walk you through this process. In addition, you can also provide the SCAs with complementary technical training using the Chalmers Center's curricula on business, home, and health (see Ministry Component #4 in chapter 7). All of these resources are available on the website associated with this book.

CHAPTER 13

THE SURPRISING CHALLENGES OF DISTRIBUTION

As a country, we direct enormous resources to and place substantial social responsibilities on the charitable sector, yet the vast majority of nonprofits can't demonstrate any commensurate return on this investment. The glossy fund-raising brochures, the moving videos, and the carefully crafted inspirational anecdotes often mask problems that range from inefficiency and ineffectiveness to outright fraud and waste. There is little credible evidence that many charitable organizations produce lasting social value.

—*Ken Stern*[1]

Donors either center an organization on its full mission or contribute to Mission Drift.

—*Peter Greer and Chris Horst*[2]

As we saw in the story of the Masai church in chapter 1, the advancement of the Great Commission in the twenty-first century is largely in the hands of some of the poorest churches on the planet, some of which are sending out their own members as missionaries. This led us to state two profound questions facing the global body of Christ at the start of the twenty-first century:

1. *How can materially poor churches and indigenous missionaries in the Global South advance the Great Commission in the context of widespread poverty inside their congregations and communities?*
2. *What are the roles of financially prosperous churches, mission agencies, Christian relief and development organizations, church-equipping ministries, and donors in this process?*

As we have seen throughout this book, microfinance ministries can be part of the answer to the first question. Indeed, the past fifteen years have shown that, with a little bit of training, poor churches and indigenous missionaries can implement microfinance ministries that powerfully communicate—using both restorative words and deeds—that Jesus Christ is making all things new. Indeed, this is already happening all across the Global South, but it could happen on a much larger scale if the global body of Christ could get this training into the hands of more poor churches and indigenous missionaries.

And that leads to the second question, which is the focus of this chapter. More specifically, this chapter explores how the global body—including financially prosperous churches, mission agencies, relief and development organizations, church-equipping ministries, and donors—can help to scale up the equipping of poor churches and indigenous missionaries to use microfinance ministries for integral mission.

Unfortunately, this is much, much harder than it looks.

It is actually surprisingly difficult to get such training—or any poverty-alleviation intervention, for that matter—into the hands of the right people in a way that is consistent with long-term, sustainable development. Economist William Easterly describes the challenge as follows:

> ... the West spent $2.3 trillion on foreign aid over the last five decades and still [has] not managed to get twelve-cent medicines to children [that would] prevent half of all malaria deaths. The West spent $2.3 trillion and still [has] not managed to get four-dollar bed nets to poor families.... It's a tragedy that so much well-meaning compassion did not bring these results for needy people....
>
> In a single day, on July 16, 2005, the American and British economies delivered nine million copies of the sixth volume of the Harry Potter children's book series to eager fans. Book retailers continually restocked the shelves as customers snatched up the book. Amazon and Barnes & Noble shipped preordered copies directly to customers' homes.... It is heartbreaking that global society has evolved a highly efficient way to get entertainment to rich adults and children, while it can't get twelve-cent medicine to dying poor children.[3]

Why is the world able to distribute entertainment on a massive scale but unable to get medicine to dying children, despite massive amounts of foreign aid? The question is both agonizing and perplexing. And if we can't get medicine—which should be relatively easy to distribute—to poor people, how will we ever get nuanced microfinance training to poor churches and indigenous missionaries in remote regions of the Global South?

This chapter explores these questions, explaining why the challenges of distribution are so great. As we shall see, although there are many obstacles, researchers and practitioners are discovering new and innovative ways to distribute microfinance training to poor people, including to poor churches and indigenous missionaries in the Global South. Indeed, perhaps God is going to use you, the reader, as part of the solution to this distribution problem.

The Key to Sustainable Ministry: Effectively Delivering What They Really Want

The global body of Christ faces two challenges as it seeks to distribute training, curricula, and other resources to enable poor churches and indigenous missionaries in the Global South to implement microfinance ministries—or any ministries for that matter:

1. How does the global body of Christ know what poor churches and indigenous missionaries really want?
2. How can the global body of Christ deliver the answer to question 1 in an efficient and high-quality manner?

Answering the first question is *absolutely crucial* if we want to see sustainable and effective ministries established. If churches and indigenous missionaries in the Global South do not really want the training, curricula, and other resources that are being provided to them, they will not use them to establish effective ministries and to sustain those ministries over time. Indeed, stories abound of the waste that has resulted from providing things to people in the Global South that they did not really want: donated tractors that sit idle in fields, wells that are not maintained, and malaria nets that are not used.[4] In this light, the challenge is not just one of getting training, curricula, and other resources to poor churches—as difficult as that is—but also of having the churches and indigenous missionaries actually utilize what has been delivered to them, when they did not really want those things in the first place. Unfortunately, as discussed below, discerning what poor churches and indigenous missionaries really want is much harder than it appears at first glance.

And even once we know what they want, addressing the second question is also quite challenging. Indeed, as the quote from William Easterly describes, it is surprisingly difficult to get even something as simple as medicine distributed to poor people in an effective and efficient manner.

In order to understand the difficulties that are involved in addressing these two distribution questions, it is helpful to consider the different ways that businesses and nonprofit organizations produce and distribute goods and services. As we shall see, nonprofits face some unique challenges, which the global body needs to understand as it seeks to equip poor churches and indigenous missionaries to use microfinance ministries. For whether the equipping is being done by a financially prosperous church, a mission agency, a church-equipping ministry, a Christian relief and development organization, or even an individual expatriate missionary, the equipping organization will necessarily be using nonprofit structures to do this training. Hence, in the remainder of the chapter, we shall refer to all of these varied organizations as "nonprofits."

Businesses Versus Nonprofits

The Harry Potter books mentioned by William Easterly were produced and distributed by businesses, while the medicine that did not get to the dying children was distributed by governments and nonprofit organizations. That truth is not meant to imply that businesses are inherently superior in some way to governments and nonprofits. In fact, businesses could not get this medicine to these dying children either. No, the difference has to do with the extent to which the end users—i.e., the customers—were able to pay for the products in each situation.

Scenario #1: When the Customers Can Pay the Full Cost

When customers can pay the full amount that it costs for a business to produce and distribute a good or service, it is possible for them to harness the world's resources in such a way that they can get what they want at an acceptable quality. How does this work?

When customers are able to afford to purchase the product, they are able to use their money to do two very important things:

1. Send a credible message to businesses and investors that they want the product.
2. Hold businesses accountable to provide this product at a quality level that is acceptable to them.

For example, because they were able to afford to buy books, customers used their money to "vote" for Harry Potter books to be produced and shipped to them over any other books that could have been produced and shipped to them. The customers did this by paying money to order the Harry Potter books and by not paying money to order the other books. These actions provided a credible message to producers and their investors that more resources should be allocated to producing Harry Potter books and that fewer resources should be allocated to producing the other books.

Furthermore, the customers were able to hold the book producers and shippers accountable for delivering quality books to them. If the books were falling apart when the customers received them, the customers could take their money elsewhere the next time that they wanted to buy books.

Note that serving customers well automatically generates the resources needed to cover the costs of serving those customers well. As products are produced and sold, the revenues from sales cover the costs of production. And as investors see profits rising in those businesses that are successfully serving their customers, they invest more in those businesses, thereby allowing those businesses to expand in order to reach more customers.

In summary, when customers are able to pay the full cost for a particular good or service, they are able to harness the world's resources to provide them that good or service at a sufficiently high quality. Indeed, this is the reason that on July 16, 2005, the world was able to get nine million copies of the entertaining Harry Potter book to customers who wanted to buy it.

Scenario #2: When the Customers Cannot Pay the Full Cost

Unfortunately, there are many instances in which the customer cannot pay the full cost of producing and distributing the product. Indeed, this is the situation facing the global body as it seeks to equip churches and indigenous missionaries with training and curricula to pursue a microfinance ministry: the customers of the training and curricula—that is, poor churches and indigenous missionaries in the Global South—cannot pay the full cost.

When the customers cannot pay the full cost, businesses cannot produce and distribute the goods and services to them, because there is no way for the businesses to generate enough revenues from sales to cover their costs. In such situations, governments and nonprofits must be used to produce and distribute. For the purposes of this book, the following discussion will focus on the distribution challenges facing nonprofits, for as mentioned earlier, the global body of Christ will be using nonprofit structures in one form or another to deliver microfinance training to their "customers"—that is, the poor churches and indigenous missionaries that they are seeking to serve.

Some readers might find this language disturbing. Certainly, poor churches and indigenous missionaries are our partners in the spread of the gospel and not our "customers." But it is a useful mental exercise to think about them as customers, for in so doing we can discover why it is so difficult to serve them and then try to design solutions to address those difficulties head on. And then after we have done this mental exercise, we should then revert to thinking about these poor churches and indigenous missionaries as what they really are: our dear partners in the gospel of Jesus Christ.

Unfortunately, because the customers of a non-profit cannot pay the full cost of the goods and services that the nonprofit is providing, they do not have the purchasing power to do the two important things that customers of businesses can do:

1. Send a clear and credible message to the nonprofit and its donors about what they really want.
2. Hold the nonprofit accountable to provide the goods or services that they want at a sufficiently high quality.

As a result, it is surprisingly difficult for a nonprofit to serve its customers well.

What Do They Really Want?

The lack of a clear and credible message from customers about what they want makes it difficult for a nonprofit to know which goods or services to provide. Do poor churches and indigenous missionaries really want training on microfinance, or would they prefer training on malaria prevention, or on HIV, or on nothing at all? As we saw earlier, knowing what the poor churches and indigenous missionaries really want is absolutely critical for establishing sustainable ministries.

If this is the case, then why doesn't the nonprofit just ask poor churches and indigenous missionaries in the Global South what they want? That is always a wise step, but that approach is often not as easy as it looks.

Like all of us, poor churches and indigenous missionaries are not all-knowing. They are not aware of all of the possibilities and of the pros and cons of all those possibilities. Indeed, many of them have been solely focused on preaching the Word and have never even considered the idea of integral mission, much less the idea of using microfinance or any other ministry as a part of that mission. Hence, it is often the case that a bit of education is necessary for them to be able to determine if they would like training and curricula to start a microfinance ministry.

But that immediately presents another problem. As described in the book *When Helping Hurts*, when outsiders interact with poor churches and indigenous missionaries, that interaction is colored by a long history, particularly if the outsiders are from wealthy nations or are perceived to represent organizations from wealthy nations. This history often includes colonialism, neo-colonialism, top-down mission agencies, and dole-outs of money and other resources. As a result, the outsiders are perceived—often correctly—as representing both power and wealth.

And when powerful and wealthy people make a suggestion—or even ask a question—it can be perceived as a command or even a funding opportunity.[5] As a result, the very process of educating the poor churches or indigenous missionaries about the possibility of starting a particular ministry can result in their saying that they want to start that ministry, even when they really do not want to do so.

For example, over a dozen years ago the Chalmers Center was testing the Promotion Model in a major slum in Africa. An African staff member of the Chalmers Center asked a church in this slum if it would be interested in promoting SCAs as a vehicle for ministry. For years, NGOs and Western churches had poured money into this community, often using relief approaches in a context in which development was the appropriate approach. As a result, the church had grown accustomed to easy money from foreigners, and knowing that the African staff member was employed by an organization based in the United States, the church naturally thought that this might be another funding opportunity.

The church asked one of its leaders to consider the possibility of starting a microfinance ministry. As part of his considerations, the church leader asked the Chalmers Center's staff member, "Do you have any money for us?" The Chalmers' staff member said, "No, we have no money for you, only training. We will *never, ever* have any money for you. We are a training organization, not a funding organization."

That was not the answer that the church leader wanted to hear, but he agreed to try the Promotion Model described in chapter 12. The Chalmers Center spent a lot of time training this church, but things never seemed to get moving. After many, many visits and trainings from the Chalmers' staff member, the church finally started some SCAs with some of its members, but there never seemed to be much enthusiasm for it.

After about a year of continued visits from the staff member, the church leader asked him, "Can we have some money now?" When the answer was still "no," membership in the church's SCAs immediately dropped from seventy people to about twelve. It appears that many people in the church had never really embraced the idea of starting SCAs; they were just saying "yes" in the hope of getting what they really wanted—easy money from outsiders.

When people who are perceived to be powerful or wealthy make a suggestion, or even ask a question, it can be construed as a command or as a funding opportunity.

All of these dynamics are exacerbated by the fact that many cultures in the Global South are "shame-based," meaning that public embarrassment is to be avoided as much as possible, particularly for outside guests. In such settings, it may be considered rude to tell outsiders that their ideas are not good. So when an outsider such as a nonprofit asks a poor church or indigenous missionary if they want microfinance training, they might get a "yes" answer when the real answer is "no." This problem is further complicated by the fact that many cultures in the Global South use indirect forms of communication in which people often do not speak openly about their true beliefs or feelings.

In summary, as we saw earlier, the sustainability of an intervention largely depends upon how much the local people actually wanted that intervention in the first place. Unfortunately, because poor churches and indigenous missionaries cannot pay the full cost of being trained to start a microfinance ministry, it is often very difficult to ascertain whether they want to start one or not.

What Should the Donors Fund?

Like investors in a business, donors to nonprofits need information about where to put their money in order to steward it well for the kingdom of God. Unfortunately, the inability of customers to pay the full cost of the goods and services that they are receiving from the nonprofits creates major problems for donors.

First, donors rightly want to see sustainable impact, which, as we have seen, is largely determined by the extent to which the customers actually want the good or service that is being provided. But as hard as it is for nonprofits to know what their customers truly want, it is even harder for the donors, who are typically very far removed from these customers.

And to make matters worse, the generous actions of well-meaning donors can actually undermine their ability to get the very information that they need. In particular, when donors pay the full cost of providing a good or a service, including paying for the training and curricula to start a microfinance ministry, they have very little idea if the customers actually want it or not.

Second, donors need to know which nonprofits are actually performing well. Unfortunately, because there are no profits to serve as indicators of excellent performance, it is very difficult for the donors to ascertain this. In principle, impact studies can help to offset this problem, but as discussed in the appendix, it is usually extremely difficult to measure impact.

No Automatic Fuel

As discussed earlier, when a business meets the customers' demands, the fuel necessary to operate is automatically generated from the customers' payments. In addition, as investors see profits rising in a successful business, they provide funds for that business to expand. In a business, success generates the fuel for more success. In contrast, in a nonprofit, success often generates the fuel for staff burnout!

A nonprofit that successfully meets the needs of its customers typically attracts more customers, but because these customers do not pay, success generates more costs, not more resources! To cover these escalating costs, the nonprofit needs to spend precious time and money seeking to raise more funds from donors, which puts additional strain on the nonprofit and may not yield any results.

Donor Driven Instead of Customer Driven

When the customer cannot pay the full cost, the system can become donor driven rather than customer driven. Indeed, one of the major tensions that nonprofits face is that their financial incentives are to pander to their donors, who pay their bills, rather than to truly serve their customers. This can tempt nonprofits to:

- Use marketing and fundraising approaches that tell the donors what they want to hear, whether those messages are true or not: "Your donation is having a huge impact! You are *the* key to saving poor children all over the world!"
- Select products and services on the basis of what appeals to the donors rather than on the basis of what is actually best for the customers. If the donors want them to get basketballs, then basketballs it is!

- Make operational decisions in order to meet the numerical goals or other priorities of the donors rather than to truly serve the customers.

It may be shocking to some readers, but the harsh reality is this: a nonprofit with an excellent marketing and fundraising department can thrive for many years without actually making a positive difference in the lives of the people they are claiming to serve. This is particularly true if the nonprofit organization finds a way to raise funds from many small donors, none of whom have the time or capacity to determine if the nonprofit's work is actually accomplishing anything.

Note that while a nonprofit organization might knowingly succumb to these temptations, there is a much larger danger that the nonprofit might fall into these temptations without even realizing it. Most nonprofit leaders or staff members do not consciously decide to serve their donors rather than their customers. Indeed, most employees in nonprofits are highly dedicated to serving their customers with missionary zeal. They often have a sincere desire to change the world, and many times they are making a huge difference. But over time, misaligned incentives, inadequate information about the actual impact of various interventions, and mounting financial pressures can combine to subtly undermine the mission and effectiveness of nonprofits in donor-driven systems.

Finally, donor-driven systems ultimately do not really serve the donors either. The vast majority of donors are people of integrity who truly want to steward the resources that God has entrusted to them in order to improve the lives of the nonprofit's customers. But it is very hard for the donors to accomplish this when the nonprofit's eyes are not singularly focused on achieving the right goals.

The Particular Challenge Facing Financially Prosperous Churches

It is difficult to be a nonprofit organization, and it is difficult to be a donor to a nonprofit organization. But it is even harder to be both at the same time! Unfortunately, that is the situation in which many financially prosperous churches find themselves: they are simultaneously the nonprofit that is providing goods and services, and they are the donor who is paying for those goods and services. This combination greatly diminishes the likelihood that the customers will drive the system, for the usual checks and balances between donors and nonprofits are not in place.

When the donor and the nonprofit are not the same entity, they can sometimes provide checks and balances for one another in ways that are good for the customers. For example, if a nonprofit leader absolutely loves snow skiing and decides that everybody in Africa needs snow skis, that leader will typically have a difficult time finding donors who are willing to pay for these skis. Similarly, if a donor is enamored with a crazy idea, many nonprofit leaders have the integrity and courage to refuse to cooperate, even if the donor is willing to pay for it.

But if the donor and the nonprofit are the same entity, the checks and balances are gone, increasing the likelihood that snow skis will be distributed all across Africa! Consider the following story, which, while fictional, accurately describes a dynamic that is constantly repeated within the global body of Christ.

Imagine that Deep Community Fellowship (DCF), a wealthy congregation in the United States, truly wants to help a very poor denomination in a particular country in Africa. So the senior pastor of DCF asks the leadership of the African denomination how DCF can help, and the African leadership says that their pastors need more training. This sounds perfect to DCF, for it wants to get its congregation moving, and it has both well-educated staff and laypersons who are sincerely eager for a chance to use their gifts in Africa.

The leadership of DCF believes that its ability to develop intimate fellowship within their congregation has been at the core of their church's success. So they ask the African denominational leaders if they think it would be helpful for DCF to put on a training conference for African pastors on how to develop a deeper sense of community in their churches. The African denominational leaders say that this would be a wonderful idea, and they seem truly excited about the opportunity to gather their pastors together for a week of fellowship and learning. They agree to take care of the logistics of putting on the conference, while DCF agrees to take care of providing all of the training. In addition, seeking to be generous with its vast funds, DCF agrees to pay the travel expenses, room, and board for the African pastors and their spouses.

What is wrong with this picture?

DCF is both the nonprofit that is providing the training and the donor that is paying for the training. There are no checks and balances. And because DCF generously paid for all of the costs of the conference, there is no way to determine if the African pastors actually wanted DCF's training or not. However, given that the African pastors are from a highly communal culture, it is hard to imagine that the most pressing issue facing them was how to create community! Moreover, it is rather absurd to think that a church from the highly individualistic United States would be particularly gifted at teaching Africans about this topic!

Although the DCF story is not real, its essence is repeated over and over again across the body of Christ. From training conferences, to building projects, to short-term teams, financially prosperous churches make "suggestions" to their brothers and sisters in the Global South and then offer to pay to make those "suggestions" happen. It all seems so genuine and so generous, and in some respects it is. But at the end of the day, it hinders the establishment of sustainable ministries, and it often undermines the dignity of poor churches, indigenous missionaries, and the people whom they are trying to serve.

It is time to move from dependency to dignity in the global body of Christ.

An Important Caveat

In summary, when customers are not able to fully pay for a good or service, it makes it difficult for nonprofits and donors to provide that good or service to them. As a result, the same world that is able to distribute nine million copies of Harry Potter books in a single day struggles to get medicine to save dying children. And for the same reason, the global body of Christ struggles to get appropriate training, curriculum, and other resources to poor churches and indigenous missionaries in the Global South.

That having been said, while nonprofits face some daunting challenges, readers should not conclude that nonprofits never make any positive contributions. Nonprofit staff members often bring tremendous passion, diligence, and self-sacrifice to their work, and many nonprofits have an enormous impact in situations in which businesses could not have any impact at all. The point is simply that to do their jobs well, nonprofits have to defy the currents; indeed, they typically have to paddle upstream.

In Search of Customer-Driven Microfinance Ministries: An Example from West Africa

The Problems to Be Solved

As discussed earlier, the fact that poor churches and indigenous missionaries are typically unable to pay the full cost of training, curricula, and other resources creates two problems:

1. They are unable to send a credible message about what they really want.
2. They are unable to hold their suppliers accountable to provide them what they want at an acceptable level of quality; and the end result is that it is difficult for poor churches and indigenous missionaries to harness the world's resources to serve them effectively.

In addition, there is an additional problem that needs to be solved:

3. At present, the primary funding sources for promoting SCAs are governments and other secular donors, who are unwilling to pay for training and curricula that is infused with evangelism and discipleship in a biblical worldview, thereby undermining the pursuit of integral mission (see Ministry Components #3–#4 in chapter 7).

An Experiment in West Africa

There is no way to completely solve all three of these problems, but partial solutions can sometimes be found by mimicking as much as possible the features of a customer-driven system. Toward that end, the Chalmers Center has been trying some possible solutions in its field project in West Africa. By no means does the Chalmers Center have all three of these problems solved. In fact, there are far more unresolved issues than answers at this point. However, the hope is that by describing this project, readers' thinking can be stimulated about possible ways for the global body to serve poor churches and indigenous missionaries in the Global South more effectively. In addition, because the Chalmers Center's strategy is to design and field-test solutions and then to train others to use those solutions on their own, the Center is eager to help organizations and churches to use the system described here to equip churches in the Global South for more effective ministry.

The distribution system being tested is pictured in figure 13.1. The Chalmers Center equips two indigenous trainers to launch a Mobile Training Center (MTC), which they own and operate as self-employed entrepreneurs.[6] The MTC then equips volunteers, called "church-based facilitators" (CFs), to promote SCAs and to provide complementary training in business, home, and health (see Ministry Component #4 in chapter 7). The CF is a member of their local church and serves as the point person for launching their church's microfinance ministry.

The MTC typically trains a group of CFs in a particular region all at the same time. The CFs gather together in one place, often a local church, for several days of training. The CFs then go back to their churches to facilitate the formation and operation of the SCAs and to provide ongoing training on relevant topics in microfinance and

FIGURE 13.1 Chalmers Center's Distribution Model in West Africa

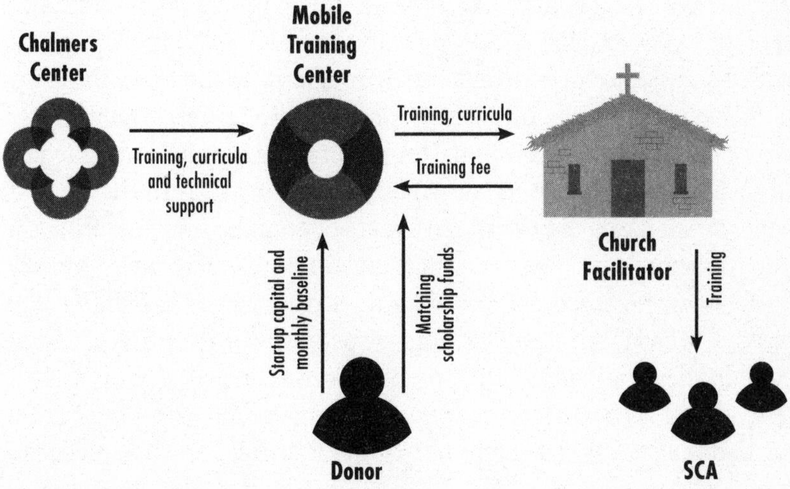

in business, home, and health, all from a biblical worldview perspective (see Ministry Components #3–#4 in chapter 7). The MTC returns to the region across time in order to provide additional training and technical support to groups of CFs.

How does this system seek to address the three problems mentioned above?

Problem #1: Customers Cannot Send a Credible Message about What They Really Want

With respect to the first problem, a partial solution is to require the customers of the MTC's training and curricula—the churches, the CFs, and the SCA members themselves—to contribute something toward the costs of being trained and of implementing a microfinance ministry. As a result, these customers are able to send a credible message that they are serious about starting such a ministry and that they want to be trained to do so. In addition, they are able to order the particular training and curricula that they would like to receive from a menu of options.[7]

Many people doubted that this approach could work, for the prevailing culture in the global body of Christ is one in which churches in the Global South are accustomed to having all of their costs covered by outsiders. In particular, when it comes to training, the expectation is often that travel, room, board, and even an honorarium is to be provided to the pastors and others who are being trained. In addition, it is often expected that those attending any training will be provided with operational funds to enable them to implement a new ministry.

Believing that this culture could change, the Chalmers Center asked very poor churches, CFs, and SCA members in Benin, Cote d'Ivoire, Ghana, Mali, and Togo to contribute something toward the costs of being trained and to bear the full costs of actually implementing the microfinance ministry. As a result, it is truly *their* microfinance ministry.

It should be noted that it is not always clear who is bearing various costs: the churches, the CFs themselves, the SCA members, or some combination thereof. In fact, it probably varies from one church to the next. Hence, we shall refer to the entire combination of the church, the CF, and the SCA as the "customer" of the MTC, all the while recognizing that in each case different subsets of this "customer" may be contributing different amounts. From the perspective of the distribution system as a whole, the "customer," i.e., the church-CF-SCA combo, is bearing the following costs:

- The venue in which the MTC trains the CFs, which is often a local church.
- The cost of the CFs' food and lodging at a MTC's training, along with the costs of the CFs' travel to and from the training.
- A fee charged by the MTC for training the CFs. The MTCs are allowed to determine what this fee will be, and a number of factors go into the setting of this price, including what the "market will bear" and the personalities of the MTC operators and the customers. A typical fee is about $1 per day of training per CF, although sometimes the MTC simply asks a CF to bring whatever they are able to contribute.
- The travel expenses for the CF to and from the weekly SCA meetings. This could be negligible, but in some cases an individual CF starts multiple groups in more than one church or location.
- Supplies for the SCAs such as flip chart paper, pens, record books, lock boxes, locks, etc.
- The value of the SCA members' and CFs' time that is spent in group meetings, in holding one another accountable, and in ministering to one another in all sorts of non-programmed ways.
- The risk of any loss of the members' savings contributions.
- The risk of any damage to the reputation of the church or of the group members.

There is no magic formula for determining how many costs the customer should bear in order for a delivery system to be customer-driven rather than donor-driven. Indeed, the Chalmers Center does not yet know if we are asking too much or too little of the customers in West Africa. The world is full of mystery! But the general principle is that in a ministry partnership, the various ministries involved should each make a contribution that is a sacrifice *from their perspective*, thereby signaling that they truly want the ministry to happen. We shall call this the **Ministry Partnership Contribution Principle**, a principle that readers can apply across many different types of training, ministries, and distribution systems.[8]

> ***Ministry Partnership Contribution Principle***
>
> All of the ministries in a collaborative partnership must contribute something of value to themselves.

Problem #2: Customers Cannot Hold Providers Accountable to Give Them What They Want at an Acceptable Level of Quality

Solving the second problem mentioned above is actually much harder. Although the MTC is receiving some payment from its customers for the services it is providing, the reality is that the vast majority of the MTC's revenues are coming from donors, who are covering most of the MTC's costs. How can the system incentivize the MTC to be productive and to serve its customers well?

The key is to mimic how a business works by tying the MTC's revenues to its actual performance in serving its customers. In other words, the money from donors should be released to the MTC only if the MTC actually performs well in the eyes of the customers, not just in its own eyes or just in the eyes of the donors. Toward that end, the MTC is given some start-up capital and a monthly baseline, but beyond that donor funds are only released when the MTC performs. In particular, in addition to the training fee that the MTC receives from each CF, the MTC also receives a payment from the donors for each day of training that the MTC provides to each CF. This payment from donors amounts to a scholarship in which donors are matching the CF's own "tuition" payments to be trained by the MTC. In addition, the MTC also receives payments from donors when an SCA is formed and when it meets certain benchmarks.

The payments to the MTC for training and for SCA formation and performance provide the MTC with the incentives to provide its customers what they want at an acceptable level of quality, thereby addressing Problem #2. If the MTC is not serving enough customers at a sufficiently high quality, over time the MTC will not have many CFs to train or many SCAs formed and performing well. And this will result in low revenues for the MTC, because the payments from the donors to the MTC are conditional upon these things. Conversely, if the MTC has a growing number of customers and is serving them well, it will automatically generate the fuel that it needs to operate, just as a business does.

In order for this system to work properly, there is a need for monitoring and auditing the MTC. Toward that end, Chalmers has created a customer relationship management (CRM) platform into which the MTC loads various financial reports, training records, and data. In addition, the MTC is required to take a picture of the CFs at each training event using a GPS-enabled camera. The GPS pinpoints the date, time, and location in which the photo was taken, all of which is shown on Google Maps once the photo is uploaded to the CRM.[9] This data is cross-referenced with training data on each CF that the MTC enters into the CRM platform. As a result, the Chalmers Center is able to verify that the MTC provided training at the date, time, and location to the CFs that they reported and then to release the scholarship funds to the MTC. Follow-up visits by Chalmers Center staff to the CFs and SCAs in various locations provide audits of the pictures, reports, and data that have been filed.

Some readers might be concerned that using performance incentives might turn a ministry into a money-making venture for the MTCs. That temptation certainly exists, just as it does for Christians in other types of ministries: authors who get book royalties; speakers who earn fees for giving a speech; and musicians who get paid per performance. Thus far, it does not appear to have been an issue, as the MTC operators were selected for their deep commitment to ministry. In this light, the incentives simply reinforce the MTC operators' desire to focus their attention on serving the church-CF-SCA combo, which is preferable to the usual situation in which the incentives are for nonprofits to focus their attention on their donors. Thus, while different types of ministries and contexts might require different approaches, we believe there is general merit in the **Incentive Alignment Principle**.

Incentive Alignment Principle

Although money should never be the primary motivation in ministry, it is generally helpful if incentives are structured in such a way that they reward staff and volunteers for doing the right things.

Problem #3: Secular Donors Do Not Want to Fund Distribution of Biblically Based Training and Curricula

The church is called to pursue integral mission: communicating the good news of the Kingdom of God through an intimate connection of restorative words and deeds (see the **Integral Mission Principle**). Unfortunately, most of the funding for microfinance, including the funding for promoting SCAs, is from governments and other secular donors who are unwilling to pay for training and curricula that incorporate a biblical worldview (see Ministry Components #3 and #4 in chapter 7). As a result, Christian organizations that use such funding are often forced to separate "spiritual" matters from the technical training in microfinance and related topics, thereby undermining the very message that the church is to be delivering: King Jesus is Lord of all. Moreover, as discussed in chapter 7, communicating that Jesus is separate from his world is devastating to traditional religionists, for it provides them with no solution to their most pressing problem: how to manipulate spiritual forces in order to gain some control over their lives. These considerations lead to the **Integral Mission Funding Principle**.

> ***Integral Mission Funding Principle***
>
> Funding sources must permit an integral connection between the proclamation and the demonstration of the good news of the kingdom of God.

In order to address problem #3, the Chalmers Center is exclusively using funding from Christian foundations, churches, and individuals, but there is still much work to be done on creating a sustainable funding strategy for the MTCs. Indeed, as the responses in the sidebar on the next page indicate, a lack of funding is one of the primary challenges facing a number of Christian organizations that would like to increase their equipping of churches to use microfinance ministries in order to pursue integral mission.

Results

Between July 2011 and September 2014, the Chalmers Center launched a total of six MTCs with a variety of starting dates: one each in Benin, Cote d'Ivoire, Ghana, Mali, and two in Togo. The MTCs in Benin and Cote d'Ivoire did not experience many customers due to a combination of

The Challenges of Scaling Up

A number of international organizations are equipping churches to promote SCAs, as described in the Promotion Model in chapter 12. We asked leaders from some of these organizations what their biggest challenge is in trying to increase the scale of their church-equipping efforts.

As with most nonprofit organizations, the biggest challenges we face includes securing funding and managing human resources.

Suzanne Schultz-Middleton, program director Five Talents International

Perhaps the biggest (and most exciting!) challenge for HOPE is building the capacity of our church partners—journeying with them as they grow in vision and expertise to ultimately take ownership of their savings group ministry. Believing that this is indeed a church-centered ministry (rather than a project operated by HOPE International, with the church serving as an efficient distribution channel), our focus is on engaging and equipping the church. Our mutual end goal with partners is that the church's role would become one of primary ownership and responsibility for all aspects of their savings ministry—spiritual, technical, and operational. We are therefore committed to designing and refining our programs so that they are as cost effective as possible and are in line with the structure and operational capacity of our church partners. For HOPE International and our partners, this continues to be an incredibly rewarding journey!

Phil Smith, director of savings and credit associations for HOPE International

The biggest challenge is to spread without losing quality. For that to happen, Tearfund needs to raise the right type of funding to help scale up. Supporting successful SCAs is a long-term undertaking. However, many financial sources are short-term. Tearfund is piloting an SCA-sponsorship model for our work in Ethiopia as a means to raise long-term funding.[10]

Donald Mavunduse, head of east and southern Africa team for Tearfund

Funding! We have very strong monitoring and evaluation standards including a set ratio of staff to church-based volunteers as well as volunteers to groups. All groups are monitored closely in their first year with quantitative data collected in a management information system to ensure both the financial success of the group as well as the group's decreased dependency on the trainer. We want to ensure that our groups are operating by the highest standards: quality savings and loan services; self-sufficiency for the group; empowered group members; and solid relationships in the group, in the church, and with Christ. Because of our desire to scale up without sacrificing any of these dimensions of quality, our scale-up is dependent on receiving adequate funding.

Courtney O'Connell, Savings for Life senior technical advisor for World Relief

factors: a civil war in Cote d'Ivoire; other demands on the MTC operators' time; and lack of receptivity on the part of churches. As a result, these two MTCs were allowed to go out of business, just as they would in a for-profit world. The Center believes that allowing these MTCs to close is actually a success of the model, as it is preferable to a donor-driven system in which money continues to be poured into settings that do not actually want the goods or services that are being offered.

The four remaining MTCs report that the CFs they have trained have started 958 SCAs reaching an estimated 12,454 people.[11] Figure 13.2 shows the time line of SCAs started for each of the four MTCs. Although there are many factors that influence the rate at which SCAs are formed, some of the differences are likely due to the very different contexts in which the MTCs are operating:

- Northern Togo's MTC was launched in partnership with the Assemblies of God (AG) denomination, which has many churches in the region. The AG leadership selected the MTC operators and publicly gave them their blessing, giving this MTC instant credibility with a large network of like-minded churches.
- The MTCs in Southern Togo and Ghana are focused on the churches in a defined geographic region, but they were not launched in partnership with any denominations. Hence, these MTCs have to engage in far more marketing and trust building than the MTC in northern Togo.
- The MTC in Mali is working in a country that has been ravaged by civil war and in which the churches are sparsely scattered over a wide geographic area. As a result, this MTC has the largest challenges in terms of marketing, trust building, and even getting to the churches it is training.

The rate of SCA formation has been most rapid for the MTC in northern Togo, which is not surprising, given that it started with a ready-made customer base. At the other end of the spectrum, it is to be expected that things are going more slowly in Mali, given that the churches are geographically quite dispersed and that there has been considerable civil unrest.

FIGURE 13.2 Timeline of SCAs Promoted by Mobile Training Centers

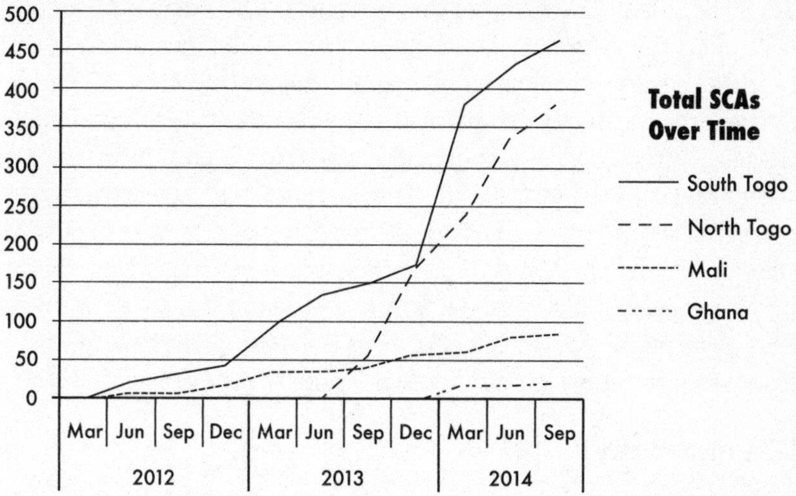

Although no formal impact studies have been conducted, surveys of SCA members suggest that the churches' microfinance ministries have had considerable spiritual, social, and economic impact in ways that are consistent with the theory of change presented in chapter 7.

In addition, there are some indicators that the model can be efficient. Large-scale secular programs that promote SCAs in poor communities report an average cost of $20–$25 per member, although there is considerable variation in how different organizations report overhead expenses and other types of costs.[12] It is to be expected that the church-centered model in West Africa would be more expensive than secular programs, for it has a number of attributes that create additional costs:

- Equipping the local church for ministry is more time consuming than simply starting SCAs, but it has the potential for more transformative and sustainable impact.
- Using more participatory approaches is more expensive but can be more empowering.
- Evangelism and discipleship in a biblical worldview slow things down, but the rewards are eternal.

In this light, it is very encouraging that the estimated costs are $15.50 per member for the MTCs in southern Togo and $12.26 for the MTC in northern Togo. Because these figures do not include *any* of the overhead costs of training, launching, and supporting the MTCs, these figures are not directly comparable to the $20–$25 industry standard. However, although it is not our primary goal to achieve the efficiency standards set by the secular industry, the estimates suggest that if two more MTCs were launched with costs per member that were similar to the two Togolese MTCs, sufficient scale would be reached to achieve industry cost standards even if all the overhead costs were included. And, as mentioned above, it is very likely that these SCAs have far more transformative impacts than those promoted by the secular industry.

Is It Customer Driven?

Although the model that is being developed in West Africa is far from perfect, there is some evidence that it is exhibiting at least some of the features of a customer-driven system:

- MTCs go out of business when, for whatever reason, they do not have sufficient "sales" of their product.
- MTCs have identified and introduced new products and services that have creatively met their customers' needs. For example, one of the MTCs designed, produces, and sells a lockbox for the SCAs' money that is shaped after the House of Principles in figure 9.3. And MTCs have also developed and delivered training on new topics to meet the specific requests of pastors, who often lack formal training.
- The CFs did not attend some phases of the MTCs' training because they felt the costs to them outweighed the benefits. The MTCs expressed this problem to the Chalmers Center, which is now being forced to shorten and simplify the training and curricula. This amounts to the customer (the CF) rejecting the products of the retailer (the MTC) and forcing the manufacturer (the Chalmers Center) to change the products.

Variations on the Model

The Chalmers Center has recently started testing a variation of this model. In some settings there are church-equipping organizations already in place; therefore, rather than launch an MTC, the Chalmers Center is equipping staff members in these organizations to provide training and curricula to the CFs. The incentive and payment structure is very similar to the one being used with the MTCs in hopes of creating a customer-driven system.

Summary

It is surprisingly difficult to equip poor churches and indigenous missionaries with the training and curricula they need to establish sustainable ministries, including microfinance ministries. One of the key determinants of sustainability is delivering to these churches and missionaries what they really want. Unfortunately, because they cannot pay the full costs of the training and curricula, it is often very difficult for donors and nonprofits to determine what these churches and missionaries truly desire. The problem is exacerbated by nonprofit delivery systems whose incentives do not always reward the proper things. By following the **Ministry Partnership Contribution Principle**, the **Incentive Alignment Principle**, and the **Integral Mission Funding Principle**, the global body can seek to overcome these problems.

Application Questions

1. Think about any partnerships that your church or organization has with poor churches or indigenous missionaries in the Global South. How do you know that they really desire what you are bringing into this partnership?

2. Missions expert Daniel Rickett describes a partnership as a "complementary relationship driven by a common purpose and sustained by a willingness to learn and grow together in obedience to God."[13] In what ways are your partnerships consistent with this quote, and in what ways could your partnerships be improved?

3. Daniel Rickett has developed a tool for evaluating the health of ministry partnerships entitled *Checklists for Building Strategic Relationships*, which can be downloaded from the website associated with this book. Consider how you might work with your partners to carefully evaluate your relationship using this tool.

4. Are there any ways that you could apply the **Ministry Partnership Contribution Principle**, the **Incentive Alignment Principle**, and the **Integral Mission Funding Principle** in your current or future ministry partnerships, including any partnerships related to spreading microfinance ministries?

APPENDIX 1
ESTIMATING THE IMPACT OF MICROFINANCE

RANDOMIZED CONTROLLED EXPERIMENTS

As described in chapter 4, it is inadequate to focus on anecdotal stories about the success of MFIs' programs, or of any programs for that matter, as MFIs have strong incentives to report only the positive stories. What is really needed to determine the impacts of an MFI is to examine the impacts of its loans on all of its borrowers. Unfortunately, this is harder than one might think.[1]

For example, assume that Marco, a poor person living in Bolivia, has entrepreneurial talents that are much greater than that of the average microentrepreneur in Bolivia. Then, all else equal, Marco would be both more willing to apply for a loan and more likely to be granted a loan by an MFI than the average microentrepreneur.[2] Now suppose that one year after the loan, a researcher finds that Marco's profits increased more rapidly than those microentrepreneurs who did not get loans. It is tempting to claim that the microloan caused Marco's profits to increase more rapidly, but it is actually impossible to know if Marco's increased profits were due to the microloan or to Marco's superior talents.

As figure A1.1 illustrates, what is really needed to determine the effects of an MFI's loans is a counterfactual—that is, the researcher needs to know what would have happened to Marco if he had not received the loan. The difference between Marco's actual profits with the loan and the profits he would have experienced had he not received the loan, i.e., the counterfactual, would then enable the researcher to

FIGURE A1.1 Actual Impact of MFI Loan on Marco

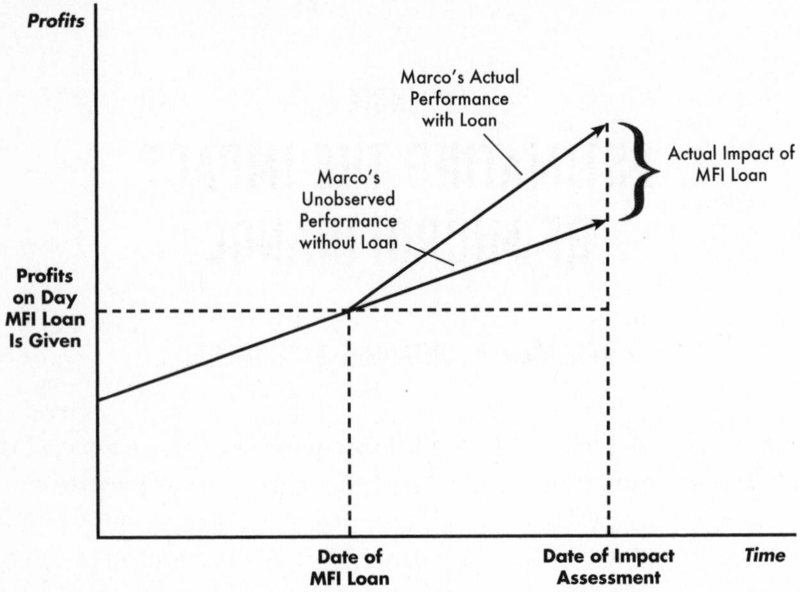

determine if the MFI loan had any impact on Marco's profits. Of course, no such counterfactual exists. It is not possible to observe what would have happened to Marco if he had not taken the loan over the same time period in which he actually did take the loan!

However, there is a potential solution to this problem. In recent years, economists have started using randomized controlled trials (RCTs) to examine the effects of MFIs' loans on borrowers. Mimicking the approach of pharmaceutical testing procedures in the medical field, researchers *randomly* assign potential borrowers to either a "control" group or a "treatment" group. Members of the treatment group are given microloans, while members of the control group are not. Because the potential borrowers are randomly assigned, there should be no systematic differences between the members of the treatment group and the control group. In other words, for statistical purposes, the control group can be considered identical to the treatment group before the loans are given. In essence, the control group provides the counterfactual that is needed, enabling the researcher to examine

FIGURE A1.2 Randomized Controlled Experiments Estimate Impact of MFI Loan

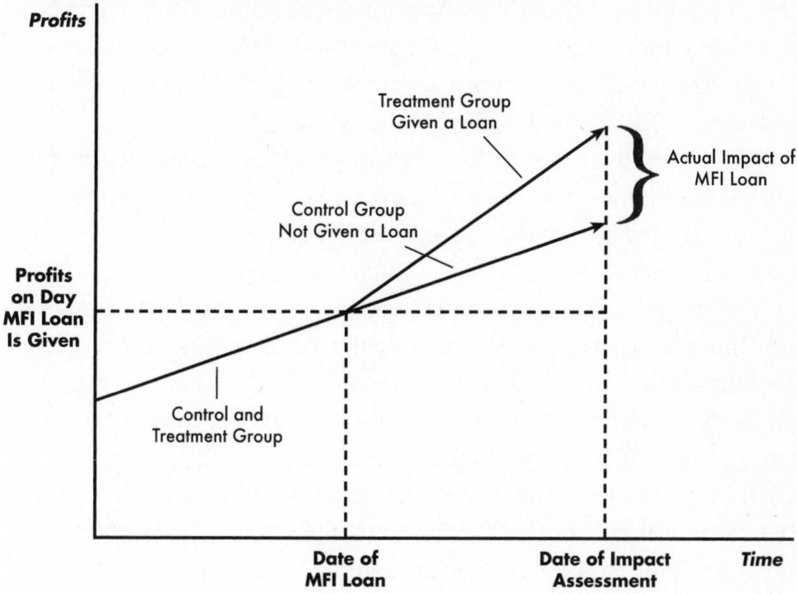

the difference between the outcomes from getting the loans to those that would have occurred if no loans had been given. As illustrated in figure A1.2, researchers then compare the profits between the treatment group and the control group, attributing any difference to the effects of the loan.

What do RCTs find about the effects of microcredit? The few studies that exist suggest that microloans do have small, positive impacts on microenterprises (investment, profits, and new starts), but there is no measured impact on household income, food quality, and a number of other measures of well-being.[3]

RCTs are also being conducted on other forms of microfinance, e.g., savings and credit associations. At present, these studies have examined the impacts of the savings and credit associations on the village as a whole rather than on just the members in the association, making it less likely that they will pick up any effects. Overall, the RCTs confirm that savings and credit associations increase savings levels and the use of credit, and they reduce consumption volatility (see figure 4.5). But in contrast to studies that use different methodologies, the RCTs find that the savings and credit associations have minimal effects on business, education, social, or health outcomes for the village as a whole.[4]

Although RCTs have some advantages over other types of empirical research, RCTs are also subject to many problems.

First, like all studies, RCTs are plagued by the substantial problem of measurement error. Hence, when an RCT fails to find an impact, it could simply be due to inadequate data rather than to there being no real impact.

Second, RCTs are only likely to detect very quantifiable changes—e.g., business profits—that can be easily measured in relatively short periods of time, like 6–24 months. More complex changes—e.g., overall family stability—and changes that unfold over longer periods of time—e.g., multigenerational impacts—are very difficult to discern with RCTs. For example, even if loans do not dramatically increase business profits over the time period of the RCT, they might reduce the overall fluctuations in those profits, thereby providing a greater sense of stability for the microentrepreneur's household. Such stability might enable the parents to keep their kids in school, resulting in positive impacts on the next generation that will not be observable for several decades.

Third, like all research, there are questions as to how generalizable the results of an RCT are beyond the immediate program and population that is being studied. Thus, the finding that a microcredit program run by a particular NGO in Peru was successful may tell us very little about the effectiveness of a microcredit program run by a different NGO in India.

Fourth, some experts have suggested that only weaker programs agree to submit to an RCT. Programs whose work is widely recognized as being effective have no incentive to undergo an RCT, for if the RCT provides evidence that the program is effective, it merely confirms what everybody already believed. On the other hand, if the RCT suggests that the program is ineffective, the MFI could lose its financial support. Indeed, there is some evidence that the MFIs that have submitted to RCTs are quite different from the typical MFIs.[5]

Fifth, RCTs can only study things that are easily quantifiable, but there are some very important things—e.g., spiritual growth—that are very difficult or even impossible to measure.

Finally, RCTs measure the average impact of the program, but they do not look at the entire range of results. Some people might be greatly helped by the program, while others may be greatly hurt. But RCTs only tell what happened on average.

RCTs are just one of many tools that researchers should use to study the impacts of microfinance. By using a range of qualitative and quantitative methods, it is possible to get a fuller picture of the complexity of the situation. For example, using a range of methods, recent research has found that savings and credit associations appear to have positive impacts on a variety of important economic, psychological, and social factors.[6]

APPENDIX 2
KEY PRINCIPLES

Integral Mission Principle

The *global* body must function in such a way that the *local* church is able to use its gifts to engage in integral mission: proclaiming and demonstrating among people who are poor the good news of the kingdom of God in a contextually appropriate way.

Church and Parachurch Principle

Parachurch ministries must be "rooted in and lead back to" the local congregation(s) that minister in the same location.

Nature of Poverty Principle

Poverty is the inability for a human being to live in right relationship with God, self, others, and the rest of creation. This poverty is due to broken individuals, broken systems, and demonic forces.

Poverty-Alleviation Principle

Poverty alleviation is the ministry of reconciliation, seeking to restore people to living in right relationship with God, self, others, and the rest of creation.

Union with Christ Principle

Being united to King Jesus—and his body, the church—is God's theory of change for addressing the broken individuals, broken systems, and demonic forces that cause poverty. This union is received and nurtured through faith as the Holy Spirit applies the church's "ordinary means of grace" to people's lives.

Asset-Based, Participatory-Development Principle

Focus on local *assets* not just on *needs*; as much as possible, use *participatory* rather than *blueprint* approaches; do not use *relief* when the context calls for *development*.

Microfinance for Households Principle

Poor households need convenient, flexible, and reliable financial services for:

1. Consumption Smoothing
2. Business Investments
3. Household Investments
4. Lifecycle Needs
5. Emergencies

Financial Systems Design Principle

In order to be successful, a financial system must maintain all of the following features:

1. Trust
2. Discipline
3. Financial Sustainability
4. Leadership, Management, and Governance
5. Transparency
6. Fit the Target Population

Savings Principle

Poor people can and do save, but they need more effective systems for doing so.

Ministry Partnership Contribution Principle

All of the ministries in a collaborative partnership must contribute something of value to themselves.

Incentive Alignment Principle

Although money should never be the primary motivation in ministry, it is generally helpful if incentives are structured in such a way that they reward staff and volunteers for doing the right things.

Integral Mission Funding Principle

Funding sources must permit an integral connection between the proclamation and the demonstration of the good news of the kingdom of God.

A FINAL WORD FROM THE AUTHORS

A Learning Journey

We have come a long way together, but the journey is really just beginning. The field of microfinance is very dynamic, so there are always exciting new things to learn. In addition, the Triune God is actively engaged with his world, so engaging in his work always reveals new truths and possibilities.

We believe that learning and practice go hand in hand. Thus, while we want you to prayerfully and carefully consider whether God is calling you to start or to improve a microfinance ministry, we don't want you to be paralyzed. Work with your ministry partners to do the best that you can to design an effective ministry: survey the financial landscape in your target community; talk to existing organizations and ministries; get lots of input from the target population; and pray really hard! And if you still believe that God is calling you to move forward, start something small. And then after trying this, step back, evaluate, improve, and try again. Eventually you might find something that really works and that can grow bigger. But as the saying goes: "Start small and grow up; start big and blow up!"

One place to take the next step in learning is to create an account at the website associated with this book: www.chalmers.org/dignity. The tools, resources, and curricula there can help you to move forward into effective ministry.

Acknowledgments

The authors are deeply grateful to the board and staff of the Chalmers Center, who have labored side by side with us for fifteen years. Indeed, in many ways this book is a diary of countless meetings, trips, conversations, prayers, training events, distance learning courses, successes, failures, joys, and sorrows.

We wish to thank Covenant College (www.covenant.edu), which birthed the Chalmers Center and where the authors teach in the Department of Economics and Community Development. We are deeply grateful to the board, administration, faculty, staff, and students who have created a rich learning community that seeks to faithfully bear witness to the coming King.

We are deeply grateful to the many organizations and individuals that have walked with us on this journey and that have taught us so many things. Although there are too many to mention by name, the following are deserving of special recognition: Anglican Church of Kenya, Rwanda, and Uganda; Chalmers' Global Fellowship of Trainers and Lead Trainers; Five Talents International; Food for the Hungry; Free Pentecostal Fellowship of Kenya; Freedom from Hunger; HOPE International; Lifechurch.tv; Mission to the World; Mobile Training Center Operators in Benin, Cote d'Ivoire, Ghana, Mali, and Togo; Saddleback Church/The Peace Plan; Tearfund UK; Urwego Opportunity Bank; World Relief; World Vision; and thousands of trainers, churches, and facilitators across the Global South, whose shoes we cannot possibly fill.

We are extremely grateful to the faithful financial supporters of the Chalmers Center, who have provided the resources for the fifteen years of research, training, and curricula described in this book. In particular, we are deeply thankful for First Fruit Inc. and The Maclellen Foundation Inc., who took significant risks in providing the initial funding for the Chalmers Center and for its initial field tests of SCAs with churches in Africa, Asia, and Latin America, long before anybody thought the church could even be involved in microfinance. Looking back, we have no idea why you thought we could do this.

We are very grateful for the trust funds donated by Dick and Ruth Ellingsworth in support of the writing of this book.

We have received very helpful comments on this book from the following staff at the Chalmers Center: Michael Briggs, Gregg Burgess, Smita Donthamsetty, Laura Hunter, Andy Jones, and Sam Moore. Helpful theological insights were provided by Kelly Kapic, Allen VanderPol, and Herb Ward. Input on some microfinance topics were provided by Will Kendall, Luke Kinoti, Donald Mavunduse, Suzanne Middleton, Courtney O'Connell, and Phil Smith.

Thanks to the following for generously providing the cover photos: Ryan Estes, Jonathan Meisner, Tom Waddell, and Andy Warren.

Thanks to Karis Tucker for her outstanding work on the figures and diagrams. "Karis, can we please change this one more time? I promise this is the last time!"

Thanks to Ryan Pazdur and the entire team at Zondervan for their outstanding support and encouragement.

I (Brian) would like to express my deep gratitude to Russell Mask for teaching me nearly everything I know about microfinance. In particular, thanks for introducing the entire Chalmers Center and me to the possibility of using the savings, knowledge, and talents of the poor themselves as the basis for microfinance. Russell, you have made a huge impact on the lives of millions of poor people around the world. And you have made a huge impact on me.

Words cannot express my love for my dear wife, Jill. As I type these words, she is massaging out the stress-induced knots in my neck and shoulders, as she has done nearly every evening for the twenty-three years of our marriage. She has enabled me to pursue my dreams and calling at tremendous personal cost and is the unsung hero in the work of the Chalmers Center. Thanks also to my incredible children—Jessica, Joshua, and Anna—who have supported, loved, and encouraged me in so many profound ways.

Without my wife, Yeyen, I (Russell Mask) would probably know almost nothing about microfinance. Over twenty years ago, as I was collecting data for my doctoral dissertation, she helped me with eighteen months of participant observation of Grameen Bank client groups in Manila and with hundreds of interviews of microfinance clients. Without her patient presence in almost all of these interviews, it would have been impossible to complete them. And then, after our three children had grown up and left home, Yeyen once again agreed to go back to the same families for follow-up research in July 2014. Thank you to the two Philippine microfinance institutions and *mga nanay* that made all of this possible. And to my kids—Caleb, Elizabeth, and

Hannah—thanks very much for your patience with all of my trips to Asia and Africa.

Most importantly, both Brian and Russ want to thank our faithful Lord and Savior, Jesus Christ, who has fully paid for all of our sins, and who is in the process of transforming two very broken authors into his glorious image.

Brian Fikkert
Russell Mask
Lookout Mountain, Georgia, USA

NOTES

Chapter 1: Masai Missions

1. Interview with staff of the Chalmers Center, 2014.
2. This story is adapted from Brian Fikkert, "Proverbs 31 Women in Tribal Dress," *Mandate*, no. 2 (2007), *https://www.chalmers.org/news/entry/proverbs-31-women-in-tribal-dress*.
3. Philip Jenkins, *The Next Christendom: The Coming of Global Christianity* (Oxford: Oxford University Press, 2002), 92.
4. "What Is the 10/40 Window?" *The Joshua Project*, *http://joshuaproject.net/10-40-windo.php*.
5. Andrew Walls, "Demographics, Power, and the Gospel in the Twenty-first Century" (presentation, SIL International Conference and WBTI Convention, June 6, 2002), 6.
6. Jenkins, *Next Christendom*, 1–2.
7. Glenn J. Schwartz, *When Charity Destroys Dignity: Overcoming Unhealthy Dependency in the Christian Movement, A Compendium* (Bloomington, IN: Author House, 2007); Jean Johnson, *We Are Not the Hero: A Missionary's Guide for Sharing Christ, Not a Culture of Dependency* (Sisters, OR: Deep River Books, 2012); Robert Reese, *Roots & Remedies: Of the Dependency Syndrome in World Missions* (Pasadena, CA: William Carey Library, 2012).
8. Steve Corbett and Brian Fikkert, *When Helping Hurts: How to Alleviate Poverty Without Hurting the Poor... and Yourself* (Chicago: Moody, 2012).
9. For a helpful analysis of the role of the North American church in twenty-first century missions, see Paul Borthwick, *Western Christians in Global Mission: What's the Role of the North American Church?* (Downers Grove, IL: InterVarsity, 2012).
10. Corbett and Fikkert, *When Helping Hurts*.
11. Roy Mersland, "Innovations in Savings and Credit Groups—Evidence from Kenya," *Small Enterprise Development* 18, no. 1 (2007): 50–56.
12. Larry R. Reed, *Resilience: The State of the Microcredit Summit Campaign Report, 2014* (Washington, DC: Microcredit Summit Campaign, 2014), 8.

Chapter 2: What Is the Mission of the Church?

1. Rick Warren as quoted in Ed Stetzer and David Putman, *Breaking the Missional Code: Your Church Can Become a Missionary in Your Community* (Nashville: Broadman, 2006), 173–74.
2. Interview with staff of the Chalmers Center, 2012.

3. This section has been adapted with permission from Corbett and Fikkert, *When Helping Hurts: How to Alleviate Poverty Without Hurting the Poor… and Yourself* (Chicago: Moody, 2012), 31–32.
4. Timothy J. Keller, *Ministries of Mercy: The Call of the Jericho Road*, 2nd ed. (Phillipsburg, N.J.: P&R, 1997), 52–53.
5. For a helpful discussion of this point, see Timothy J. Keller, *Center Church: Doing Balanced, Gospel-Centered Ministry in Your City* (Grand Rapids: Zondervan, 2012), 267–71.
6. For fuller presentations on the nature and role of the church see Charles Van Engen, *God's Missionary People: Rethinking the Purpose of the Local Church* (Grand Rapids: Baker, 1991); Edmund P. Clowney, *The Church* (Downers Grove, IL: InterVarsity, 1995); Keller, *Center Church*.
7. The Lausanne Movement, *The Capetown Commitment: A Confession of Faith and Call to Action*, 2011, Part 1, Section 10.B.
8. Louis Berkhof, *Systematic Theology* (Grand Rapids: Eerdmans, 1941), 575.
9. See Van Engen, *God's Missionary People*, 101–18; Keller, *Center Church*, 228–30.
10. See Lesslie Newbigin, *The Gospel in a Pluralistic Society* (Grand Rapids: Eerdmans, 1989); Van Engen, *God's Missionary People*; Darrell L. Guder, ed., *Missional Church: A Vision for the Sending of the Church in North America* (Grand Rapids: Eerdmans, 1998); Christopher J. H. Wright, *The Mission of God: Unlocking the Bible's Grand Narrative* (Downers Grove, IL: InterVarsity, 2006); Michael W. Goheen, *A Light to the Nations: The Missional Church and the Biblical Story* (Grand Rapids: Baker, 2011); Craig Van Gelder and Dwight J. Zscheile, *The Missional Church in Perspective* (Grand Rapids: Baker, 2011); Bryant L. Myers, *Walking with the Poor: Principles and Practices of Transformational Development*, rev. ed. (Maryknoll, NY: Orbis, 2011); Corbett and Fikkert, *When Helping Hurts*; Keller, *Center Church*.
11. Keller, *Center Church*, 89.
12. Ibid., 94.
13. See Newbigin, *The Gospel in a Pluralistic Society*; Walls, *Demographics, Power, and the Gospel*.
14. Newbigin, *The Gospel in a Pluralistic Society*, 141. Andrew Walls makes a similar point when he says that the Christian faith must be "translated" into each local culture just as Jesus's incarnation involved "translating" God into humanity. See Andrew Walls, "The Mission of the Church Today in the Light of Global History," *Word & World* 20, no. 1 (2000): 17–21.
15. Keller, *Center Church*, 264.
16. The Integral Mission Principle is consistent with the concept of a "missional church." See Keller, *Center Church*.
17. Because savings and credit associations are indigenous to the local culture, the Masai microfinance ministry is an example of the "conversion" rather than the "proselytization" of local culture. See Walls, "The Mission of the Church Today in the Light of Global History."
18. This is simply the idea of "sphere sovereignty" developed by Abraham Kuyper. For a brief introduction, see Keller, *Center Church*, 294–95.
19. Richard Stearns, "Solving Poverty Is Rocket Science," *Christianity Today* (July 8, 2013), *http://www.christianitytoday.com/ct/2013/july-web-only/solving-poverty-is-rocket-science.html*.

20. Myers, *Walking with the Poor*, 79.
21. Tim Chester, ed., with C. Rene Padilla, Tom Sine, and Elaine Storkey, *Justice, Mercy, and Humility: Integral Mission and the Poor* (Carlisle, UK: Paternoster, 2002), 8.
22. Newbigin, *The Gospel in a Pluralistic Society*, 227.
23. Note that while the Bible indicates that the local church is called to care directly for the poor, this task is not given exclusively to the local church. In fact, the Bible indicates that the family, businesses, and even the state have roles to play in helping the poor. It takes wisdom in each situation to discern exactly which tasks the church should undertake directly with respect to the poor and which tasks should be left to other organizations, including parachurch ministries. For a fuller discussion of this issue, see Keller, *Center Church*, 322–28.
24. For a helpful discussion of this point, see Keller, *Center Church*, 267–71.
25. Myers, *Walking with the Poor*, 192.
26. Ibid.; Corbett and Fikkert, *When Helping Hurts*.
27. Corbett and Fikkert, *When Helping Hurts*.

Chapter 3: Integral Mission: Avoiding Unhealthy Dependencies

1. Jean Johnson, *We Are Not the Hero: A Missionary's Guide for Sharing Christ, Not a Culture of Dependency* (Sisters, OR: Deep River Books, 2012), 17.
2. Integral mission was also part of the people of God under the Old Covenant, as Israel's words and deeds proclaimed the good news of the coming King and his kingdom to the Gentile nations. See Christopher J. H. Wright, *The Mission of God: Unlocking the Bible's Grand Narrative* (Downers Grove, IL: InterVarsity, 2006).
3. John Rowell, *To Give or Not to Give? Rethinking Dependency, Restoring Generosity, and Redefining Sustainability* (Tyrone, GA: Authentic, 2007).
4. Glenn J. Schwartz, *When Charity Destroys Dignity: Overcoming Unhealthy Dependency in the Christian Movement, A Compendium* (Bloomington, IN: Author House, 2007).
5. Rowell, *To Give or Not to Give?* 23.
6. The Marshall Plan refers to the large-scale initiative that the United States used to fund the rebuilding of Europe following World War II.
7. Schwartz, *When Charity Destroys Dignity*, xvii.
8. For a helpful summary of the debate between Rowell and Schwartz, see Daniel Rickett, "Lean on Me (Part 1): The Problem of Dependency," *EMQonline.com*, January 2012, *http://www.emqonline.com*.
9. Ronnie Hahne and Wouter Rijneveld, "Dependency," unpublished manuscript, available from World Mission Associates, *http://www.wmausa.org*, 2005, 21.
10. See Schwartz, *When Charity Destroys Dignity*; Reese, *Roots and Remedies*; Borthwick, *Western Christians in Global Mission*; Johnson, *We Are Not the Hero*; Steve Corbett and Brian Fikkert, *When Helping Hurts: How to Alleviate Poverty Without Hurting the Poor... and Yourself* (Chicago: Moody, 2012).
11. Ajith Fernando, "Some Thoughts on Missionary Burnout," *Evangelical Missions Quarterly* 35, no. 4 (1999): 442.
12. Chalmers Center for Economic Development at Covenant College, "Listening Well: West Africans Speak on Poverty and the Global Church," *Mandate* (August 27, 2013).

13. From the website: *www.lausanne.org*.
14. See Section 2.3 of The Lausanne Movement, *The Lausanne Standards: Giving and Receiving Money for God's Work*, available at *http://www.lausanne.org/content/the-lausanne-standards*.
15. Acts 11:29–30 also discusses an offering taken by the church in Antioch for the church in Judea.
16. Chuck Bennett, "Two Christian Leaders Discuss Dependency," *Mission Frontiers* (January/February, 1997): 1.
17. Luis Bush and Lori Lutz, *Partnering in Ministry: The Direction of World Evangelization* (Downers Grove, IL: InterVarsity, 1990); Glenn Fretz, "Toward Interdependent Ministry Partnerships: Fueling Ministry without Fostering Dependency," *EMQonline.com*, April 2002, *http://www.emqonline.com*; Andrew Walls, "Demographics, Power, and the Gospel in the Twenty-first Century" (presentation, SIL International Conference and WBTI Convention, June 6, 2002); Paul Borthwick, *Western Christians in Global Mission: What's the Role of the North American Church?* (Downers Grove, IL: InterVarsity, 2012); Daniel Rickett, "Walk with Me (Part 2): The Path to Interdependency," *EMQonline.com*, April 2012, *http://www.emqonline.com*.
18. Rickett, "Walk with Me (Part 2)," 2.
19. Ibid., 3.
20. Lesslie Newbigin, *The Gospel in a Pluralistic Society* (Grand Rapids: Eerdmans, 1989); Charles Van Engen, *God's Missionary People: Rethinking the Purpose of the Local Church* (Grand Rapids: Baker, 1991); Andrew Walls, "The Mission of the Church Today in the Light of Global History," *Word & World* 20, no. 1 (2000).
21. Some excellent advice on how to do this is in chapter 9 of Borthwick, *Western Christians in Global Mission*.
22. Corbett and Fikkert, *When Helping Hurts*, 109–13 and 119–31.
23. Newbigin, *Gospel in a Pluralistic Society*, 227.
24. For an elaboration of these points, see Johnson, *We Are Not the Hero*.
25. Roy Mersland, "Innovations in Savings and Credit Groups—Evidence from Kenya," *Small Enterprise Development* 18, no. 1 (2007).
26. Once group members have been trained to form a savings and credit association, it is very common for them to help others to start groups. In fact, in some regions such self-replication is considered the "norm." See Paul Rippey and Hugh Allen, "Making It Happen: Approaches to Group Formation," in *Savings Groups at the Frontier*, ed. Candace Nelson (Rugby, UK: Practical Action, 2013), 65–82.

Chapter 4: Microfinance: So Much Less . . . and So Much More

1. Interview with staff of the Chalmers Center, 2012.
2. David Roodman, *Due Diligence: An Impertinent Inquiry into Microfinance* (Washington, DC: Center for Global Development, 2012), 6.
3. Data are through June 2014 as featured in report of July 7, 2014, from the Grameen Bank website: *www.grameen-info.org*.
4. As will be discussed later, many MFIs are now seeking to offer additional financial services, including savings and insurance.

5. Larry R. Reed, *Resilience: The State of the Microcredit Summit Campaign Report, 2014* (Washington, DC: Microcredit Summit Campaign, 2014), 8.
6. Two dollars per day is commonly used as the global poverty line. People whose incomes fall below this line are considered "poor," and those whose incomes are higher than this are "non-poor." The roughly 1.2 billion people whose incomes fall below $1.25 per day are commonly called the "extreme poor."
7. Abhijit V. Banerjee and Esther Duflo, "What Is Middle Class about the Middle Classes Around the World?" *Journal of Economic Perspectives* 22, no. 2 (2008): 14.
8. Ibid.
9. Martin Ravallion, Shaohua Chen, and Prem Sangraula, *New Evidence on the Urbanization of Global Poverty* (Washington, DC: World Bank, 2007), Policy Research Working Paper 4199.
10. Daryl Collins, Jonathan Morduch, Stuart Rutherford, and Orlanda Ruthven, *Portfolios of the Poor: How the World's Poor Live on $2 a Day* (Princeton, NJ: Princeton University Press, 2009).
11. Ibid., 40–43.
12. She typically buys $5 worth of raw sheep intestines per day, so that would be the maximum amount she would need to borrow for the next day. In principle, she could borrow a larger amount of money from an MFI and keep that larger amount in a safe place to use for working capital. Unfortunately, poor people lack access to safe places to store money.
13. Ibid., 153.
14. Ibid., 20.
15. Dropout rates in some East African MFIs have exceeded 30 percent per year.
16. Two caveats are in order. First, some program participants are in their first loan cycle, so they are still discovering whether or not they will be successful. Second, some borrowers who had negative outcomes from their previous loans may still be hoping for positive outcomes from future loans. Such borrowers may still be in the program. Nonetheless, these caveats do not change the basic point that those hurt by the program will be underrepresented in the pool of current program participants.
17. For a helpful review of these studies and of the overall empirical literature on the impact of microcredit, see Roodman, *Due Diligence*.
18. See also the "whistleblowing" book by Hugh Sinclair, *Confessions of a Microfinance Heretic: How Microlending Lost Its Way and Betrayed the Poor* (San Francisco: Berrett-Koehler, 2012).
19. Jan P. Maes and Larry R. Reed, *State of the Microcredit Summit Campaign Report 2012* (Washington, DC: Microcredit Summit Campaign, 2012).
20. Roodman, *Due Diligence*, 28–29.
21. Banerjee and Duflo, *What Is Middle Class?* 18–19. These authors define "middle class" as those earning between $2–$10 per day.
22. See William R. Easterly, *The Elusive Quest for Growth: Economists' Adventures and Misadventures in the Tropics* (Cambridge, MA: MIT Press, 2002).
23. See especially David Hulme and Paul Mosley, *Finance Against Poverty, Volume 1* (Oxford, UK: Routledge, 1996); Stuart Rutherford, *The Poor and Their Money* (New York: Oxford University Press USA, 2000).

24. This section summarizes the story from chapter 2 of Collins et al., *Portfolios of the Poor.*
25. Ibid., 29.
26. The "vulnerability line" is different for every family, depending on its circumstances, but it would typically be lower than the official poverty line of $2 per day.
27. Ibid., 17.
28. Rebecca M. Vonderlack and Mark Schreiner, "Women, Microfinance, and Savings: Lessons and Proposals," *Development in Practice* 12, no. 5 (2002): 602–12.

    For a recent review of savings amongst materially poor people in the Global South, see Dean Karlan, Aishwarya Lakshmi Ratan, and Johnathan Zinman, "Savings by and for the Poor: A Research Review and Agenda," *The Review of Income and Wealth* 60, no. 1 (2014): 36–78.
29. Collin et al., *Portfolios of the Poor*, 54–57.
30. Ibid., 53.
31. Ibid., 153.
32. See Rutherford, *The Poor and Their Money*; Collins et al., *Portfolios of the Poor.*
33. Anirudh Krishna, *One Illness Away: Why People Become Poor and How They Escape Poverty* (New York: Oxford University Press USA, 2010); Collins et al., *Portfolios of the Poor*, 68.
34. Collins et al., *Portfolios of the Poor*, 3–4.

Chapter 5: What Is Poverty? The True Nature of the Problem

1. Deepa Narayan, Robert Chambers, Meera K. Shah, and Patti Petesch, *Voices of the Poor: Crying Out for Change* (New York: Oxford University Press, 2000), 28.
2. HOPE International, "A Father's Second Chance," online client stories, June 13, 2014, *www.hopeinternational.org*.
3. For an elaboration of this point, see Steve Corbett and Brian Fikkert, *When Helping Hurts: How to Alleviate Poverty Without Hurting the Poor... and Yourself* (Chicago: Moody, 2012).
4. Bryant L. Myers, *Walking with the Poor: Principles and Practices of Transformational Development*, rev. ed. (Maryknoll, NY: Orbis, 2011).
5. Corbett and Fikkert, *When Helping Hurts.*
6. Abhijit V. Banerjee and Esther Duflo, *Poor Economics: A Radical Rethinking of the Way to Fight Global Poverty* (New York: PublicAffairs, 2012), 43.
7. Indonesia has since begun to slowly roll out a national health insurance program that might begin to address access to healthcare.
8. Robert Chambers, *Rural Development: Putting the Last First* (London, UK: Longman Group, 1983).
9. Adding to the challenge is the fact that the Bible does not always use language precisely or in the same way that philosophers, natural scientists, or social scientists do.
10. For example, see Fred Sanders, *The Deep Things of God: How the Trinity Changes Everything* (Wheaton, IL: Crossway, 2010), 112–17; Kelly M. Kapic, *Communion with God: The Divine and the Human in the Theology of John Owen* (Grand Rapids: Baker, 2007), 35–66.

This framework corresponds to the "substantive perspective" of the "image of God." See Robert Peterson, "Humanity, Christ, and Redemption," a course at Covenant Theological Seminary, St. Louis, MO, Summer 2006; Anthony A. Hoekema, *Created in God's Image* (Grand Rapids: Eerdmans, 1986), 68–73.

11. See Malcolm Jeeves, *Minds, Brains, Souls, and Gods: A Conversation on Faith, Psychology, and Neuroscience* (Downers Grove, IL: InterVarsity, 2013); Timothy R. Jennings, *The God-Shaped Brain: How Changing Your View of God Transforms Your Life* (Downers Grove, IL: InterVarsity, 2013); James E. Zull, *From Brain to Mind: Using Neuroscience to Guide Change in Education* (Sterling, VA: Stylus, 2011); James K. A. Smith, *Desiring the Kingdom: Worship, Worldview, and Cultural Formation* (Grand Rapids: Baker, 2009); Dennis P. Hollinger, *Head, Heart, and Hands: Bringing Together Christian Thought, Passion and Action* (Downers Grove, IL: InterVarsity, 2005); James E. Zull, *The Art of Changing the Brain: Enriching the Practice of Teaching by Exploring the Biology of Learning* (Sterling, VA: Stylus, 2002).
12. See Smith, *Desiring the Kingdom*.
13. Volumes have been written about the meaning of the term "image of God." Helpful surveys can be found in Peterson, "Humanity, Christ, and Redemption"; Hoekema, *Created in God's Image*.
14. Richard L. Pratt Jr., *Designed for Dignity: What God Has Made It Possible for You to Be*, 2nd ed. (Phillipsburg, NJ: P&R, 2000); J. Richard Middleton, "The Liberating Image? Interpreting the Imago Dei in Context," *Christian Scholars Review* 24, no. 1, 8–25.
15. Kelly M. Kapic, "Anthropology," in *Mapping Modern Theology: A Thematic and Historical Introduction*, eds. Kelly M. Kapic and Bruce L. McCormick (Grand Rapids: Baker, 2012), 121–48; Peterson, "Humanity, Christ, and Redemption"; Hoekema, *Created in God's Image*.
16. Michael Reeves, *Delighting in the Trinity: An Introduction to the Christian Faith* (Downers Grove, IL: InterVarsity, 2012).
17. For a helpful discussion of image bearing in these relationships, see Hoekema, *Created in God's Image*, 75–111. Hoekema treats the "relationship with self" in a slightly different manner than the other three, but the distinction he is making is not relevant for the purposes of this book.
18. See the first question and answer in the *Westminster Shorter Catechism*.
19. There is a sense in which the first spoke should be pictured as more important than the other three. No analogy is perfect!
20. J. Todd Billings, *Union with Christ: Reframing Theology and Ministry for the Church* (Grand Rapids: Baker, 2011), 48.
21. This is the essence of the "neoclassical growth model" developed in the 1950s by Robert Solow, Nobel Laureate in Economics. The subsequent literature on "endogenous growth" has added "human capital" to physical capital and technology as sources of long-run growth, but human capital is very closely related to the generation of new technology and does not change the basic assertions made here. For a helpful discussion of these topics, see William Easterly, *The Elusive Quest for Growth: Economists Adventures and Misadventures in the Tropics* (Cambridge, MA: MIT Press, 2001).

22. Commission on Children at Risk, *Hardwired to Connect: The New Scientific Case for Authoritative Communities* (New York: Institute for American Values, 2003), 68.
23. Ibid., 6.
24. Clearly, Wilberforce was operating in a fallen world, so this example is not ideal to illustrate the effects of humans on systems in a world without sin.
25. Darrow L. Miller with Stan Guthrie, *Discipling the Nations: The Power of Truth to Transform Cultures* (Seattle: YWAM, 2001). See also Corbett and Fikkert, *When Helping Hurts*, 87–93.
26. Smith, *Desiring the Kingdom*.
27. E. J. R. David, ed., *Internalized Oppression: The Psychology of Marginalized Groups* (New York: Springer, 2013); E. J. R. David, *Brown Skin, White Minds: Filipino-/American Postcolonial Psychology* (Charlotte, NC: Information Age, 2013).
28. For a similar definition, see Corbett and Fikkert, *When Helping Hurts*; Myers, *Walking with the Poor.*
29. See Gailyn Van Rheenen, *Communicating Christ in Animistic Contexts* (Pasadena, CA: William Carey Library, 1996).
30. For example, when farmers in Bolivia's Alto Plano experienced an increase in their agricultural production, it deepened their worship of Pachamama, the goddess of fertility. See Corbett and Fikkert, *When Helping Hurts*, 80.
31. David, *Internalized Oppression*; David, *Brown Skin, White Minds*.
32. For example, see John D. Kammeyer-Mueller, Timothy A. Judge, and Ronald F. Piccolo, "Self-Esteem and Extrinsic Career Success: Test of a Dynamic Model," *Applied Psychology: An International Review* 57, no. 2 (2008), 204–24; Avshalom Caspi, Richie Poulton, Richard W. Robins, Terrie E. Moffitt, Brent M. Donnellan, and Kali H. Trzesniewski, "Low Self-Esteem During Adolescence Predicts Poor Health, Criminal Behavior, and Limited Economic Prospects During Adulthood," *Developmental Psychology* 42, no. 2 (2006): 381–90; Eirini Flouri, "Parental Interest in Children's Education, Children's Self-Esteem and Locus of Control, and Later Educational Attainment: Twenty-Six Year Follow-Up of the 1970 British Birth Cohort," *British Journal of Educational Psychology* 76, no. 1 (2006), 41–55.
33. See Corbett and Fikkert, *When Helping Hurts*.
34. Christopher Blattman and Edward Miguel, "Civil War," *Journal of Economic Literature* 48, no. 1 (2010), 3–57; Paul Collier, "Economic Causes of Civil Conflict and Their Implications for Policy," in *Leashing the Dogs of War: Conflict Management in a Divided World*, eds. Chester A. Crocker, Fen Osler Hanson, and Pamela Aall (Washington, DC: United States Institute of Peace, 2007), 197–218.
35. Pieter Serneels and Marijke Verpoorten, "The Impact of Armed Conflict on Economic Performance: Evidence from Rwanda," *Journal of Conflict Resolution* 53, no. 1 (2013), 3–29.
36. William Easterly, *The Elusive Quest for Growth*.
37. For example, see World Bank, *World Development Report 2010: Development and Climate Change* (Washington, DC: The World Bank, 2010); World Bank, *World Development Report 2003: Sustainable Development in a Dynamic World: Transforming Institutions, Growth, and Quality of Life* (Washington, DC: The World Bank, 2003).
38. For an example of this with the Pokomchi people of Guatemala, see Corbett and Fikkert, *When Helping Hurts*, 82.

39. Joel Mokyr, *The Enlightened Economy: An Economic History of Britain 1700–1850* (New Haven, CT: Yale University Press, 2012); Deirdre N. McCloskey, *Bourgeois Dignity: Why Economics Can't Explain the Modern World* (Chicago: University of Chicago Press, 2010); Robert E. Lucas Jr., *Lectures on Economic Growth* (Cambridge, MA: Harvard University Press, 2002).
40. Lucas, *Lectures on Economic Growth*, 17–18.

Chapter 6: A Trinitarian Theory of Change

1. Interview with staff of the Chalmers Center, 2012.
2. J. I. Packer, *Knowing God* (London: Hodder & Stoughton, 1973), 224.
3. Interview with staff of the Chalmers Center staff, 2012.
4. See Marcus Peter Johnson, *One with Christ: An Evangelical Theology of Salvation* (Wheaton, IL: Crossway, 2013); Robert Letham, *Union with Christ: In Scripture, History and Theology* (Phillipsburg, NJ: P&R, 2011); J. Todd Billings, *Union with Christ: Reframing Theology and Ministry for the Church* (Grand Rapids: Baker, 2011), 48; Fred Sanders, *The Deep Things of God: How the Trinity Changes Everything* (Wheaton, IL: Crossway, 2010); Kelly M. Kapic, *Communion with God: The Divine and the Human in the Theology of John Owen* (Grand Rapids: Baker, 2007).

   See John 6:56; 15:4–7; Romans 8:10; 1 Corinthians 15:22; 2 Corinthians 12:2; 13:5; Galatians 2:20; 3:28; Ephesians 1:4; 2:10; 3:17; Philippians 3:9; Colossians 1:27; 1 Thessalonians 4:16; 1 John 4:13. These passages were found in the very helpful article by Justin Taylor, *Union with Christ: A Crash Course*, The Gospel Coalition website, February 9, 2011, *thegospelcoalition.org/blogs/justintaylor/2011/02/09/union-with-christ-a-crash-course*.
5. Johnson, *One with Christ*, 40–57.
6. Anthony A. Hoekema, *Created in God's Image* (Grand Rapids: Eerdmans, 1986); Richard L. Pratt Jr., *Designed for Dignity: What God Has Made It Possible for You to Be*, 2nd ed. (Phillipsburg, NJ: P&R, 2000).
7. J. Todd Billings, *Union with Christ: Reframing Theology and Ministry for the Church* (Grand Rapids: Baker, 2011), 33.
8. For a helpful discussion of the relationship of the church to the kingdom, see Charles Van Engen, *God's Missionary People: Rethinking the Purpose of the Local Church* (Grand Rapids: Baker, 1991), 101–18.
9. See the discussion in the previous chapter; and E. J. R. David, ed., *Internalized Oppression: The Psychology of Marginalized Groups* (New York: Springer, 2013); and E. J. R. David, *Brown Skin, White Minds: Filipino-/American Postcolonial Psychology* (Charlotte, NC: Information Age, 2013).
10. Vern S. Poythress, "Territorial Spirits: Some Biblical Reflections," *Urban Mission* 13, no. 2 (1995): 37–49.
11. The Lausanne Movement, *The Capetown Commitment*, Part 2, Section IIE.5.
12. David W. Jones and Russell S. Woodbridge, *Health, Wealth, and Happiness: Has the Prosperity Gospel Overshadowed the Gospel of Jesus Christ?* (Grand Rapids: Kregel, 2011); Lausanne Theology Working Group, *A Statement on the Prosperity Gospel*, *http://www.lausanne.org/content/a-statement-on-the-prosperity-gospel*.

Chapter 7: Restoring Broken People: Transformative Ministry

1. Bryant L. Myers, *Walking with the Poor: Principles and Practices of Transformational Development*, rev. ed. (Maryknoll, NY: Orbis, 2011), 312–13.
2. Some ecclesiastical traditions would add several other items to the list, and some would subtract "prayer." For a helpful introduction to this topic, see Luke Stamps, "Especially Preaching: The Ordinary Means of Grace and Christian Spirituality," Gospel Coalition website, February 10, 2011, *http://thegospelcoalition.org/article/especially-preaching-the-ordinary-means-of-grace-and-christian-spirituality*.
3. Tim Chester, ed., with C. Rene Padilla, Tom Sine, and Elaine Storkey, *Justice, Mercy, and Humility: Integral Mission and the Poor* (Carlisle, UK: Paternoster, 2002), 8.
4. As quoted in Myers, *Walking with the Poor*, 313.
5. Ibid.
6. Traditional religionists largely conceive of "sin" as any action that brings disharmony to the community of both the living and deceased members of the tribe or family, rather than as offenses against a holy God. Hence, there are some nuances in how to best present the gospel in such contexts. See Gailyn Van Rheenen, *Communicating Christ in Animistic Contexts* (Pasadena, CA: William Carey Library, 1996).
7. Ibid.; Gailyn Van Rheenen,"Modernity Sweeps Africa," Missiology.org, Missiological Reflection #32, November 15, 2004, *http://www.missiology.org/?p=183*.
8. James F. Engel and William A. Dyrness, *Changing the Mind of Missions: Where Have We Gone Wrong?* (Downers Grove, IL: InterVarsity, 2000); Van Rheenen, *Communicating Christ in Animistic Contexts*.
9. James K. A. Smith, *Desiring the Kingdom: Worship, Worldview, and Cultural Formation* (Grand Rapids: Baker, 2009); Dennis P. Hollinger, *Head, Heart, and Hands: Bringing Together Christian Thought, Passion and Action* (Downers Grove, IL: InterVarsity, 2005).
10. Ibid.
11. James E. Zull, *The Art of Changing the Brain: Enriching the Practice of Teaching by Exploring the Biology of Learning* (Sterling, VA: Stylus, 2002).
12. Malcolm S. Knowles, Elwood F. Holton III, and Richard A. Swanson, *The Adult Learner: The Definitive Classic in Adult Education and Human Resource Development* (Oxford, UK: Elsevier, 2011).
13. Jane Vella, *On Teaching and Learning: Putting the Principles and Practices of Dialogue Education into Action* (San Francisco: Jossey-Bass, 2008); Jane Vella, *Learning to Listen, Learning to Teach: The Power of Dialogue in Educating Adults* (San Francisco: Jossey-Bass, 2002). Global Learning Partners provides a host of additional training and tools to equip trainers in all aspects of dialogue education, and readers are encouraged to visit their website for more information: *www.globallearningpartners.com*.
14. Darlene M. Goetzman, *Dialogue Education Step by Step: A Guide for Designing Exceptional Learning Events* (Montpelier, VT: Global Learning Partners, 2012).
15. A good place to start is Paul Rippey and Ben Fowler, *Beyond Financial Services: A Synthesis of Studies on the Integration of Savings Groups and Other Developmen-*

tal Activities, Aga Khan Foundation, April 2011, *https://www.microlinks.org/sites/microlinks/files/resource/files/2011_akf_beyond_financial_services.pdf.*

16. In particular, see chapters 4–6 in Steve Corbett and Brian Fikkert, *When Helping Hurts: How to Alleviate Poverty Without Hurting the Poor... and Yourself* (Chicago: Moody, 2012).
17. See the discussion in chapter 5; and E. J. R. David, ed., *Internalized Oppression: The Psychology of Marginalized Groups* (New York: Springer, 2013); and E. J. R. David, *Brown Skin, White Minds: Filipino- / American Postcolonial Psychology* (Charlotte, NC: Information Age, 2013).
18. Acts 1:15–16; Romans 8:28–30; Galatians 6:10; 1 Thessalonians 4:9–11; Hebrews 2:11; 1 Peter 2:17; 5:9. Similarly, the church is also referred to as God's "household": Ephesians 2:19; 1 Timothy 3:15; Titus 1:7; 1 Peter 4:17.
19. Abhijit V. Banerjee and Esther Duflo, *Poor Economics: A Radical Rethinking of the Way to Fight Global Poverty* (New York: PublicAffairs, 2012), 42.
20. Ibid., 41–70.
21. Ibid., 64–65.
22. Helen Coster, "Peer Pressure Can Be a Lifesaver," *New York Times*, Opinion Pages, May 14, 2014. For additional experiments by behavioral economists, see Innovations for Poverty Action (*www.poverty-action.org*) and J-Pal Poverty Action Lab at Massachusetts Institute of Technology (*www.povertyactionlab.org*).
23. Megan Gash, "Pathways to Change: The Impact of Group Participation," in *Savings Groups at the Frontier*, ed. Candace Nelson (Rugby, UK: Practical Action, 2013), 101–25. It is important to note that this research focused on savings and credit associations, not on groups started by MFIs, although it is reasonable to expect somewhat similar effects in MFIs' programs as well.
24. Ibid., 106–18.
25. Ibid.
26. United Nations Development Programme, *Human Development Report 2014, Sustaining Human Progress: Reducing Vulnerability and Building Resilience* (New York: United Nations Development Programme, 2014), iv.
27. The World Bank, *World Development Report 2014, Risk and Opportunity: Managing Risk for Development* (Washington, DC: The World Bank, 2013).
28. Eldar Shafir and Sendhil Mullainathan, "On the Psychology of Scarcity," presentation to the 2012 Social Enterprise Leadership Forum, Columbia Business School, New York, NY, May 18, 2012, quoted in Larry R. Reed, *Vulnerability: The State of the Microcredit Summit Campaign Report, 2013* (Washington, DC: Microcredit Summit Campaign, 2013), 20.
29. Ibid., 21.

Chapter 8: ROSCAs, ASCAs, and MFIs: A Primer on Microfinance

1. Arthur Lewis, *The Theory of Economic Growth* (Homewood, IL: Richard D. Irwin, 1955), 225–26.
2. David Roodman, *Due Diligence: An Impertinent Inquiry into Microfinance* (Washington, DC: Center for Global Development, 2012), 115.

3. Prudence's story is taken from Brigit Helms, *Access for All: Building Inclusive Financial Systems* (Washington, DC: The World Bank, 2006), 19.
4. Stuart Rutherford, *The Poor and Their Money* (New York: Oxford University Press USA, 2000); Susan Johnson and Ben Rogaly, *Microfinance and Poverty Reduction* (Oxford, UK: Oxfam, 1997).
5. Daryl Collins, Jonathan Morduch, Stuart Rutherford, and Orlanda Ruthven, *Portfolios of the Poor: How the World's Poor Live on $2 a Day* (Princeton, NJ: Princeton University Press, 2009).
6. Rebecca M. Vonderlack and Mark Schreiner, "Women, Microfinance, and Savings: Lessons and Proposals," *Development in Practice* 12, no. 5 (2002).
7. Rutherford, *The Poor and Their Money*; David Hulme and Paul Mosley, *Finance Against Poverty, Volume 1* (Oxford, UK: Routledge, 1996); Graham Wright, M. Hossain, and Stuart Rutherford, "Savings: Flexible Financial Services for the Poor (and Not Just the Implementing Organization)" in *Who Needs Credit? Poverty and Finance in Bangladesh*, ed. G. D. Wood and I. Sharif (Dhaka: University Press Ltd., and England: Zed Books, 1997).
8. Syed Hashemi, "Building Up Capacity for Banking with the Poor: The Grameen Bank of Bangladesh," in *Microfinance for the Poor?* ed. H. Schneider (Paris: IFAD, OECD, 1997).
9. Gailyn Van Rheenen, *Communicating Christ in Animistic Contexts* (Pasadena, CA: William Carey Library, 1996); Darrow L. Miller, *Discipling the Nations: The Power of Truth to Transform Cultures* (Seattle: YWAM, 2001).
10. For a helpful discussion of biblical teaching with respect to debt and interest, see Kershaw Burbank, "A Christian Perspective on Micro-Enterprise Loans and the Payment of Loan Interest," unpublished paper at Eastern University, St. Davids, PA, undated.
11. For an overview of the key issues in providing microinsurance services to poor households, see Craig Churchill, "Insurance," in *The New Microfinance Handbook: A Financial Market System Perspective*, eds. Joanna Ledgerwood, Julie Earne, and Candace Nelson (Washington, DC: The World Bank, 2013), 249–70.
12. Ibid., 250.
13. Roodman, *Due Diligence*, 116–7.
14. Collins et al., *Portfolios of the Poor*, 92.
15. Ibid., 93–94; Roodman, *Due Diligence*, 282.
16. World Bank, *Migration and Development Brief* 20 (Washington, DC: The World Bank, 2013), 1.
17. Ibid., 7.
18. Nicole Woolsey Biggart, "Banking on Each Other: The Situational Logic of Rotating Savings and Credit Associations," *Advances in Qualitative Organizational Research* 3 (2001): 129–53.
19. Rutherford, *The Poor and Their Money*.
20. Ibid.
21. The pot may also grow due to fines that are often imposed on members for missing meetings, failing to make their savings contribution, or being delinquent on loan repayments.

22. ASCAs usually charge lower interest rates on their loans than the 240 percent to 360 percent typically charged by the moneylenders.
23. Jeffrey Ashe and Lisa Parott, "Impact Evaluation: PACT's Women's Empowerment Program in Nepal: A Savings and Literacy-Led Alternative to Financial Institution Building," working paper at Institute for Sustainable Development, Heller School, Brandeis University, 2001.
24. William Grant and Hugh Allen, "Care's Mata Masu Dubara (Women on the Move) Program in Niger: Successful Financial Intermediation in the Rural Sahel," *Journal of Microfinance* 4, no. 2 (2002): 189–216.
25. Collins et al., *Portfolios of the Poor*, 153.
26. Rutherford, *The Poor and Their Money*.
27. Ibid.
28. Lien-sheng Yang, *Money and Credit in China: A Short History* (Cambridge, MA: Harvard Press, 1952).
29. Sudanshu Handa and Claremont Kirton, "The Economics of Rotating Savings and Credit Associations: Evidence from the Jamaican 'Partner,'" *Journal of Development Economics* 60, 1 (1999): 173–94.
30. Gertrude R. Schrieder and Carlos E. Cuevas, "Informal Financial Groups in Cameroon," in *Informal Finance in Low-Income Countries* by Dale W. Adams and Delbert A. Fitchett (Boulder, CO: Westview Press, 1992).
31. SAVIX website: *www.savingsgroups.com*.
32. Reported to the authors in private correspondence, August 1, 2014.
33. Hugh Allen, email to VSL constituents, September 10, 2014.
34. Rutherford, *The Poor and Their Money*.
35. SAVIX website: *www.savingsgroups.com*.
36. Historically, MFIs focused on providing loans, but in recent years there has been a dramatic increase in their provision of savings services. As of 2012, MFIs were reporting 72 million microsavings clients, compared to 94 million microcredit clients. See the Microfinance Information Exchange, MIX Database, available at *www.mixmarket.org*.
37. Neal Johnson and Steven Rundle, "Distinctives and Challenges of Business as Mission," in *Business as Mission: From Impoverished to Empowered*, eds. Tom A. Steffen and Mike Barnett (Pasadena, CA: William Carey Library, 2006), 26.
38. Ibid.
39. F. J. A. Bouman and Otto Hospes, "Financial Landscapes Reconstructed," in *Financial Landscapes Reconstructed: The Fine Art of Mapping Development*, eds. F. J. A. Bouman and Otto Hospes (Boulder, CO: Westview Press, 1994); Graham Wright, *Understanding and Assessing the Demand for Microfinance* (Nairobi, Kenya: Microsave, 2005).

Chapter 9: The Three Cs: Making Financial Systems Work

1. As quoted in David S. Gibbons ed, *The Grameen Reader* (Dhaka, Bangladesh: Grameen Bank, 1994), 46.
2. As quoted in Soutik Biswas, "India's Microfinance Suicide Epidemic," *BBC News online*, December 16, 2010.

3. Readers interested in more discussion of risk, trust (confidence), and value are strongly encouraged to read J. D. Von Pischke, *Finance at the Frontier: Debt Capacity and the Role of Credit in the Private Economy* (Washington, DC: World Bank, 1991).
4. The story of Riverbend and Mount Zion is fictional; however, it is a composite of the actual experiences of the people with whom the Chalmers Center has interacted over many years.
5. In economists' language, Grameen's methodology helped to overcome the "adverse selection" and "moral hazard" problems due to "asymetric information." Readers interested in learning more about the underlying economic issues are encouraged to read Beatriz Armendariz and Jonathan Murdoch, *The Economics of Microfinance*, 2nd ed. (Cambridge, MA: MIT Press, 2010).
6. There are many variations on how strictly this is enforced in actual practice. For example, sometimes MFIs will allow well-performing borrowers to start a new group that excludes the borrowers who did not repay their loans. See Dean Karlan and Jacob Appel, *More Than Good Intentions: Improving the Ways the World's Poor Borrow, Save, Farm, Learn, and Stay Healthy* (New York: Plume, 2012), 113.
7. Both theoretical and empirical research is ongoing about the importance of groups in general and of the joint-liability incentive structure that characterized the original Grameen methodology, with some doubting that the joint-liability feature is essential. See Karlan and Appel, *More Than Good Intentions*, 109–41; Jeffrey Carpenter, *Moral Hazard, Peer Monitoring, and Microcredit: Field Experimental Evidence from Paraguay*, working paper at the Federal Reserve Bank of Boston, no. 10-6 (June 28, 2010); Niels Hermes and Robert Lensink, "The Empirics of Microfinance: What Do We Know?" *Economic Journal* 117 (February 2007): 1–10.
8. At a theological level, as depicted in Figure 2.1, the local church is called to directly perform a limited number of tasks, with other tasks left to the parachurch and to other institutions in society. This is simply the idea of "sphere sovereignty" developed by Abraham Kuyper. For a brief introduction, see Timothy J. Keller, *Center Church: Doing Balanced, Gospel-Centered Ministry in Your City* (Grand Rapids: Zondervan, 2012), 294–95.
9. As discussed in Steve Corbett and Brian Fikkert, *When Helping Hurts: How to Alleviate Poverty Without Hurting the Poor... and Yourself* (Chicago: Moody, 2012), the materially non-poor's broken "relationship with self" is typically manifested in a sense of pride and superiority.
10. See Joanna Ledgerwood with Julie Earne and Candace Nelson, eds. *The New Microfinance Handbook: A Financial Market System Perspective* (Washington, DC: The World Bank, 2013).
11. We are thankful to Ed Jimenez for this suggestion.
12. For more on this topic, see Kershaw Burbank, *A Christian Perspective on Micro-Enterprise Loans and the Payment of Interest*, unpublished paper at Eastern University, St. Davids, PA.
13. A 36 percent "flat rate" interest. Please see *http://www.mftransparency.org/* to learn how "flat rate" interest translates into much more transparent annual percentage rate (APR) figures. A 36 percent "flat rate" loan translates to an APR

of 65.7 percent. These high interest rates are needed to cover the very high costs of making small loans, particularly loans less than $100.

14. Microfinance Transparency, *http://www.mftransparency.org/*, is leading the way in encouraging financial systems, particularly MFIs, to publish transparent pricing using the APR method of interest rate calculations.
15. Ledgerwood et. al., *The New Microfinance Handbook*; Brigit Helms, *Access for All: Building Inclusive Financial Systems* (Washington, DC: The World Bank, 2006); David Hulme and Paul Mosley, *Finance Against Poverty, Volume 1* (Oxford, UK: Routledge, 1996).
16. Claudia McKay and Mark Pickens, *Branchless Banking 2010: Who Is Served? At What Price? What's Next?* (Washington, DC: CGAP, 2010), Focus Note 66, September 2010.
17. Aude de Montesquiou and Tony Sheldon with Frank F. DeGiovanni and Syed M. Hashemi, *From Extreme Poverty to Sustainable Livelihoods: A Technical Guide to the Graduation Approach* (Washington, DC: CGAP, 2014).
18. The House of Principles appears in various forms in the curricula available from the Chalmers Center on the website associated with this book.

Chapter 10: The Provider Model of Microfinance

1. Confidential conversation with one of the authors, July 30, 2014.
2. As quoted in Dean Karlan and Jacob Appel, *More Than Good Intentions: Improving the Ways the World's Poor Borrow, Save, Farm, Learn, and Stay Healthy* (New York: Plume, 2012), 112.
3. Data are through June 2014 as featured in report of July 7, 2014, from the Grameen Bank website: *www.grameen-info.org*.
4. Stuart Rutherford, *The Poor and Their Money* (New York: Oxford University Press USA, 2000).
5. Larger providers, such as MFIs like Grameen, also obtain loan capital from investors or even other lenders.
6. A few Christian MFIs in Asia and Africa now serve over 100,000 clients, putting them in the category of Large-Scale MFIs.
7. Individual loans work better for those who are above the poverty line, as these people sometimes have more of a credit history and can often provide physical collateral.
8. Comment made by a student in a distance course on Christian microfinance offered by the Chalmers Center in 2009.
9. Efficient providers now have operational costs of 12–18 cents per dollar of loan portfolio. See David Bussau and Russell Mask, *Christian Microenterprise Development: An Introduction* (Oxford, UK: Regnum, 2003).
10. To learn how the "flat rate" translates into the more transparent "annual percentage rate," see *http://www.mftransparency.org/*.
11. Centre for the Study of Financial Innovation, *Microfinance Banana Skins 2008: Risk in a Booming Industry* (UK: Centre for the Study of Financial Innovation, 2008).
12. Personal interview with one of the authors. The country and date of this interview are being withheld to preserve anonymity.

13. It is expensive to lend very small amounts of money to a high-risk population, so MFIs have to charge relatively high rates of interest to cover their costs. Because the non-poor can borrow larger amounts of money and are less risky, it is less costly to lend them money. Hence, they are able to obtain loans with lower interest rates than those charged by MFIs.
14. Philip Smith and Eric Thurman, *A Billion Bootstraps: Microcredit, Barefoot Banking, and the Business Solution for Ending Poverty* (New York: McGraw-Hill, 2007); Steven L. Rundle and Thomas A. Steffen, *Great Commission Companies: The Emerging Role of Business in Missions* (Downers Grove, IL: InterVarsity, 2003); Tetsunao Yamamori and Kenneth A. Eldred, *On Kingdom Business: Transforming Missions Through Entrepreneurial Strategies* (Wheaton, IL: Crossway, 2003).
15. Even without this donor pressure, increasingly competitive markets make it difficult for Christian MFIs to include evangelism and discipleship. If, for example, a secular MFI is charging 36 percent, why would a poor person who is not a believer pay 40 percent in order to cover the additional costs of evangelism and discipleship from a Christian MFI?
16. Confidential conversation with one of the authors, July 30, 2014.

Chapter 11: The Partnership Model of Microfinance

1. David Larson, *A LEAP of Faith for Church-Centered Microfinance*, working paper (Baltimore, MD: World Relief, 1999), 14.
2. Interview with one of the authors, 2006.
3. Daniel Rickett, *Building Strategic Relationships: A Practical Guide to Partnering with Non-Western Missions*, 3rd ed. (Minneapolis: STEM Press, 2008), 13.
4. This section briefly summarizes Larson, *LEAP*; additional examples of the Partnership Model can be found in Lanie Andres, *New Century Church Partnership with TSPI Development Corporation in the Philippines*, working paper (Lookout Mountain, GA: Chalmers Center for Economic Development at Covenant College, 2005); Russell Mask, *Missionary, Local Churches, and MFI Partnership: A Case from Metro Manila, Philippines*, working paper (Lookout Mountain, GA: Chalmers Center for Economic Development at Covenant College, 2004); Russell Mask, *Grameen Banking in Metro Manila, Philippines: Religion and Other Factors in Borrower and Program Performance*, unpublished doctoral dissertation at the University of Wisconsin-Madison, 1995.
5. Larson, *LEAP*, 10.
6. Ibid., 17.
7. Ibid., 15.
8. See Ministry Component #4 in chapter 7.
9. See figure 8.2 and the related discussion in chapter 8.
10. Andres, *New Century Church*.
11. Daniel Rickett, *Making Your Partnership Work* (Enumclaw, WA: Winepress, 2002).
12. Ibid.
13. Rachel Blackman, *Partnering with the Local Church* (Teddington, UK: Tearfund, 2007).

14. David Bussau and Russell Mask, *Christian Microenterprise Development: An Introduction* (Oxford, UK: Regnum, 2003).
15. For more on culture changes in NGOs partnering with churches, see Blackman, *Partnering with the Local Church*.

Chapter 12: The Promotion Model of Microfinance

1. Report from Joel Assaraf, Leader of the Poverty Initiative of Saddleback Church/The PEACE Plan, July 20, 2014.
2. Sarah Tan, "Reconciliation Through Saving," online client stories of HOPE International, August 12, 2014.
3. This story about one of the Chalmers Center's pilot projects with Food for the Hungry International in the Philippines has been adapted with permission from Malu Garcia, "Light Rising in the Darkness," *Mandate* (Spring 2003): 1. It also appeared in Brian Fikkert, "Fostering Informal Savings and Credit Associations" in *Attacking Poverty in the Developing World: Christian Practitioners and Academics in Collaboration*, eds. Judith M. Dean, Julie Schaffner, and Stephen L. S. Smith (Federal Way, WA: Authentic Media in partnership with World Vision, 2005), 77–94.
4. See chapter 10.
5. See Ministry Component #4 in chapter 7.
6. See figure 8.2 and the related discussion in chapter 8.
7. See chapters 4 and 8 of this book for an introduction to this research. Many people were introduced to the savings-led approach by Stuart Rutherford's book entitled *The Poor and Their Money* (New York: Oxford University Press USA, 2000). The savings-led approach was then given much greater visibility by a 2002 symposium published in the *Journal of Microfinance* 4:2, which reported on the large-scale promotion of SCAs by CARE in Niger and Pact in Nepal.
8. The VSLA materials can be freely downloaded from the website of VSL Associates: *www.vsla.net*
9. Email from Hugh Allen of VSL Associates, September 10, 2014.
10. Sometimes they used credit unions, which are non-time-bound ASCAs. See Rachel Yousey, *The CRWRC Paluwagan Model: Fostering Poverty Alleviation through Income Generation and Sanitation Projects*, unpublished master's thesis at The American University, Washington, DC, 2002; Jack Shaffer, *Historical Dictionary of the Cooperative Movement* (Lanham, Md.: Rowman and Littlefield, 1999); John H. Magill, "Credit Unions: A Formal-Sector Alternative for Financing Microenterprise Development," in *The New World of Microenterprise Finance: Building Healthy Financial Institutions for the Poor*, eds. Maria Otero and Elizabeth Rhyne (West Hartford, CT: Kumarian Press, 1994), 140–55.
11. Lien-sheng Yang, *Money and Credit in China: A Short History* (Cambridge, MA: Harvard Press, 1952).
12. See Rutherford, *The Poor and Their Money*.
13. A list of the local names of ROSCAs in many countries can be found at *http://www.gdrc.org/icm/rosca/rosca-names.html*.

14. Lesslie Newbigin, *The Gospel in a Pluralistic Society* (Grand Rapids: Eerdmans, 1989), 227. See the discussion in chapter 2.
15. See the discussion of this point in chapter 7.
16. If we have overlooked any organizations, we sincerely apologize. It was not our intent to leave anybody out of this list.
17. The VSLA materials can be freely downloaded from the website of VSL Associates: *www.vsla.net*.
18. Ibid. Data accessed on August 27, 2014.
19. Tearfund refers to its SCAs as "Self-Help Groups."
20. In reality, the "savings" services of many MFIs are really deposits of collateral that must be made before loans can be taken from the MFI. In contrast, at least some of the money saved in an ASCA can be withdrawn when the participant needs it.
21. Hugh Allen, "CARE's Village Savings and Loan Programmes: Microfinance for the Poor that Works, Powerpoint retrieved July 10, 2007, from SEEP Network: *www.seepnetwork.org*.
22. As of May 2014. Data provided by HOPE International.
23. Hugh Allen and William Grant, "Care's Mata Masu Dubara (Women on the Move) Program in Niger: Successful Financial Intermediation in the Rural Sahel," *Journal of Microfinance* 4, no. 2 (2002): 189–216.
24. Website of VSL Associates, accessed on September 3, 2014, *www.vsla.net*.
25. Jessica Murray and Richard Rosenberg, *Community-Managed Loan Funds: Which Ones Work?* (Washington, DC: CGAP, 2006), Focus Note 36.
26. For a further discussion of the absence of a kingdom theology in churches and missions, see chapter 1 of Steve Corbett and Brian Fikkert, *When Helping Hurts: How to Alleviate Poverty Without Hurting the Poor... and Yourself* (Chicago: Moody, 2012).
27. Roy Mersland, "Innovations in Savings and Credit Groups—Evidence from Kenya," *Small Enterprise Development* 18, no. 1, 50–56.
28. Roy Mersland and Tuiname Team, "Tuiname: Internal Evaluation," December 2011, downloadable at *www.norad.no/en/tools-and-publications/publications/reviews-from-organisations/publication?key=394975*.

Chapter 13: The Surprising Challenges of Distribution

1. Ken Stern, *With Charity for All: Why Charities Are Failing and a Better Way to Give* (New York: Doubleday, 2013), 15.
2. Peter Greer and Chris Horst, *Mission Drift: The Unspoken Crisis Facing Leaders, Charities, and Churches* (Minneapolis: Bethany House, 2014), 115.
3. William Easterly, *The White Man's Burden: Why the West's Efforts to Aid the Rest Have Done So Much Ill and So Little Good* (New York: Penguin Press, 2006), 3–4.
4. See, for example, the article by Jonathan Mitchell, "How to Be a Savvy Investor in Water and Gospel," *Mission Frontiers* (September/October, 2013): 20–22.
5. See the "Donald Trump Effect" in Steve Corbett and Brian Fikkert, *When Helping Hurts: How to Alleviate Poverty Without Hurting the Poor... and Yourself* (Chicago: Moody, 2012), 239–41.

6. A number of organizations promoting SCAs on a large scale are also experimenting with various "fee-for-service" delivery models. While there is a need for much more research, there is some evidence that SCAs started by "fee-for-service" trainers have higher performance than SCAs started by salaried staff members. See Paul Rippey and Hugh Allen, "Making It Happen: Approaches to Group Formation," in *Savings Groups at the Frontier*, ed. Candace Nelson (Rugby, UK: Practical Action, 2013), 65–82.
7. The menu of potential curricula is described in Ministry Components #3–#4 in chapter 7.
8. A similar point is made by Daniel Rickett, *Building Strategic Relationships: A Practical Guide to Partnering with Non-Western Missions*, 3rd ed. (Minneapolis: STEM Press, 2008), 34.
9. A randomized controlled experiment has found that requiring teachers to take digital photos of themselves with their students reduced teacher absenteeism and increased students' test scores in India. See Esther Duflo, Rema Hanna, and Stephen P. Ryan, "Incentives Work: Getting Teachers to Come to School," *American Economic Review* 102, no. 4 (2012): 1241–78.
10. Tearfund refers to its SCAs as "Self-Help Groups."
11. Surveys have found that the SCAs in this field project have an average of thirteen members.
12. Rippey and Allen, *Making It Happen*, 75–77.
13. Daniel Rickett, *Building Strategic Relationships*, 13.

Appendix 1: Estimating the Impact of Microfinance

1. See David Roodman, *Due Diligence: An Impertinent Inquiry into Microfinance* (Washington, DC: Center for Global Development, 2012).
2. This assumes that both Marco and the MFI are aware of Marco's superior entrepreneurial talent.
3. Robert Cull, Tilman Ehrbeck, and Nina Holle, *Financial Inclusion and Development: Recent Impact Evidence*, Consultative Group to Assist the Poor, no. 92 (April 2014); Roodman, *Due Diligence*.
4. Megan Gash and Kathleen Odell, *The Evidence-Based Story of Savings Groups: A Synthesis of Seven Randomized Control Trials* (Arlington, VA: The SEEP Network, 2013).
5. Eldar Shafir and Sendhil Mullainathan, "On the Psychology of Scarcity," presentation to the 2012 Social Enterprise Leadership Forum, Columbia Business School, New York, NY, May 18, 2012, quoted in Larry R. Reed, *Vulnerability: The State of the Microcredit Summit Campaign Report, 2013* (Washington, DC: Microcredit Summit Campaign, 2013), 20.
6. Megan Gash, "Pathways to Change: The Impact of Group Participation," in *Savings Groups at the Frontier*, ed. Candace Nelson (Rugby, UK: Practical Action, 2013), 101–25.